About these books . . .

Neither Robert Ozment nor Dale Evans Rogers need introductions to Guideposts' readers. Both have been members of our "family" for some time. Dale and her husband Roy have each written articles which have appeared in the magazine and Dr. Ozment's faith affirming book "But God Can" was a previous Guideposts book selection. Now it is your privilege to hear from them again.

Dale Evans Rogers' latest book, "The Woman at the Well," is another milestone in this unusually talented lady's life. After such highly praised and widely distributed books as "Angel Unaware," "Salute to Sandy," "Christmas Is Always," and "Dearest Debbie," Dale has penned what many feel is her greatest effort yet in this exceptionally candid autobiography. In it, she traces her life from fragmented childhood to a starring role in films. She tells of her search for a meaningful, real life in the sometimes unreal setting of show business; her rising career, her first meeting of Roy; their marriage; their exciting adventure together in faith; their joys; their heartaches; victories and failures.

Without polish or paint, Dale relates her story fully, openly, honestly, warmly. It's a warts and all book, which can only be told by a mature Christian who realizes, "There but for the grace of God go I."

In the second half of this 2-in-1 selection is Robert Ozment's marvelously helpful, practical book "Love Is the Answer." At a time when we see all too little compassion and caring around us, Dr. Ozment comes forth with a book of promise and hope. And instead of just lamenting the state of things, he offers specific suggestions as to how we can change our behavior and thinking and how this can change others around us. Loneliness, alienations, self-pity, doubt, fear, trials and setbacks are all dealt with positively, creatively and victoriously by this talented minister-author.

We believe Dr. Ozment's words will, like Dale Evans Rogers', strengthen you and make your faith come alive. Both have lived the Christian life and have tested it in the marketplace. Their joint message is: you can too.

—The Editors

The Woman at the Well

Dale Evans Rogers

LOVE

IS THE

ANSWER

Robert V. Ozment

GUIDEPOSTS ASSOCIATES, INC.

Carmel, New York

The Woman
at the Well

Dale Evans Rogers

GUIDEPOSTS ASSOCIATES, INC.

Carmel, New York

Copyright © 1970 by Fleming H. Revell Company

Old Tappan, New Jersey

All right reserved

*Guideposts edition published by arrangement with
Fleming H. Revell Company*

Printed in the United States of America

TO MY WONDERFUL PARENTS, to whom I shall ever be grateful for the early Christian training in my life.

TO MY SON, Tom, whose shining example of unswerving loyalty to his Lord led me to the foot of The Cross.

TO ALL THOSE WHO BEFRIENDED and helped me in my chosen career as an entertainer.

TO MY HUSBAND, Roy Rogers, for his understanding, his love, and for his generous heart that was big enough to allow me the large, wonderful family so vital to my development as a Christian wife and mother.

TO FLEMING H. REVELL COMPANY, especially to Dr. Frank S. Mead, who believed in me enough to publish my first book, the subsequent ones and now my personal Christian testimony.

And he must needs go through Samaria. Then cometh he to a city of Samaria, which is called Sychar, near to the parcel of ground that Jacob gave to his son Joseph. Now Jacob's well was there. Jesus therefore, being wearied with his journey, sat thus on the well: and it was about the sixth hour. There cometh a woman of Samaria to draw water: Jesus saith unto her, Give me to drink. (For his disciples were gone away unto the city to buy meat.) Then saith the woman of Samaria unto him, How is it that thou, being a Jew, asketh drink of me, which am a woman of Samaria? for the Jews have no dealings with the Samaritans. Jesus answered and said unto her, If thou knewest the gift of God, and who it is that saith to thee, Give me to drink; thou wouldst have asked of him, and he would have given thee living water. The woman saith unto him, Sir, thou hast nothing to draw with, and the well is deep: from whence then hast thou that living water? Art thou greater than our father Jacob, which gave us the well, and drank thereof himself, and his children, and his cattle? Jesus answered and said unto her, Whosoever drinketh of this water shall thirst again: But whosoever drinketh of the water that I shall give him shall never thirst; but the water that I shall give him shall be in him a well of water springing up into everlasting life. The woman saith unto him, Sir, give me this water, that I thirst not . . . (John 4:4–15).

Prologue

$\mathcal{T}$ he Bible tells us that we are always to be ready to give reason for the hope that is within us. The greatest joy and privilege of my life has been to do just that—to give my personal Christian testimony wherever and whenever it seemed good or necessary. Especially since *Angel Unaware,* the little book about our retarded baby, was published in the spring of 1953, I have been witnessing to the saving grace and power of Jesus Christ in my life, to literally thousands of people. I was sadly conscious of all the people I could not reach with these spoken testimonies. Time and working schedules made it impossible for me to accept all of the warm and wonderful invitations I have had to speak of my faith.

Hence this book, which has a double purpose: it is intended to be my autobiography, but I am more anxious to have it be my Christian witness.

It is astounding to me that so many people do not understand the meaning of "Christian witness" and "Christian testimony." A dear friend once asked me, "How can you stand up there in front of all those people and flay yourself in such a personal way?" My answer was and is, "I, personally, do not count, for my life is crucified with Christ. He counts, and I 'flay' myself only that others may see what He has done for me."

In the telling, I must be as honest as I know how to be, without embarrassing others with whom I have been concerned or involved. There have been many experiences in my life, from ages seventeen to thirty-five, which have burned deeply and

9

left scars on me and possibly on others. Many were self-inflicted, due to the bitter disillusionment of my first marriage. Had I turned when that marriage failed, in submission to God, and had I asked Him *then* to take over my messed-up life, things might have been vastly different. Instead, I made a pact with and within myself that never again would anyone hurt me, that I would be completely independent of everybody, asking no quarter, and that *on my own* I would reach the top rung of the ladder of success and insure my own future. Little did I realize that the only security worth fighting for is our spiritual security in Christ!

Out of respect for the feelings of others, I shall not go into detail about the many mistakes I made in my attempt to find the perfect husband and father for my child (after that first marriage went on the rocks). Let me say just that I failed miserably. Nothing turned out right, no matter how hard I tried. Fighting in the blindness of disillusionment, I struck out in all directions, hurting myself and often hurting others— never realizing what an emotionally immature and insecure and selfish person I was—always rationalizing my sense of guilt, always trying to justify my wrongdoing.

When I finally "came to myself" early in 1948, soon after my marriage to Roy Rogers, I asked the Lord to take over my life, and I set about making restitution wherever possible. Unfortunately, it is often impossible to make full and just restitution in such situations, and (this is excruciatingly painful) to get rid of one's guilt *only* in recognizing the fact that Christ died to relieve us of guilt. He died to cover every sin through His atonement. When neither of the partners in a marriage is committed all the way in the matter of faith, that marriage is on a precarious footing. Only when we realize that *all* have sinned and come short of the glory of God, and that it is a privilege to love and serve our mates *in the Lord,* do we have a chance for real wedded bliss. In the best of marriages there

10

are squalls and sometimes tempests. If Christ is the head of the house, that house may creak and shake in the storms *but it will stand!* I know—from personal experience. The marriage will stand even if only one partner to it is committed to the Lord, because a committed Christian will not only go the extra mile but go until he drops, or is knocked out!

In the spring of 1968, my mother was in the hospital with a fractured hip; one of her nurses asked me, skeptically, if I had really written *Angel Unaware,* or whether someone else had ghost-written it for me. After all, she said, I was "just an entertainer." When I told her how God had inspired me and directed me in the writing of that little book, she said, "OK. But being in show business and publicly professing faith in Jesus Christ does make you something of a spectacle to people, doesn't it? How do you feel about being thought of as a sort of freak?"

I had to stop and count ten before I could answer that one for, to me, there is nothing freakish about a show person giving a witness. I repeated to her the words of Paul in I Corinthians 4:9–10:

> . . . for we are made a spectacle unto the world and to
> angels and to men. We are fools for Christ's sake. . . .

I am willing and privileged to be thought a fool, or a spectacle, for His sake, if through my halting efforts one searching soul might find Him as I searched and found, and in whom is life— abundant!

DALE EVANS ROGERS

There was a woman at a well, one day
Near a city of Samaria, in a land far away.
There she met a Stranger, who changed her life that day,
For He gave her living water—from
    The Truth, the Life, the Way.
She left her waterpot, there by the well,
Ran into the city—*for she must tell*
    That she had met the Messiah at the well!

DALE EVANS ROGERS

1

*T*here have been many women at the well. I am one of them. In the spring of 1948, with a great thirst already in my heart, I went to a place called The Fountain Avenue Baptist Church seeking the Water of Life—and Life, in the Person of Jesus Christ, met me there. Let me tell you who and what I was, and why I was so thirsty.

I was born in Uvalde, Texas, just when I am not sure. It was either on October 30th or October 31st, 1912. I don't know, even yet, which day it was, and frankly I don't much care. I have settled on Halloween as my birthday, and more than once I have said to myself, "No wonder I have had so much trouble; I was born a witch!"

The confusion over the date really came to mean something when Roy Rogers, my good husband, and I were packing for a personal appearance theater tour in England—and incidentally to be with Billy Graham in the first week of his London Crusade for Christ, in 1954. The only record of my birth was an affidavit from my parents, which said that I had been born on October 31st, and I had lost that somewhere. The affidavit also said that I had been named Frances Octavia Smith. Nobody had any doubt about either the date or the name during all those years.

Imagine the shock—and the chagrin!—when I asked the vital statistics people in Austin, Texas, for a copy of my birth certificate, and was told that I had been born on October 30th, and that I had been named Lucille Wood Smith! I was speechless, and my mother was mad. Someone, she said, had

15

made a stupid mistake. It could only have been the doctor who presided at my debut—and he had long since departed this vale of tears, so he wasn't much help. Mother was *sure* I was Frances Octavia, so Frances Octavia it has remained.

Frances had a difficult time arriving; my mother said that she had been given an anesthesia called twilight sleep, which not only anesthetized her, but her baby as well. For three days I made scarcely a sound. The doctors and the nurses were sure that I was an abnormal child. When I finally came to, I made up for lost time with a racket that upset the whole hospital. Mother says I have been making myself heard ever since.

My parents lived on a farm belonging to my grandfather, near Italy, Texas. (Population, 1183 in 1950; what must it have been in 1912?) My father and my mother's brother ran a hardware store in Italy, in addition to farming (mostly cotton). I was the first grandchild in the family, which meant that I never lacked attention—and I loved *that*. I learned very early to watch for the mail man, who brought presents; when he didn't, I didn't like him any more. My mother says I was quite vain, especially when someone gave me new clothes; I pirouetted in front of the mirror, à la the greatest actress in the world. I also loved to sing; I would burst into song at the drop of a hat—anyone's hat, anytime, anywhere. At times it became embarrassing. When I was taken to church, I would swish my little skirt and more than once I broke away from my parents when the lively gospel songs were sung, and danced down the aisle of the church. On those occasions my father would escort me to the fire station next door, where a laying on of hands that had nothing to do with religion was firmly and not gently applied.

Mother played the piano in Sunday school, and took me along. I was interested more in what I was wearing and in what the other children were wearing than I was in the lesson for the day. Once after Sunday school my father asked me what I had

16

learned about Jesus that day, and still thinking of those clothes, I replied, "Oh, he wasn't there today." (There's food for thought in that! How often isn't Jesus there?)

When I was three I was told that God was going to send us a baby. I enthusiastically approved. It was decided that I was to accompany one of my aunts to Uvalde, to my grandparents' home, while mother was "busy" at the hospital. Aunt was on her way home from college at the time, and her train was to pass through Italy where it made a water stop. All dressed up in my Sunday best, I was driven to the station. I was beside myself with joy when I saw the train coming, its headlight lighting up the track and its whistle blowing like mad. Alas! It didn't stop! Someone had forgotten to tell the conductor to stop at Italy. It roared past us, and I had a fleeting glance of my aunt standing on the platform between the cars with her arms outstretched. For one agonizing second they thought of throwing me into her arms, but the train was going too fast. My face fell six feet as I watched the form of my aunt receding in the distance, and I cried nearly all night. How *dare* anyone treat me like this? (But we made it the next day to Uvalde, and I forgave everybody.)

When they brought the new baby boy home to Italy, I loved him. It wasn't long before I hated him. I can vouch for the trauma that occurs in the firstborn child in a family when the secondborn enters his world. I was being left out! All the bustling, all the whispering in low tones, and (I thought) all the love that had been lavished on *me*, as the only grandchild, was now lavished on *him*. My nose went definitely out of joint. It was so awful that I decided to run away. If they didn't want me any more, OK, I could take care of myself somewhere else! I got as far as the wooded glen behind the farmhouse, where my grandmother caught up with me, switch in hand.

That should have cured me, but it didn't; they went right on pampering the baby, and I was even more convinced that

17

nobody loved me and that all was lost. I hied myself out to the pigpen behind the barn to assuage my grief and my feeling of neglect by cuddling the litter of newly born little pigs. When they missed me, my father came; he stepped gingerly into the pen, between me and the distrustful old sow who was working up a storm and emitting grunts of disapproval. My father was terrified with fear that one of the little porkers would squeal before he could lift me away from the fiercely protective mother. Lift me he did, just in time; he hugged me in relief, and then there was more of the laying-on-of-hands business.

We moved into town, into Italy, where my father could give more time to the hardware store, and where I caught, in turn, just about all the sicknesses of childhood. I had mumps, chicken pox and the flu. I escaped measles, though my brother did not. I caught diphtheria, and it left me with a paralyzed palate. They cut something to loosen my speech, and after that they had a time trying to silence me! A huge evil-looking egg appeared on my neck (a glandular disturbance) which was lanced; the tonsils came out at six. There was a sprained hip in the interim, caused by jumping off the running board of the family car while it was still in motion.

Double, double, toil and trouble! It was to stay with me all my life.

I was an extrovert, in these early days—extrovert, but also extremely sensitive. I was lucky enough to have relatives around me who understood that. I visited in their homes many times during my childhood, for my brother was afflicted with more than his share of sickness, and I was a handful that mother must have been glad to be rid of as often as possible. My aunt tells me that on one of my visits to her home, I had disobeyed her orders and run down the street to see a little friend. When I came back she locked me in solitary confinement in a clothes closet. This had never happened to me before, and I was badly frightened. Under this strange discipline, my wailing and weep-

18

ing and gnashing of teeth was so bad that my aunt got into the closet with me. I suppose that didn't help the discipline very much, but as mercy and forgiveness and understanding, it registered deeply in my subconscious mind. She loved me enough to take the punishment with me. It was, I believe, Christlike mercy and understanding. He was compassionate enough to identify with us, to suffer with and for us. My aunt probably never knew it, but that's what she was doing.

My great-grandfather I remember as a crusty, unconventional and completely lovable old rebel who went his own way and stood on his own feet—no matter what. When his eyesight began to fail, he refused to be driven to prayer meetings on Wednesday nights and went it alone down the middle of the village street with his trusty cane. People laughed at him and loved him. I remember that he used to reach out with that cane and hook me around the neck. I didn't like it, but inside I had to smile with him. I'm sure that I inherited a lot of my love of fun from him, and I *know* that his non-conformity rubbed off on me—generously. Even when he was wrong, there was something delightful about his refusal to conform, or to do whatever everybody else did and expected him to do. Once, on the tracks near the railroad station, for some reason known only to God and to him, he paused right in the middle of the track in front of a train about to pull out of the station. The brakeman walked up to him and asked him please to get off the track; he refused to budge until his good friend the stationmaster came out and somehow moved him out of the way. He might have been arrested, but I think that even the threat of that would not have made him change his mind, or his ways.

I idolized my Grandfather Wood. We spent every Christmas and part of every summer with him in Uvalde, and from the start there was between us that rare spark of understanding and affection that adds such richness to life. He was old, but he never lost his youthfulness or his love for children and young

19

people. Days after my birth when he looked at me in my crib, he said, "She will die hard, with her head up!" That was prophetic, but he saw clearly. And he was right. Many the time adversity has struck at me and bowed my head, but from *somewhere* strength has always flowed into me to take it, and to bring the head up again.

My paternal grandparents lived in Centerville, Mississippi, in one of those big old rambling southern houses. Grandfather Smith owned a "mercantile" store in the town, in addition to a cotton plantation called Oleo. There were open Bibles in both grandparents' homes, well-worn and always open. Family prayers were as regular as the meals on the table. How grateful I am for that! And how I pity the child who doesn't have it! There's no telling how far I would have fallen, later, without this undergirding of Christian love and teaching. (Children, I think, *must* have this religious training while they are yet children because if they don't get it then, they may never get it at all; the chances are that they will not search for it at all until they get in a very bad way, and by that time it may be too late.) "Remember . . . thy creator in the days of thy youth . . ." (Ecclesiastes 12:1). As the twig is bent, so grows the tree.

My father grew up in the old home in Centerville, along with four sisters and two brothers, under a strict discipline mixed with a great amount of love. That love rubbed off from him upon everyone he knew, and it was especially strong in his family circle. His mother's (my Grandmother Smith's) health was poor when he was born, and he was nursed through infancy and into childhood by a wonderful black mammy whose parents and grandparents had been slaves on the Smith plantation. When slavery was abolished, she chose to stay with the family that her parents had served and loved—and who had been loved in return. I think my father loved Aunt Lethie almost as much as he loved his own mother. After his marriage to my mother he would go back to the old home in Mississippi for an oc-

20

casional visit, and he always brought a hug and a present for Aunt Lethie. I remember the house as being full of fun and laughter and literally jumping with family, friends and neighbors. My father loved to dance—and dance he did, though it was forbidden by his (Baptist) church and family. (*Another* nonconformist!) His family was not rich, but it was what people then called "well off"—which probably meant comfortable. He was educated in (Baptist) Hillman College. (When he was born he was named Hillman for the founder of that college.)

My mother's family was Baptist, too, but something slipped somewhere, and she was graduated from Texas Presbyterian College. Her father loved music and always wanted a musician in the family, so she and her sisters were forced to study piano all through grammar, high school and college. That isn't a good way to produce a good musician, or a good anything else! Today she can hardly play a C scale, and hardly ever goes near a piano. Whatever musical talent she may have had was forced out of her. I have often heard her say, "If I was given a talent, I never found it—unless it was for washing dishes." But she *did* have a talent—the superb talent of being a good wife and mother. There was and is a great music in my mother, and it has been expressed in her ability to "train up a child in the way he should go" (Proverbs 22:6). It was a talent, almost instinctive, to instill in her children a strong sense of right and wrong and a desire to do what was right. God gave her that talent, and she has used it well.

I rebelled and drifted often from my moorings across the next twenty-five years, but that did not make her discipline wrong; nor did it diminish her love for her strong-headed little rebel, no matter what I did nor where I went. In all those turbulent, floundering years her example was always before me and her influence strong within me, no matter how much I tried to rationalize and to justify what I knew was wrong. Mother

21

often remarked, "Frances is too impulsive; she means well, but she rushes into things before she thinks them through."

She knew me like a book—and still does. I am thankful that she does, just as I am thankful that the Lord "knoweth our frame; he remembereth that we are dust" (Psalm 103:14); and that He is always there waiting for His rebellious child to accept His mercy and forgiveness and come home. She loved me and stayed with me, regardless of my waywardness—suffering with me in my self-imposed dilemmas—keeping the faith that some day I would come to myself and back to Him. Had she lost her faith in God and in me . . . I can't even bear the thought of what might have happened to me. (This is why I go up and down the land "witnessing." I urge Christians, young and old, to be faithful to God, persevering in prayer in behalf of those they love—never despairing, never doubting that God, like a good parent, is willing and able to do abundantly more than we ask.)

When I was seven we moved to Arkansas. Father's brother had a farm in Arkansas, where they raised long staple cotton for a ready and lucrative market. He wrote, urging Dad to "come over into Macedonia" (Acts 16:9), and help work the farm and enjoy the sure-fire profits of what looked like an unusually good year. Dad was one of those men who always thought the grass was greener somewhere else, so he turned the farm in Texas back to my grandfather, sold the hardware business, and off we went to Arkansas.

It wasn't a good year. It was a year of unusually long and flooding rains, boll weevils and the worst crop ever. We lost everything, but I am still thankful for the year we lived in that small frame house; it was good experience. It was primitive, but the smell of the good earth was wonderfully pungent, and there was a big vegetable garden and plenty of fresh milk and butter—and there were playmates. Near us lived a family of tenant sharecroppers—a black family with two children near my age. We had great fun together, playing cowboys 'n Indians, and hide-and-seek, and building castles in the air. There was one firm rule laid down by our parents that we never disobeyed: we could play together outside all we wished, but that was it, and all of it. They never came into our house, and we never went into theirs; when company came we separated and shut the doors of our respective homes. We children never discussed this; we knew that it was expected of us, and we accepted it; but it was hard for me to understand why we were so different at times like these, and so much alike playing in God's out-of-doors. I finally said that it was unfair to have to separate just because company came. Dad told me, "Hush! When you're older, you will understand." I still don't!

It rained, and it rained, and it rained. The roads were impossible, knee-deep in mud and slippery even for a car with chains, so we were seldom on the road. We had no electricity in that house—only oil lamps and an oil burner for heat. My brother and I had a few toys—very few, but enough to enjoy them. I am glad for that—glad that we didn't have so many toys that we wouldn't really enjoy any of them. I found fun in simple things; my greatest kick came when I pulled a few mustard greens from the garden and cooked them on my toy iron stove. The stove smoked furiously, but the aroma was heavenly!

One dark morning a man drove up to our house and slid into the muddy front yard in a horse-drawn buggy. He handed my mother a telegram which told her that my grandmother, "Mama Wood," was critically ill in a San Antonio hospital. We left the following day. How well I remember walking into that hospital room—I was only seven—and seeing my beloved grandmother lying there close to death. She was so pale! Her lovely iron-gray hair was piled atop her head, and she wore an expression of perfect peace and submission to whatever her Lord had in store for her. It was so clear: *she was not afraid.* She knew that she was to be on the operating table early the next morning; she didn't know that the surgeon was fearful that she couldn't survive the long operation to remove unbelievably large gallstones, and that he was afraid that peritonitis had already set in. I doubt that she would have been afraid, even if she had known. Like the Apostle Paul, she had learned to be content in whatever state she found herself.

She smiled, and asked me to rub her aching arms. As I rubbed, the nearness of her and the faith that was within her filled me with a strange new feeling of love and peace that I did not understand at the time. There were huge beads of perspiration on her serene forehead. Young as I was, I sensed that she was in pain.

My brother and I were taken to the family home in Uvalde, where we were to wait until the operation was over, and Mama Wood could come home again. Waiting there was almost as bad as it would have been in the hospital, for the shadow of death was over the place. The family talked in hushed voices of Mama and her love and her life—about how she looked up from the stretcher on which they had carried her out of the house and said with a smile, "Whatever the Lord wants, I am ready for it"; of how she had said, at the door, "Take care of my baby." Her baby was fourteen years old—my youngest aunt. She worried about that at the gates of death; I think she knew she would never come home to Uvalde. She didn't. The operation came too late, and she died two days later.

They brought her back to lie in beautiful peace in the parlor of the old Texas home. She was beautiful—so beautiful that I could not keep my eyes from her face; my mother had real difficulty keeping me from just standing beside the casket and staring at her. I can still see her today, fifty years later, sleeping so quietly, smiling faintly, in a white crepe-de-chine-and-lace dress with a wide pink satin sash and with a look of utter serenity on her face. Somewhere, recently, I read in a book or

24

a magazine, "The two most beautiful things in life are to be seen at the extremes of life: the laughter of a child and the look of peace on the face of one who has just died in faith." That look was on her face; it was the product of long years of love. She had known the travail and trouble of a mother with seven girls and one boy, but with it all she brought them up in faith and she left her faith in their hearts. She was never demonstrative with them in her affection; it was subtle, but tremendously real and powerful. One day Grandfather said to her, "Mama, I hardly ever see you hugging and kissing the children." She said quietly, "Never mind that, Papa. Still waters run deep." The spiritual "deep" in her called unto the deep in her children; it called out the best in them—and in me.

This was my first brush with death, and it was beautiful— so beautiful that it gave me a strength to face far-distant encounters with death, of which, then, I knew nothing.

We went back to Arkansas, and life began again. I got to know my cousins better after this, and spent more time with them in their big two-story house. We wrestled with each other and chased each other up and down the great stairway in the front hall. We had a lot of fun with Liney, their boisterous, rollicking and very religious cook. Liney could neither read nor write, but the Christian faith that was in her put many a "superior" white adult and child to shame. I can still hear her singing hymns and rattling pans in the kitchen. Her favorite was my cousin Quentin, who used to read the Bible to her every day. In the evenings he would sit at the side of her bed and read the Scriptures to her, and she would nod her head and cry yes! in assent to the great truths of the Book. Many years later, after her chicks had left the house, she was found dead on her knees beside the bed; apparently she had died in prayer. What a way to go! She had a great, direct, influence on Quentin, as he grew to the status of manhood, and I know now that— indirectly—she had influence on all of us. I think of her whenever I hear someone say or sing, "No man is an island. . . ." We are *all* a part of each other and of God; every move we make has its influence, for good or ill.

Soon my brother and I were enrolled in school; our first-grade teacher was Miss Blanche, who was held in high respect by her small charges. She loved us, and she demanded—and received—implicit obedience. She won our love, and the love and cooperation of our parents. How different it is today, when the kids have so little respect for the teacher, and when so many parents defend the misbehaving child against the correction of the teacher! I wonder sometimes how such a situation ever got going!

Miss Blanche had a paddle, and she *used* it. We eyed her weapon with awe. We knew what to expect when we sassed Miss Blanche, or showed her any discourtesy. What's wrong with that, anyway? Have you ever watched an old mother bear cuff her cubs? She does it in the interests of survival; she knows that if she doesn't teach them the rules of bear life, they will *die*. The same thing goes for *our* cubs! I'm for a limited, careful, merciful use of the paddle. We've spared the paddle too much, and the result is that we have reared a generation of hard-boiled, insolent youngsters who, never having known the paddle, do not hesitate to use a gun or a Molotov cocktail to get what they think they want. Today we reap the whirlwind of our lack of discipline, and we wonder why!

Miss Blanche's paddle looked—and sounded—worse than it was. Each day she lined up the little trespassers and applied the penalty; it was never severe; neither was it ever forgotten. According to their need, they got it, some one stroke, some two, some five, but never a hundredfold. None of us, so far as I can remember, ever experienced any emotional conflicts from it, but all of us refrained from telling our parents about what teacher had done to us; we knew too well that we'd get *another* going over from them if we did. Believe you me, we were care-

26

ful—and hesitant to sin in that classroom. Frances Smith was *very* careful, so she suffered few chastisements, but one day Frances stepped out of line, and was called for the lineup. Trembling in my Buster Browns, I stepped up to Miss Blanche and said in a trembling voice, "If you spank me, I'll get another spanking when I get home!" Mercy conquered justice in that good and wise teacher. She hid her laughter behind her hand and said, "All right, Frances; you deserve it, but I think you have suffered enough already," and she hung up the paddle. Heaven only knows how relieved I was that day—but today I think she did me no favor. She could have gone a little easier than usual, but she really should have spanked me. It might have helped me the next time I acted purely on impulse in getting out of line.

Since my parents had taught me my numbers and the alphabet before I entered the school, I skipped half of the first grade, all of the second, and went right into the third grade. I think that was wrong, too. Children are children for such a short time! We can skip too much, in human experience—skip too many valuable experiences. My mother felt the same way about it. She used to say that I was "born grown" (born more mature than most) since I always seemed to prefer the company of those who were older than I.

All in all, I loved school; I was a good student (which was good) and I knew it (which was bad). I also loved music, so I started taking piano lessons when I was eight years old. It went well for a time, until I began to get impatient with scales and with those everlasting exercises, and began to improvise and to play the way *I* wanted it! The little rebel on the piano stool produced improvisations that nearly drove her poor teacher out of her mind and finally, in anger and despair, she said bluntly that I was wasting her time and that my parents were wasting their money—and stalked out. It was too bad; Paderewski was getting old, and I might have succeeded him as the world's greatest pianist. As it turned out, I played thereafter only by ear, and only well enough to play simple hymns in Sunday school. So I turned to voice and I sang my first solo at a worship service in the church. It was "In the Garden" accompanied by the organist.

Friday nights I spent in the homes of my girl friends, or they spent the night in ours. Saturdays were given to straightening out dresser drawers and helping with the household chores. Sundays we went to Sunday school, to church services and the meetings of the Baptist Young Peoples' Union. There was an evangelistic service at 7:30 in the evening, and I was expected to be there, too. All this was not so much demanded as expected, and it never occurred to me to goof off on any of it until I reached my early teens. Then the usual generation gap became evident. (We talk of the generation gap as though it were something new. It isn't. It has *always* been there!)

Our church nearly disbanded while I was still going to BYPU; there was a marital scandal that tore the place apart. I was badly upset by it, and so were all the others; it took years to rebuild the faith and confidence of the whole membership. An almost desperate attempt was made to hush-hush the whole business; the older members just didn't want the young people —like me—to know anything about it (which of course was silly), lest they get the idea that there were anything but 100-percent-perfect Christians in the church. It's too bad that such scandals happen in such places; it's also too bad that we tend to put Christians on pedestals, and that we refuse to acknowledge that we *all* have feet of clay. That goes for the best of them. Of course it is no small thing for a Christian to fall into grievous sin, but it seems to me a greater sin to refuse to get up out of the ditch through repentance and confession and restitution. The rest of us must continue in faith in the presence of such sin and scandal and go on behaving like Christians. Too many Christians are fringe Christians, people-watchers instead of

28

Christ-watchers. We need to remember Christ's words about sinning in thought as well as in deed—and to remember that none of us can stand spotless. If more of that spirit had been present in that congregation at that time, it would not have been so traumatic—especially for me. It took a long time to get over it.

Church and school were quite close in those days; what we learned in one carried over into the other. Each school day, for instance, began with a short prayer. We had school chapel every Friday morning, to which different ministers from all the churches in town brought a short talk; we called it "the sermon." It was tremendously effective. There were children in that school whose parents never darkened the door of any church—but there were seeds planted in their children, those Friday mornings, that blossomed and flowered into fine Christian character in later days. I loved it; we all loved it. I still believe it was good, and I think it was a tragic mistake in American education to make any religious emphasis illegal in the schoolroom. How could we be so blind and apathetic as to permit one atheist to bar prayer from the schools? Our children need this God-given power in their lives, if they are to survive in today's jungle of desperate, vicious, dog-eat-dog existence.

If this sounds harsh, let's face it: we are living in times when every decent anchor we have known on the sea of life is being cut loose or thrown overboard, leaving us helplessly adrift. Is it any wonder that we have so much tragedy in the lives of our confused youngsters? The basic needs of these youngsters have not changed. The same situations have occurred in generation after generation—only to different people. Young people have always been self-centered; they have always thought that *their* generation was the only one to experience the growing pains of maturity. They are always surprised to discover that their parents *do* understand their problems. This is one reason why I have faith in this generation. In spite of us, in spite of themselves, they will mature into adults able to cope with their world—*if* we parents and grandparents do everything we can to preserve human freedom and the right to worship the eternal God Who guaranteed this right and freedom in His Word, the Holy Bible.

When I was ten, an itinerant evangelist came to town and our church had a revival. Again I heard the old, old story of Jesus and His love—but this time it was presented in such a dramatic and straightforward way that it really shook me up. That evangelist opened the gates of hell and I had a good look at it; I was so thoroughly frightened at the prospect of spending eternity in such a miserable and terrifying place that I reached out desperately for the hand of the Saviour. I *reached*, but I did not *dedicate*. I reached, in fear, but I was not really ready to hand over control of my life to Him. I was like a child who cannot swim but who wants to learn in the ocean all by himself: he asks his father, an experienced swimmer, to stand on the shore and, if the waves overpower him, to jump in and save him. I thought I'd like to have God nearby, if I got into trouble, but . . . ! I made my way down the aisle of the church and stretched out my hand to Jesus Christ. In honest and complete truth, it was no soul-shaking experience; it was only a matter of laying hold upon eternal security. A few weeks later I was baptized by immersion, and then I felt that I really had it made. Not for years did it occur to me that what I had done was not enough—that in addition to this faith in Christ to save me from peril and even from death, I had to turn over my whole life to Him—to be used as He saw fit.

Furthermore, being gregarious, aggressive and self-assertive, and with a consuming zest for colorful adventure, I still had the notion that God might hold me back from something I wanted to do on my own. With such an attitude, my spiritual life hardly got off the ground, in spite of my march down the

30

aisle! True, I read my Sunday school lessons and the BYPU materials, but that was about it—about *all* of it. I never thought of really seeking the Lord, and more often than not I would fall asleep at night repeating the Lord's Prayer with no thought at all of really talking with Him about the questions that bothered me and about the guilty feeling I had about my questionable thoughts and behavior. I just didn't give myself a chance to know the One who cared most about me and my future.

At eleven, I discovered that I had nerves. Because of overwork in school due to my skipping the seventh grade and participating in too many extra-curricular activities, I had a nervous breakdown, plus a spot on a lung. I spent the whole summer vacation in bed. I had tried to do more than my physical body could take, and I had to pay the piper in enforced idleness.

As an adolescent, boys had fascinated me, as they fascinate most adolescent girls. My family often laughed at my performances with the boys, and that stung me; I was oversensitive to ridicule of any sort, and I wanted to grow up quickly. I was *sure* I was old enough to do what I was doing. My parents tried to stem this feeling, so that I could enjoy my childhood as long as possible, and I resented that and began to strain at the leash. There were public dances at the courthouse attended by "everybody in town," and I cajoled my mother into accompanying me to those dances as one of the mother-chaperons for younger girls who were too young to date. I loved dancing, though it was frowned upon by our church, so I went to the courthouse hops, and before long I was dancing every dance. Here I met my first steady—a boy from a neighboring town.

He was quite handsome, and in his late teens. I was fourteen. We went everywhere together—to the dances, to parties, everywhere. Poor Mother couldn't stop it, even when she realized that it was getting out of hand. She forbade me to see him—but I still saw him. Had I really known what the honor-thy-father-and-thy-mother commandment meant, I would have stopped; as

31

it was, rebellion flared inside me and I met the boy secretly at the homes of friends. Came the night when I was supposed to be at a play rehearsal and spending the night with a girl friend—we eloped. He had obtained a marriage license that afternoon in the Gretna Green of our area, lying about his age and mine. We drove to his town, were married in the home of a minister and sped away across the line into Tennessee to his mother's home, where we spent the weekend.

I knew that my parents would be frantic, and I was conscience-stricken at the heartbreak I had caused them. I called my mother long-distance, and told her I was married. Never will I forget the awful, throbbing silence that followed, but it didn't last long. She forgave me and asked us to come home. We went home the next day; he went to work for his father, and we moved in with his father and stepmother.

My mother pleaded with me to go back to high school, since I was in the junior class and would graduate in another year. I refused. All I wanted, then, was to be a good wife and to start a home of my own.

The marriage turned out to be a dismal failure—but God sent me a son who did not become a failure. My boy Tom was to become the shining light of my life. He seemed so much like the little boy Samuel, in the Bible—quiet, thoughtful, bright. When he was six months old his father announced that our marriage had been a mistake, that he was too young to be tied down with a wife and baby, and that he wanted a divorce. I loved him, and I pleaded with him to give our marriage a chance, but—no!

My blessed mother said she would help me raise the boy, and help me get on my feet as a provider. I knew that I would have to do most of it myself, so to prepare myself for a business career I enrolled in a business school. Because of my good grades in high school, the business school accepted me without a high school diploma—at the age of sixteen and a half.

My days were busy enough, but at night I was lonely and I wept a sea of tears before applying for a divorce a year later. The court awarded me complete custody of our son on grounds of desertion. I asked no support from Tom's father. My pride had been trampled in the dust, and I wanted nothing from him, nothing, ever again.

2

*W*e moved to Memphis, and that was good for me. It was a change of scene—new environment, new friends, new activities. I started attending church regularly now, singing in the choir and working in various church groups in the effort to forget. For the first time I read the Bible from cover to cover. I found much that I could not understand, but what I did understand I made a real effort to retain. I was still in my teens.

Mother looked out for Tom as though he were *her* child! Once she suggested that she adopt him legally, since I was still so young—and so busy. I couldn't bring myself to do that, even for my dear mother. Tom called her Mom and he called me Sassie; he still couldn't pronounce Frances.

My first job after business school was with a bus company in Memphis. I was there just three weeks when I was offered another job, as a secretary in an insurance firm. It was a good job, and I grabbed it, but I was more interested in show business than I was in the insurance business. I spent a great deal of time singing and accompanying myself on the piano. I also wanted to write short stories. I did write several—all flops. They all came back from the publishers accompanied by the dreaded rejection slip. It dawned on me that millions would never read me as they read O. Henry, so I tried song writing. This was easier. I wrote several that were just plain terrible, and then one that I thought was good enough to submit to a music publisher. I submitted it in person, sang it in the publisher's office

34

and was flattered by a vague promise that they would consider it. For several months I waited—while they considered; one day I was in a music store and I heard my tune, slightly altered, on a phonograph record bearing the name of another composer.

As I said, nothing was turning out right for me. As I look back at it now, I think of that great and profound truth in Francis Thompson's poem, *The Hound of Heaven:* "All things betrayeth thee who betrayest Me." It was really happening.

One day I sat at my desk in the insurance office staring vaguely at an accident claim form in my typewriter. Actually I was trying to think up words to fit a tune I had just composed, when the boss walked in. He stood there looking at me for a moment, and then he exploded, "Young lady, I think you are in the wrong business!" My fingers flew to the keyboard and I typed like a maniac. He walked away, turned, came back to me, and said, "How would you like to sing on a radio program?" The heavens opened! Bells rang and trumpets sounded! *Would* I? He asked me if I could accompany myself on the piano; if I could, he might just get me on as a guest on a radio program in which he had a sponsor's interest.

The next Friday night Frances Fox made her radio debut, playing and singing "Mighty Lak a Rose." In those days you were permitted to dedicate your song to anyone you chose, and so my first dedication—the first of many to come—was to my son Tommy. Someone must have liked it for they offered me a regular spot at the radio station.

I held onto the secretarial job; radio offered only experience but with no pay. How I loved it! Civic organizations in town began inviting me to sing at luncheons and banquets. Once in a while I got paid for these appearances in real money (as much as twenty dollars); mostly I was paid in chicken croquettes and peas. The experience was good. I learned to meet and face the public, and within a few months' time I had moved up from

35

that first small radio station to the most powerful one in Memphis.

When the big dance bands came to town I would go with an escort to hear them, and sometimes I would be asked to sing a number with the orchestra, using a big, old-fashioned megaphone. My name began to get up there in popular demand. I reasoned that if I could crack Memphis, I could crack Chicago, and off I rushed to subdue the Windy City.

I didn't crack Chicago; it cracked me. After a few short years I wound up with a case of severe anemia due to overwork as a secretary. Nothing worked—no matter how hard I tried. I just couldn't make the grade. Finally, with my money gone and my health broken, I wired my folks for money enough to get home. My parents had moved back to Texas and were living on a farm. We were a miserable pair, Tommy and I, as we rode the train back to Texas. After two weeks in the hospital and much intake of liver and iron, I was released for three months' rest on the farm.

In the fall of that same year I landed a job in Louisville, Kentucky—my first job with really good pay. The program director at Station WHAS there gave me my professional name, Dale Evans, when I joined the staff. It was designed primarily for the ease of announcers (it rolls off the tongue easily), and is almost impossible to mispronounce or misspell. (And, I might add, it stuck!)

Tommy went with me, just as he had gone with me to Chicago, but he didn't stay. I came home from work one day and the lady who was caring for him told me that he had been vomiting all day, and that he had severe pains in his legs and arms. I was nearly frantic with fear; there was an epidemic of infantile paralysis raging in Kentucky. In agony I prayed when they took Tommy to the hospital for a spinal tap. I promised God, tearfully, that I would put Him first in my life if Tom's test proved to be negative. It was negative, and for a few weeks

36

I prayed and read my Bible every day, but . . . my musical ambition was too strong—stronger than my spiritual devotion, and strong enough to make me forget my promise to God. Back to Texas and the farm we went, beaten again!

My boy loved that farm, and the small community life surrounding it. The first day there he chased the poor hens all over the place, until both he and the chickens dropped from sheer exhaustion. His cheeks bloomed with health, and for the first time I was secure in the knowledge that he was safe and happy.

But I still had to find work—somewhere. I couldn't let my parents do it all. I found a job singing on the staff of Station WFAA, in Dallas, on the Early Bird program; I also found a husband. One day in Dallas I had a long-distance call from a pianist and orchestral arranger with whom I had worked in Louisville. We had dated frequently there, but when we said good-by I never expected to see him again. He said he was on his way to make a fortune in California and intended to stop over in Dallas. If he could find work there, he might stay awhile before going on to the Coast. He was offered a job playing piano and arranging for the staff band at WFAA in Dallas, and our dates began and multiplied. A year later we were married.

Two years later I found myself back in Chicago with my musician husband. ("She'll die hard, with her head up!") My dreams *did* die hard.

I registered with several booking agencies in Chicago, and auditioned like mad. One audition finally paid off: I was engaged as a jazz singer with an orchestra at the Edgewater Beach Hotel. It was a step up, but not too pleasant a step. Another girl did all the pretty ballads and got most of the applause; the Edgewater was a dignified ballroom, and jazz wasn't popular there. It was tough.

Anson Weeks' orchestra was playing at the Aragon Ballroom at the time, and he was looking for a female vocalist. I was

37

hired. For the next year I sang on the proverbial dance band one-nighters and hotel engagements, driving hundreds of miles from date to date. I finally left the band so that I could have Tom with me; he was now ready for junior high school. A job opened on the staff of WBBM (CBS network); I auditioned, and got it. At the same time I sang every night at the Blackstone, Sherman and Drake hotels, and I made it to the top spot—the then famous Chez Paree Supper Club. Things did seem to be picking up, at last.

I went to church regularly now with Tom; I wanted him to have what I would not take for myself—a solid relationship with the Lord. The minister was a bit disturbing. Every now and then he would say something about "the claims of Jesus Christ," and I would feel myself drawn toward the Cross. After the church services were over, I would rationalize again my feelings of guilt for not making a definite stand for Christ and for not following His commandments. I would reckon that the Lord might demand something that would cost more than I could pay—that He might ask something that would jeopardize my precious career. I wanted nothing that would deter me from making a name for myself in show business—from making a lot of money and being independent and in a position to guarantee a good future for Tom by way of college or in whatever he wanted to do. One part of me wanted to be married and a good housekeeper and mother, and the other part wanted to be an entertainer. It was like trying to ride two horses at once and not being able to control either one of them.

Suddenly, right out of the blue, I got a telegram from an agent in Hollywood who had heard me sing on a broadcast that reached California. I laughed long and loud when I read it. He asked for photographs of me. If he liked the photographs, he would arrange a screen test for me. Me! I had no desire whatever to go to Hollywood; I was aiming at musical comedy in New York, thank you, and besides, I did not think I was pretty enough to be in pictures. I wasn't an actress—and I was twenty-eight years old. So I ignored the telegrams which kept coming. Finally, I took them to my program director who said that I should give it a whirl. Still laughing and still not believing in it, I had the inevitable glamour photos taken, and sent the best of them to the agent, Mr. Rivkin, in Hollywood.

He wired me to take a plane immediately for a screen test at Paramount Studios. And I did.

My heart was pounding fast, as I boarded the sleeping plane for Hollywood. It was my first long flight. I had never crossed the country in a plane before, and I got an earache ten feet off the ground and suffered with it all night long. (In those days, there was no adjustable pressure system to compensate for high altitudes.) The stewardess dropped warm oil in my ears, but it didn't help much. I couldn't eat any breakfast because of nausea, and as the plane started descent for the landing in Burbank I wished with all my heart that I could have been anywhere but *there*. I wished I had never heard of any Hollywood agent, but I had to meet him. Lucky for me, I thought, that I can wear dark glasses to hide the ravages of the painful night. I looked out of my window and saw a man pacing up and down, looking nervously at the plane. This had to be the one. I'd read in a book that all agents were nervous.

I got down the steps to the ground somehow; I'll never know how. I walked over to him and quavered, "Are you Joe Rivkin?"

He stopped pacing, stood there with an incredulous look on his face, sized me up (and down) and he said, "My God! Are *you* Dale Evans?" I never felt so put down in my life!

I said, "Oh, Mr. Rivkin, I had a terrible night." He didn't seem to hear it. He kept staring, and suddenly he spoke again.

"Take off those glasses!"

I pulled them off as slowly as possible; he caught his breath, and turned pale. Finally he said, "Well, you don't look like your pictures!" I wanted to run back into the plane and take off for almost anywhere in the world but Hollywood. What a welcome!

I thought the worst of it was over as we piled into his car, baggage and all, and started down the road for Hollywood. Then looking down he saw the wedding ring on my finger, and howled: "You didn't tell me you were married."

"You didn't ask me."

Silence. A long, stabbing silence.

"How old are you?"

I had been told to say that I was twenty-two. I said that.

"No," he said. "You are twenty-one. Got it? And you are *single*. Understand?"

I understood, and I didn't like it. I didn't like the whole set-up. I didn't even answer him, but in my mind I had decided to go through the screen test, enjoy the vacation, see Hollywood and then get back to Chicago and resume my musical career. I was sure that nothing would develop from this venture in the flicks.

He drove like he wanted to get nowhere fast, and from time to time he looked me up and down and he seemed more disgusted every time he looked. I got the idea that he didn't like anything about me, but I held my chin up and pretended to be enjoying the scenery—which I wasn't.

"I don't like your lipstick. Don't wear it any more. I don't like your hair, either. We'll have to do something about it." Sure enough, when we reached the Hollywood Plaza Hotel he rushed me downstairs to the beauty salon, introduced me to an operator and said, "See what you can do with her. And step on it. We have to be at Paramount in an hour." I felt like a prize pig being groomed for exhibition at a small-town fair. I didn't care what might happen at Paramount. All I wanted was a little rest.

The operator gave me a stinging facial massage. ("Get a little blood in that face," Rivkin told her.) She tinted my light brown hair with auburn rinse, and sent me off to dress for a luncheon with a Mr. Meiklejohn, a casting director at Paramount. Now, for luncheon in Chicago, a dark dress with furs and gloves was the proper thing, so I put on a sheer dark dress, selected a fur (my *only* fur!), pulled on a pair of spotless white gloves and walked into the lobby with all the pride and confidence of Cleopatra on her barge. Rivkin saw me coming, and he put his hands over his eyes.

"Who's dead?" he asked, "your agent? What's the black dress for?" I could have popped him, then and there, but for once I kept control of my temper, and replied haughtily, à la Cleopatra, "In Chicago, sir, this is proper dress for a business meeting at noon."

"Well, you're not in Chicago now. You're in Hollywood, and in Hollywood you wear bright colors, with flowers—casual. But it's too late now. Come on!" By the time we reached the office of the casting director, I was shaking like a leaf, inside and outside.

Mr. Meiklejohn was gentle and kind as we smiled at each other and shook hands. He said, "Dale, you remind me a lot of my wife when she first came to Hollywood." I liked that, and I liked him. He took my arm and led me through the maze of people in the dining room; they all stopped eating and craned their necks to see "the new one." I wished the floor would open and swallow me up—away from those eyes. At the table, I felt like a tennis ball in a very fast game.

"Dale," Mr. Meiklejohn asked, "how old are you?"

"Twenty-one," shouted Joe Rivkin. The director looked long and hard at my face, and then he said, "I'm a little worried about the nose. A trifle too long for the chin." I felt like saying that the good Lord had given me the nose, and if he didn't mind, I'd keep it, but I never had the chance to say anything. Rivkin beat me to it with, "Don't worry about the nose; we'll have some of it taken off."

Mr. Meiklejohn: "Dale, do you dance?"

41

Mr. Rivkin: "Dance? She makes Eleanor Powell look like a bum!"

Miss Evans: "No, I can't dance, Mr. Meiklejohn. I can't even do a time step." I explained that I had turned down a chance at a part in the stage musical, "Hold Onto Your Hats" because I was not a professional dancer. I could do ballroom well enough, but not solo.

Bill Meiklejohn almost blew his top when he heard that. He looked at Joe Rivkin with an icy stare that would have frozen a polar bear into silence, reminded him in a few well-chosen words that his ancestry was in doubt and that he was suspicious of the whole deal. But Joe wasn't frozen; he promised quickly and glibly that I could pick up the dancing in no time at all.

The director turned to me and explained that I had been summoned for a screen test with an eye to the ingenue lead in the picture *Holiday Inn,* starring Bing Crosby and Fred Astaire. They were looking for a new (female) personality for the picture, but since I could not dance, they would make the screen test anyway, and perhaps something might come of it. Whereupon the luncheon ended and I was taken to the wardrobe department and introduced to Miss Edith Head, who fitted me out with a dress and a fur muff formerly worn by Barbara Stanwyck. Then the dramatic coach took me under his wing. He picked a scene from Marlene Dietrich's picture, *Blue Angel,* and told me that MacDonald Carey was to play opposite me.

I worked hard all that week and the next. Joe Rivkin watched me like a hawk watching a chicken; he saw to it that I did not stay out late and that I had plenty of time to study my part in the test. He also told me what I could and could not eat, in the interests of reducing my weight. I was getting more and more nervous about the whole business—particularly about the deception with my age, and about the fact that I had a son.

The day of the screen test I was carefully made up and gowned, and taken to the set by my agent. As I sat there waiting for

42

the crew to get the lights set up, a sense of doubt and shame swept over me. Basically I was completely honest about it all, but I hated any form of deception, and I knew that all this was not on the up-and-up. I felt as though I would blow up under the tension. I got up and walked over to Joe Rivkin and told him that I must talk to him, alone and *right now,* before things went further. We walked out into the alley behind the studio; I turned and faced him like a cornered criminal and I said, "Mr. Rivkin, I have not been completely honest with you, and I can't go on with this thing until you know the facts. I am not twenty-one; I am twenty-eight. I have a son who is twelve years old. He lives with me."

His jaw dropped as though he had been clobbered with a meat-ax. He paced up and down muttering, "Let me think, let me think." Suddenly he had the solution:

"You will have to send him away to school."

That seemed to make it worse than ever. I refused, saying that if Tom could not come to Hollywood with me, we would stay in Chicago. I could make a good living in Chicago, and my husband, who was well-placed in Chicago radio, would add to my security. Biting his nails, Rivkin tried another tack.

"Tom is your brother. Do you understand?"

I still didn't like it, but at least it gave me the chance to have Tom with me in Hollywood and that was something. So I said, "All right. It's all right with me if it's all right with Tom." It was all right with Tom. (He commented, "It sounds pretty silly, but you can do anything you want, Mother, as long as I myself don't have to lie.") I figured that with what I could make on a good Hollywood job I could send him to college and give him the musical education he so desperately wanted. Besides, my husband wanted to come to Hollywood to compose, orchestrate and score films, and that would be all to the good.

Rivkin reckoned that it would all work out—*if* I would just keep my mouth shut about having a husband and a child. In

43

my heart I knew it was wrong, but again I rationalized. Nothing would come of the screen test, anyway, so why worry?

I took the test, and flew home to Chicago to wait it out. Actually, I was still hankering for a place in a New York stage show, so I didn't worry too much. I had almost put Hollywood out of my mind when I got a call from Mr. Rivkin, who told me (excitedly) that while Paramount had not taken up their option on me, Twentieth Century Fox had bought me at a salary of four hundred dollars per week on a one-year contract.

It looked like a lot of money, after all our lean years. We (the whole family) talked it over and over and over, and decided that we should give it a whirl. I packed.

3

*M*other, Tom and I flew to Los Angeles, leaving my husband behind to work out his contract with the NBC studios in Chicago. He and his parents, who were living with us at the time, followed us a month later. We rented a house in West Los Angeles. I put on my best bib and tucker and checked in at Twentieth Century Fox for work. I was told to get ready for another screen test. Actually, *they* got me ready.

I was sent to a dentist to have my teeth capped and levelled; I was hustled off to a health club to get rid of some weight. I was pummeled, pounded, massaged, steamed and exercised until the scales reported that I had lost twelve pounds, which seemed to satisfy them—at least for the moment. Then they produced the dramatic coach of the studios—Tom Moore of the old silent film era, and a most kindly man. For the test he chose a reading of selections from *The Hound of Heaven,* by Francis Thompson. I wondered why. He said there was a spiritual quality in my face, and he wanted to project that in the test. He must have been a very perceptive and sensitive soul—a lot more perceptive and sensitive than I was. I wasn't even dimly aware of any such quality either in my face or in my heart, and no one else I had ever known had noticed it, so far as I knew. How ironic that he should choose that masterpiece! I could barely understand who the Hound of Heaven was, much less read it with any depth of feeling. Years later, after I had found God and Christ, someone sent me a copy of *The Hound of Heaven,* and this time I understood it perfectly. I saw that it

45

told my own story of running and hiding from the Hound (God) over eighteen years of sunshine and shadow, toil and pleasure, success and defeat, trying hard to get out of my ears and out of my life the sound of those steady, strong, haunting feet that followed me everywhere.

The studio announced that I would be starred in a college musical entitled *Campus in the Clouds,* and I was really on top of cloud nine. On my way at last! But I was tumbled off the cloud the day the Japanese bombed Pearl Harbor, and World War II began. The picture was shelved, and I found myself twiddling my thumbs, waiting for the next break. I started dramatic lessons with a famous British coach named Flossie Friedman. The first time she heard me read, she stared at me as though I were a visitor from Mars, and she said, "Oh, darling! You must be kidding with that accent. I'm afraid we shall never be able to kill it!" Right she was. I still have that strong Texas tone and inflection, and I think I'll die with it. But Flossie tried, and she did help, a little.

Family affairs were getting complicated, too. Tom was in junior high school, and he was developing into a very wise, Christian and considerate boy. Whenever there was any movie publicity work going on around the house he just disappeared, quietly and completely. He knew that the deception I was practicing in passing him off as my brother was hard for me to bear and to continue. He told me again that he could never lie as I was lying, even for his own mother. He couldn't, he said, because he was a Christian, and Christians don't lie. That stung me, but my ambition was strong enough to smother the lie and the guilt, and I told myself that I was doing it for him, for his future. I loved him; I was proud of his natural musical ability, of his peace and serenity.

I was beginning to be acutely aware of a deep void and emptiness in my life; nothing satisfied, nothing gave me any sense of security. I began to read books on peace of mind, eastern

46

philosophy and mysticism, looking for an escape hatch from a life that I knew was wrong. Talk about inner chaos!

I attended church every Sunday with my husband, his parents and Tom, but I didn't let it do very much for me or to me. I left my faith on the church steps after the service until the next Sunday. I kidded myself into thinking that God would understand why I couldn't go all the way with Him, and that some day, when I was really safe and secure and ready to retire with enough money, *then* I would give more time to Him and His work. (Get the money first, Dale; God can't blame you for wanting *that!*)

The minister of the church (First Baptist, in Hollywood) was Dr. Harold Proppe. He was an upsetter. He preached sermons that probed my heart. It seemed to me that he was throwing spiritual shoes at me and saying, "If they fit, put them on!" They did fit, sometimes so tightly that my toes ached. The old defenses would rise up in my heart and mind, and I would go away in a resentful pout, and the next Sunday morning I would find some excuse—any excuse—to stay home.

One Sunday he took a crack at those people who had God-given talents in music, and who refused to honor God's house by using them there, for God. I was furious; I just *knew* he had aimed that remark straight at me. I thought to myself, "Brother, if you only knew how demanding show business is, you wouldn't say that. I'm lucky to be here once a week!" Tom read my mind. After the service he looked at me in a searching, knowing way—and I knew that my son really had my number.

We were so busy, my husband and I, that we saw less and less of each other. At the studio I worked like a slave to get that four hundred dollars a week, and I did a lot of shows for the boys in the army camps; my husband went with me as often as he could, playing piano for my songs, and doing a lot of spot jobs necessary for his acceptance into the musician's union. That's the way it is in Hollywood. Schedules aren't arranged

47

for the convenience of man and wife and children; you go where you have to go and do what you have to do, and married bliss can wait. We were making money, but . . . .

All of a sudden Joe Rivkin went into the army and I was left on my own. It was a bad time for that to happen (my contract was up for renewal), and inasmuch as I had had only two small bit parts in pictures, I began to worry about it. Sure enough, one day I learned via the studio grapevine that the contract would not be renewed. In a fine frenzy I phoned Joe and told him that I was fed up with pictures and that I was going back to radio. Did he know of an agent who might help me in radio? He suggested a man named Art Rush.

Three days later, following an audition, Art took me to NBC for a tryout on "The Chase and Sanborn Hour," starring Edgar Bergen. I got it. I worked harder than hard, and things seemed to be OK until I turned down the invitation of a top executive to have dinner with him in New York. Such an invitation is usually accepted by the unwary beginner. I told him that I had a previous engagement with an old friend in the music publishing business—and the exec turned cold as ice.

I never meant to insult him, but he took it as a personal affront and days later he informed me that I would "never get anywhere in this business running around with musicians and music pluggers." He gave me another chance and another invitation to "lunch," but again I was unable to accept it. That did it. The following fall I found myself replaced after the fourth show with no hope of getting another commercially sponsored program for that season. (I tell this not to pat myself on the back for refusing to compromise my talent, but simply to say that I had too much pride in accomplishment to buy my way. I did not want to become obligated to anyone, in any way, to further my career. I had promised myself that I would never get trapped in such an involvement. I have always been infuriated with men who used their high position to acquire the

48

scalps of hapless and heedless women. This was one area where I stuck to my guns, and I have never regretted it.)

Just as I received my notice of release from the Chase and Sanborn program, Art Rush took off for New York; he had a date with his number one client, a fast-rising, singing cowboy named Roy Rogers. I had seen Roy only once, at Edwards Air Base, where he was appearing in a camp show with the Sons of the Pioneers. (I had done an audition with them in Chicago, two years earlier.) He seemed like a very nice guy—and certainly well liked by young and old.

I liked Art Rush both as an agent and as a person. I liked him a lot the day he told me that he had gone to Bethany College in West Virginia to prepare for the ministry, but halfway through he decided that he was not called for that and changed his course. That didn't dampen his faith or destroy the effects of an early Christian training in his home and his church. All through college and all through his later work in recording studios and on the radio networks, he never lost his love of God and the Bible. He talked a great deal about the Bible, and of how he was trying to apply its laws to his life and work. This impressed me deeply, and though I left him in a fit of irritation to go with another agent, we parted friends and I was really sorry to leave him.

(Agents take a beating, sometimes, but they are not as bad as they are painted. Looking back at the agents I have known, I think of them with real respect, and even affection. I think God must have had a hand in sending three of them—Joe Rivkin, Art Rush and Danny Winkler—my way. They gave me very sound advice about my career and my personal life, and I am forever grateful for that. Joe Rivkin said to me many, many times, "Work hard, go to bed early, keep yourself in good shape and don't get mixed up in your private life." How right he was! Art's inclination toward the spiritual life was a stabilizer I sorely needed. Danny Winkler guided me with a steady hand to a con-

49

tract with Republic Studios which was to mean much in my later life. God bless them all—all three!)

Actually, it was Roy Rogers who was responsible for my breakup with Art Rush. While I loved to discuss religion with Art, I just plain got fed up with his talk about that cowboy. He'd get going on Roy at the drop of a hat, and I resented it. Here I was because of the collapse of the Chase and Sanborn job, with my whole career in jeopardy, and here *he* was taking off for New York to gab with a star who already had it made! In no uncertain words I informed Mr. Rush that I'd had enough; inasmuch as he didn't seem to have time for both me and that cowboy, he could just take care of Roy Rogers and I'd take care of myself. I left him and signed with Danny Winkler, who got me a year's contract with Republic Studios. I started a picture for Republic two weeks later. It was a country musical called *Swing Your Partner,* with Lulu Belle and Scotty (of the "National Barn Dance" show) and Vera Vague from the "Bob Hope Show."

I must have been doing something right at Republic. They picked up my option at the end of the year and subsequently cast me in nine more pictures. I worked so hard that I met myself coming and going. ("Work hard, go to bed early. . . .") Near the end of the first year I took time off for a tour of the army and air bases in Texas, and with my accompanist, I worked myself into insensibility every twenty-four hours. I enjoyed it, and I think we brought a little sunshine into those soldier hearts. But today, I still flush with regret when I think of the opportunities I had to say or sing one line of spiritual hope for those boys. Since I had no spiritual awareness at the time, I couldn't share it with anyone else.

Things were going along beautifully when Herbert J. Yates, the boss at Republic, called me up to the front office. He had just returned from New York, where he had seen the musical hit *Oklahoma,* and he was planning to produce a new kind of

50

western with the *Oklahoma* treatment. I gasped when he told me that the picture would star—who else?—*Roy Rogers!* I hesitated, mumbling something about my ambition to get into a big sophisticated musical, and that I had never thought of myself doing Westerns. Still, my heart reminded me, I had loved Westerns ever since I was a kid in Texas—had *always* loved cow-pokes and horses, as a good Texan should—but my whole theatrical ambition had been on the musical comedy side. I wasn't sure.

Mr. Yates *was* sure. I was a singer, *wasn't* I? I had a definitely western (Texas) personality, *didn't* I? And, being a Texan, I could ride a horse, *couldn't* I? (I didn't tell him that I hadn't been on a horse since I was seven years old!) I just kept my mouth shut about *that,* and I did the picture. It was called *The Cowboy and the Senorita.* Art Rush's pet, Roy Rogers, was the cowboy, and I was a Mexican girl named Isabel Martinez. Joe Kane, the director, said I sounded like "Si, si, you-all!"

The first day on location was a riot—half fun and half plain misery. When I got ready to ride, I didn't even know which side of the horse to get on, and I had to be shown how to hold the reins. Roy Rogers looked at me in amazement, and his eyebrows climbed a few notches. He said, "I thought you could ride."

I said, "Well, it's been a long time since Texas."

On that set almost immediately, I *liked* Roy Rogers, in spite of all that had gone before. He was no phony Hollywood character; he was honestly down to earth, as comfortable to have around as an old shoe. He had dared to be himself, and his star was rising rapidly. I enjoyed working with him.

It wasn't easy. One day I had to come riding at a canter down a steep slope. How I stayed on that horse, I'll never know! I bounced around so hard that the temporary caps on my teeth flew off. What was worse, the horse *stepped* on them! I had the time of my life stopping the horse, and when I did Roy came ambling over to me and drawled, "Well, I never saw so much sky between a woman and a horse in all my born days." He then *allowed* that I should take some riding lessons—if I wanted to stay alive. I knew he was right; he knew a lot about riding. He sits a horse like he is glued to the saddle. I tell him that it's his Choctaw Indian blood that accounts for it, but it's probably because he learned to ride the simple but best way—bareback—on his boyhood farm in Ohio. To this day, I get a thrill every time he rides out into a rodeo arena.

Between shots on location Roy and I talked a lot. Slowly but surely he got into my heart. He told me one day about a writer on a movie magazine who asked him why he had adopted a little orphaned girl as his first child, and he told me what he had told the interviewer. He had been visiting and entertaining in an orphanage in Louisville, Kentucky, with Pat Brady and the Sons of the Pioneers. A little girl there "got hold of me and just wouldn't let me go." From the minute she saw him, this little tot, with her dark hair and deep blue eyes, grabbed hold of his pant's leg and hung on. She followed him all over the place, tugging at him until he picked her up. When he had to leave she burst into tears and held out her arms to him. For months afterward, he couldn't get her out of his mind.

Some time later he was appearing with the Sons of the Pioneers at the Centennial in Dallas. (I was appearing there at the same time, but we never saw each other!) He asked a friend, Bob O'Donnell, where he might find a little girl to adopt. Roy and his wife had just about given up hope of having a baby of their own after three years of marriage. Bob O'Donnell told him about Hope Cottage, an orphanage full of adoptable babies.

Roy told the rest of it almost wistfully, with a low-voiced intensity that reached my heart: "My wife and her mother and I came back to Dallas a few months later and we went out to look over the babies. When we had looked at a few, I stopped by a bed, looked down and saw my little girl! I knew instantly

52

she was the one for us. We named her Cheryl Darlene, and she is really something."

Kids! He loved kids. I think that was the first real spark that flashed between us, the first bond of common interest. All my life I had wanted kids, a lot of kids. As a child in Uvalde, Texas, I used to sit on the bank of the Nueces River and dream that some day I would marry Tom Mix and have six children. Every Saturday afternoon in Osceola, Arkansas, I watched old Tom and his horse and all but worshipped them. As it turned out, I came pretty close to my dream, didn't I?

He also impressed me with his lack of egotism. He never thought he could act; he didn't even think of himself as any great shakes as a singer—and he was really good at that. From the first, I felt that he had a great native talent that somebody ought to discover, and give him the break he deserved. Roy was always himself, on the screen or off; he was "The King of the Cowboys" to a tremendous audience, and that audience loved him. He was also the boy next door, a breath of clean country air, a handsome, two-fisted man sitting easy in his saddle. And he was always interested in children—particularly sick and handicapped children. My eyes would fill up when I would see him climb down from the saddle to put his hand on the head of some little crippled kid. There was no show about it; he meant it. Like everybody else who worked with him, I fell under his spell. This one was no Hollywood ham; he wore no movie facade. I liked that—and I liked the man.

I was sitting on a particularly frisky (and downright mean) horse one day on location, dressed to the teeth in city clothes and wearing high heels. Roy had warned me to watch the horse, and to watch those heels—if they ever got caught in a stirrup as I was getting aboard or getting off, I could be dragged to death. I listened, but it didn't register too well. I was thinking of other things as I sat up there listening to the wonderful Gabby Hayes read some funny offstage dialogue and twisting that wrinkled old face of his in contortions that made me roar with laughter. In my amusement, I threw my head and my body backwards, and the horse thought it was a signal to go. He bolted; I slipped from the saddle (on which I was sitting sideways); one of my heels caught in the stirrup, and I grabbed the saddlehorn hanging on for dear life. Gabby yelled, "Grab her, Roy!" Roy reached me on Trigger just as I was losing my grip on the saddlehorn and picked me up like you would pick up a sack of potatoes. Hero saves heroine! I could have been killed. I more than liked him, right then.

In those days I was an extrovert on the outside and an insecure introvert on the inside. I was as uncertain about my work and my future as Roy was, but we both kept quiet about it. He helped me to hide it with his irrepressible good humor; he could drawl a wisecrack in the face of disaster. We were doing a "two-shot" one day, standing close to each other. The producer had told me, "Always show your best face," which meant showing it at a three-quarter angle. I turned my face from Roy and jabbered away at a tree a hundred yards behind him! The producer shouted, "For the love of Mike! You're supposed to be talking to each other, not to some tree a mile away!" Roy said, "When she looks at me, I'll look at her." It almost broke up the party—and it fixed me good. From then on the public got my straight profile—good or bad.

Like I said, Roy's blunt and honest—and *helpful*. He went out of his way to help me in everything I did, and heaven knows I needed help right then. He showed me how to "take the action," in riding a horse, in my knees and forelegs, and how to lean back when I was pulling my horse to a stop. That was really helpful, for while he had Trigger, a wonderful and well-trained horse to ride, I drew horses with the disposition of a convict breaking out of jail. I always seemed to get what the cowhands call cold-jawed critters—horses who always have to be held on a tight rein. That's one of the reasons why today I seldom show

54

my upper arms in a formal gown: my biceps developed like a professional wrestler's, and no pounding or massaging has been able to knock them down! It was easy enough for Roy with Trigger; he was a natural there, but with me it was strictly a case of blood, sweat and tears. After thirty-odd films with him, I can hold my own with a horse. I'm no Annie Oakley, but I can get by. Roy compliments me, now and then, with something like, "Well, at least you don't look like a sack of meal in the saddle!" I hate to think what I might have looked like in those first films if it hadn't been for him.

We were a studio family: Roy, Gabby Hayes, Pat Brady, the Sons of the Pioneers and me. We spent most of our waking hours together. We saw the best and the worst in each other. Roy was the acknowledged head of the family, and I felt as easy with him as I did with anyone of my own flesh and blood. Little did I dream that one day in real life he *would* be the head of my family! Still, much as I liked him and the studio people, I kept telling myself that a woman could go just so far in Westerns, and that it was always the handsome cowboy who held the spotlight, never the leading lady. I still longed for a non-Western musical—and a Broadway show.

Our first picture was an instant success and I was immediately cast with Roy in another one. The exhibitors said, "They're a good team; don't change it." Before I knew it, I had filmed eight more Westerns, and I began to see that I was being typed as a Western player. I asked to be cast in some other type of picture where I could star and not be just a part of a team, but Mr. Yates turned a cold shoulder. He said that I would be suspended if I refused to go along with the Westerns. Expenses were heavy, and I couldn't afford suspension, so I decided to stay in the saddle until Danny Winkler (my agent at the time) could spring me into a different kind of film or into a radio show. He did manage to get me on the Jimmy Durante radio show, and on another one with Jack Carson, the comedian.

I struggled—and hard—to improve my performance in every picture. After the shooting was over for the day, I would look at the rushes of the film shot the day before, studying every gesture, movement and expression, looking for mistakes and bad spots that could be improved. I still had a tendency to cheat a little in getting my three-quarter angle in scenes when my face showed, and if that face didn't look just right in the rushes, I'd worry myself sick all the way home. Then I'd go to sleep thinking about it instead of saying my prayers. I could hardly wait for the next day's shooting, when I could redeem myself. My ego grew to be as big as the Empire State Building. It was a monster. It is a monster to many in show business—and I pity them! This madness for personal success unbalances the whole of one's life, if one gives it free rein. It was doing that to me; I couldn't see it then, but now I know that I was sacrificing the most precious things in life—love, marriage, children—to satisfy that unrelenting drive to establish myself. It is one of the most pernicious of sins.

Let me say here and now that show business, in itself, is not sinful. To me it is a wonderful profession, in that it brings joy and often emotional release to those participating in it and to those who watch the finished product—the show. Just as the Bible says of money: it isn't the money itself that is bad but the inordinate, consuming love of it that is sinful. So it is with show business! It is the lust to get to the top, the passion to get to where the money is that is bad—evil. It is the exclusion of all the really good and decent values of life in the effort to get your hands on the prize that destroys so many of us.

Yes, there are a lot of people in show business who are caught—burned and consumed in this flame of greed—and there are a lot of others who are *not!* There are good ones and bad ones in every line of work—even in the Christian ministry. As Roy says, "When you send for a plumber you don't always get a good one."

As my career progressed, my marriage declined. My husband was a fine, talented man; he was the first man to encourage and help me in the entertainment business, and I shall forever be grateful to him for that. But due to the demands of his profession, he was also a night person who worked with dance bands while the rest of the world was asleep. He worked in the late afternoons and the evenings, and his social life came afterwards, usually in the small hours of the morning. My work hours were exactly the opposite to his. I was often up at 4:30 A.M., worked until 7 or 8 P.M., and fell into bed after dinner in complete exhaustion. We had no life together. He scored films for Republic; I rushed here and there giving performances for the USO and the Hollywood Victory Committee in addition to my work at the studio. Perhaps, if I had quit making pictures and made a home, it would have worked out, but neither of us thought of giving up our precious jobs. It was the fault of neither of us and of both of us *and* of the relentless system to which we sold ourselves. It was Hollywood—and a typical Hollywood tragedy. In 1945 we were divorced.

I had lost another husband, but I still had Tom, and my conscience began to talk to me about him. Because of the scant time I had at home, I was giving Tom as little attention as I had given my husband and to my sorrow I knew it. I tried harder to find time to have talks with him when I got home from work, and I began to discover things in him that I had missed for too long. He had developed into a fine Christian—thanks not to me but to the training he got from my mother and my good mother-in-law, who had left us now. They did what I should have been doing through the teen years of his life. I could see a concern for me in his face, and I vowed by all that was high and holy that "when I had it made" I would be the kind of mother he deserved. But not just yet, Tom.

Roy was married to Arlene Wilkins, a very pretty girl, quiet and reserved, and a good partner. They had two children—the adopted daughter, Cheryl, and Linda Lou, their own natural daughter. Cheryl could have doubled for Shirley Temple, with her honey-colored hair and bright brown eyes. She was definitely an extrovert; she was the pet of the set, and she knew no strangers. She had been photographed almost as much as little Shirley, for the movie magazines were forever publicizing Roy and his family. She had an avid interest in everybody, and, as a true Texan, she could talk the ears off a billy goat—just like me! I used to look at her and think, "She's so much like me; she could easily have been my child."

Linda was different. She was shy—a pretty little girl with blonde hair and huge, sparkling eyes which did most of the talking for her. She was on the quiet side, like Roy and her mother. She spent a lot of time with her maternal grandparents, and she got very little publicity, and wanted less. They were a lovely family.

Roy talked a lot about them in the gab sessions between shots on the set. One day we got to talking about religion. I declared my faith in God and in Jesus Christ as the Saviour of the world, but I quickly compromised that by saying that I was not what you might call a 100 percent Christian, since I met God only at church services on Sunday. Roy sat listening, and saying nothing until I asked him if he believed in Christ, and if he was taking his little girls to church and Sunday school. His answer really cut me down.

"No," he said, "Sunday is my day to relax. Saturday nights we usually play cards with friends, and we sleep in late Sunday mornings. But aside from that, I'm not completely sold on all this business about God and Christianity. I've played a lot of children's hospitals and orphanages, all over this country, and what I've seen makes me wonder why a helpless, innocent child should be born with a bad heart, or with cancer, or with crippled legs when he hasn't done anything wrong. Why does God let that happen? Maybe His eye is on the sparrows, like

58

the Book says, but sometimes I think it isn't on those poor kids. If you can explain how God can let innocent children suffer, I'll change my mind about going to church."

He hit me with that, and it hurt—but he had more. "When I was growing up in Ohio, I used to listen to the traveling evangelists who came to our little church in Duck Run. They would preach up a storm and then a lot of town characters would go down front and get saved. In a week's time they would be back where they had always been. I didn't see any difference in them. Then another preacher would come, and these same guys would do it all over again. I don't buy that."

Wow! I just sat and stared at him. Since I had gone down the church aisle twice—once to accept Christ and again to join the church—and since that hadn't seemed to make much difference in my life, I kept my mouth shut. I didn't, yet, have the answers for all that.

The Pioneers knew I had a son, and of course Roy knew it. But the publicity department at Republic and the front office didn't know it. One day Dorothy Blair, who was on the publicity staff, came rushing out on the set with the look of a hunted animal, took me aside and whispered hoarsely in my ear, "Dale, do you have a son?" A columnist had just called, saying that the army induction center had reported that a recruit named Tom Fox had named Dale Evans as his mother. In relief I admitted it and explained to her how the deception had been set up during my first screen test. She said, "Just keep quiet." When another member of the publicity staff asked her about it she gave him a blank stare and said it was nothing but a ridiculous rumor with no foundation whatever. I wished at the time that it had all come out in the open, for I was weary of the deceit, but it didn't come out. Tom went off to play in an army band, and I went back to work—sadder, and no wiser.

Right out of the blue, Danny Winkler had a call from RKO about a western musical they were planning, and they wanted me for the ingenue lead. It was called *Show Business Out West,* starring Eddie Cantor and Joan Davis. I was beside myself with joy; this was the break into musical comedy, *at last!* It came at a good time. Republic had refused to give me a promised salary jump, so I left that studio and sat down to wait for the RKO musical. I also left the Roy Rogers' shows, since I couldn't do them and the musical, too. We regretfully said good-bye, and I waited—and waited. The picture never got off the ground, and I was left high and dry. Something or someone should have told me then that I was never meant for the musical comedy stage, but they didn't. I was about ready to quit when Republic called and asked me to come back on a very good contract. I muttered and mumbled, and went back to the saddle again.

Roy and Arlene were looking forward to the birth of another child, and Roy was sure it was going to be a boy. It was— Roy, Jr., or, as we knew him later, Dusty. Dusty was born by Caesarian section, and eight days later, a blood clot formed. The doctors were helpless, and Arlene died.

This was *real* sorrow; my troubles seemed insignificant every time I looked at Roy's stricken face.

The months that followed were terrible for him and for his children. How would he ever take care of them? He was working unbelievably long hours at Republic, and the minute he finished a picture he was off on personal appearance tours to make the extra money for publicity, wardrobe—and the family. His salary was brutally small, considering the fact that he was number one at the box office; his fan mail was astronomical, and he even had to pay the bills involved in answering it with no help at all from the studio. With all that, he had little time to think about running a home. Arlene had always done that, and here he was with the family on his back. He had a series of nurses and housekeepers and companions for the children, but it was rough going even with that help. Six months later he bought a ranch near Lancaster, California, called Sky Haven, up near the top of a mountain. Nearby was beautiful Lake Hughes.

He drove me up there one Sunday, and it was quite a ride. The mountain road wound and twisted up steep grades with no guardrails; all the way up, there were only two places where you could pull out to pass another car. My heart was in my mouth, and I almost asked him to turn around and take me home. But we made the top—and it was worth the trip. There were flowering almond trees around the small rustic ranch house, ducks swimming on the lake, and there was Cheryl and Linda and Dusty, who welcomed Daddy with a joy that hurt me in my heart. It was perfect. Being with Roy up there, I felt completely at home, and I realized that we had a rapport born of years of struggle in our work together. We were somewhat opposites in temperament, but that was all to the good; it gave us good balance with each other. He said that he felt easy with me; we seemed to know exactly where we stood with each other.

As time wore on our attraction for one another deepened. Neither of us wanted to rush into marriage; we wanted to be sure it would *work*. Roy had his family; marriage meant that I would become a part of that family, and I knew something of the problems a stepmother faced. Roy had never made any profession of Christian faith, and I had no really personal relationship to Christ; there was no real help from religious faith for either of us. I kept wondering about his children. Could I adjust to them, and would they, could they, adjust to me? Could I discipline them? I remembered my own resentment at correction, as a child, and I remembered how I resented the correction of my own son by others, when he was a child. Problems, problems, problems.

Tom had solved his part of the problem by getting engaged to Barbara Miller, a fine Christian girl. He had changed his course. Instead of pursuing the musical career I had planned for him in symphony work, he had decided to become a teacher of music in order to help children to a career—and to God. It was a stunning blow to a mother who planned not wisely but too much, but how grateful I am today for his decision!

Roy helped again. We were sitting on our horses in the chutes of a rodeo at the Chicago Stadium late that fall of 1947, waiting to be announced, when Roy asked me, "What are you doing New Year's Eve?"

I had no plans for New Year's Eve—which was months away!

"Well, then, why don't we get married?"

And what do you think I said to that?

You're right. That's exactly what I said.

4

*T*wo old friends, Bill and Alice Likins, asked us if we wouldn't like to be married in their beautiful home on the Flying L Ranch, near Oklahoma City, and we accepted the invitation almost before it was out of their mouths. This was good; it would save us from the usual spectacle atmosphere that always prevailed when movie stars had a wedding in Los Angeles. We wanted a quiet wedding, with as little publicity as possible. Art Rush (who was still Roy's agent and manager) and his lovely wife would be the only attendants, and Bill Likins would give me away.

We did get one piece of publicity, even though we thought we were keeping it all a secret. On a radio broadcast, Louella Parsons broke the news that we were to be married, and where—and she also told the world that I had a grown son. I was frightened at first, then relieved beyond words that the long deception about Tom was over at last. Tom and Roy liked it, too. These two had come to respect and admire each other deeply. Roy was impressed with the way Tom had conducted himself, with his musical ambition, his practical Christianity and his love of little children.

Thank you, Louella: you solved a real problem for me, and I'll never forget it!

New Year's Eve came—with increasingly dismaying gusts of sleet and snow. The wedding was planned for 5 P.M., and by four o'clock most of the guests had made it to the ranch, with congratulations for us and something less than congratulatory

63

remarks about the storms they had struggled through. My mother, my father and my aunts arrived from Texas. Tom and Barbara and Barbara's sister were the last to arrive, after a real ordeal with the snow—*and* a leaky radiator—from Los Angeles.

So the guests were all there, and we could get going. Then we discovered that Bill Alexander, a close friend and pastor of First Christian Church in Oklahoma City, hadn't put in an appearance. No minister, no wedding! Bill was nearly *two hours* late. The storm was bad around Oklahoma City, and he had the worst fight of all of us to get through to the Flying L. We were so glad to see him, when he *blew* in through the front door, that we didn't notice his old frontier clothes. With frock coat and string tie, he was decked out as he thought a marrying parson on the old frontier should be garbed. We didn't even notice it, until the ceremony was about to begin!

Roy was as nervous as a kitten up a tree. I laughed at him. These men! I laughed too soon.

As I was dressing for the ceremony, a strong chill of foreboding rushed over me. I suppose most brides go through the same experience, but I wasn't thinking of most brides that day—only of me. I'd been married before, and it hadn't worked. Was I sure this time? I was alone in the room, all by myself, with no one to help me, no shoulder to cry on. For the first time in my life, I knew how much I needed *God!* I ran into an empty clothes closet, shut the door and just stood there, my heart pounding like mad. It was as though I were standing on a mountain top, before an awesome, questioning God. I felt weak and inadequate—and I *knew* I couldn't go through with this marriage without His help. Haltingly, I prayed.

"Dear God, you know who I am and what I am and what I have been. You know what a great responsibility I am taking on, marrying this man with three motherless children. You know the problems that will come. Please help me. Help me with the courage and the understanding to establish a Christian

64

home for these children—the kind of home You gave me. If You don't, I'll never make it."

I didn't hear any bells, or have any blue-lighted vision as I said, "Amen," but a deep, reassuring, strengthening calm welled up in my heart. It was like the floodgates of a dam opening to set free the deep waters in which I had floundered for so long. I stepped back into the room, finished my dressing, and heard the strains of "Here Comes the Bride" from downstairs.

Bill Likins gave me his arm, and we walked into the big den and took our places before the huge fireplace. Bill Alexander was there, all set to start the ritual; Mary Jo Rush, my matron of honor, came up beside me, and we stood silently waiting for Roy and Art Rush, his best man. We waited five long, long minutes—and no Art, no Roy! I almost ran for the nearest exit. Finally they came, almost running into the room, looking a little disheveled and out of breath. I looked daggers at Roy; he just stood there and rolled his eyes toward heaven. I swear, I hardly heard Bill Alexander read the ceremony. When it was over, Roy kissed me and Art Rush exploded, "What a way to start a wedding—with the house on fire!"

It seemed that someone had thrown a smouldering cigarette into a trash basket, igniting the paper in the basket and the curtains hanging above. As Art and Roy passed the door of the room, they saw the flames, dashed in and put them out, and rushed on downstairs for the ceremony.

The storm had become a blizzard as the reception line formed; we had to send for the state troopers to help the guests find the motels in which they were to spend the night. It was wild, but nobody complained—least of all the two principals of the wedding.

It took two days to clear. The second night of our honeymoon, Roy suggested that it was a nice clear night for coon hunting. I looked out of the window at patches of snow still on the ground, and I almost said, "Man, you've got to be kidding"

—but I didn't. The minister had said "for better or for worse," and while this was definitely worse, the better was that Roy had just promised to attend church with me the next Sunday, so—I went on the hunt.

Have you ever gone coon hunting? It's something. You tramp around in the cold dark following the hounds; every once in a while they let out a yelp, as though they were hot after the coon—just to keep you interested. You stumble over rocks and stumps and holes in the ground, with only a flashlight to help you—unless you're lucky and the moon is out. It wasn't out that night. Along about midnight the men reckoned that the dogs were lost (I knew we were!) and that we should build a fire and wait for them to show up. We drank gallons of hot coffee and waited, and waited. Finally Roy suggested that he might take me and the other women home, while the other men waited for the dogs. I stumbled through the dark to the car, muttering to myself, "What have I done? I'm no sportswoman. I should have married a college professor." But when we got back safely home, I repented those words—a little. I made up my mind to try to like hunting and the out-of-doors, to please my man.

We went out again another night, and this time the dogs did better; they treed two coons in a big oak, and Roy called me to come and see them shake the coons down. There were seven dogs yelping and jumping at the base of the tree and our flashlights picked up four eyes glittering in the branches. The men shook the tree vigorously, and down came the coons, into the most sickening fight I have ever seen. I let loose a barrage of protest and accusation that made the men stare at me in open-mouthed disbelief. Roy was quiet for a moment, then took my arm and walked me away from the scene. "Maw," he said, "I'm afraid you'll never be a hunter. You'd better not come any more."

That was all right with me. Two coons against seven dogs didn't look like a fair fight to me, and I was fed up and fighting mad about the whole business. Roy explained patiently that the coons were actually faster and more savage than the dogs, and if the dogs didn't get their prey they wouldn't try on the next hunt, and coons were *very* destructive creatures, and. . . . It went in one ear and out the other. I'd had it—for keeps!

Back in California, we looked for a home. Roy's children were still living at Lake Hughes, and Tom was at my little house in North Hollywood, attending classes at USC. We found one up at the top of Vine Street, on the side of a mountain, built there by the late Noah Beery. It was a beauty—a large two-story Spanish home with a glorious winding stairway, the largest master bedroom I have ever seen, and with a wrought-iron balcony overhanging the driveway. The grounds were beautifully terraced and dotted with huge trees. There was a big basement: this would be our den.

We moved in. I'll never forget that day. Furniture and "fixin's" poured in from Roy's house and mine, plus Marion (our housekeeper) and Virginia (our nurse), and a pack of hunting dogs who were parked in a huge pen Roy had started building the day after he bought the place. We opened barrel after barrel, argued where to put this furniture, this silver, this glass, until we could do no more. I cooked a huge pot of spaghetti for supper. What a day! What a home!

But it took more than moving in to make it a home. I knew that, and planned for it. When we had announced our engagement, the studio had said that the public would not be interested in a married couple doing westerns, so I would have to devote my time to running the home while Roy got himself a new leading lady. This was quite an adjustment for me—and for the children, who naturally resented me in the role of mother.

One day while I was arranging the furniture in the living room, little Linda Lou stopped me with this remark: "That isn't your furniture. It's my Mommy's!" I started to rebuke her, held my tongue for a second or two, and then said, as gently as I could, "Honey, your Mommy has gone to heaven, and she doesn't need this furniture anymore. So now you and Daddy and I will have to use it." She turned and walked away without a word. I knew this would happen. Roy was working long hours, and I was alone with the children—as *step*mother. I was on the defensive—edgy, and a little frightened. It would have gotten worse if Tom had not walked in one day to suggest that I start taking them to Sunday school and church—that God could help me do what I was unable to do for myself. I thought it over, carefully. The next Sunday I attended the evening service with Tom.

Tom denies it, but I will always believe that he conspired with Dr. Jack MacArthur on the sermon that night. His sermon topic, "The House That Is Built on the Rock," didn't mean very much to me until he began to explain that *any* house built on the rock of faith in Jesus Christ *could and would* survive anything that came up against it—illness, death, poverty, suspicion, greed, selfishness, deceit, lies—you name it! It was as though he had known I was coming to church that night, as though he were throwing his rocks right at me. They hit me square in the middle. I twisted and dodged and squirmed under the barrage, but there was no escaping it; I sat there looking into my heart and hearing it shout "Guilty, guilty, *guilty!*"

When he finished the sermon and extended an invitation to the congregation to accept Christ as Saviour, the invitation had my name on it, and I knew it. I felt a pull from that altar, but—no, not yet. I still fought it off. Tom read the story in my eyes and he said, "Why don't you go? Why not make it right with the Lord now? Give Him your life, and let Him give you the peace I've watched you struggling for—for so long?"

68

I was defensive with him: "Tom, I *am* a Christian. I've been a Christian since I was ten years old. Isn't that enough?"

"No," said Tom. "You don't really know Christ. I've watched you reading all those 'Peace of Mind' books, and all that 'Eastern philosophy' stuff, and it hasn't helped you one little bit. If you really knew Him, all you would need would be your Bible and your faith in Him. *You won't find peace until you understand that.*"

I *wanted* to go down that aisle, but I just didn't have the courage. There were voices whispering to me, "All these people will know you're a no-good sinner, if you do that. They'll talk about it, and it will be all over Hollywood in twenty-four hours. . . . Don't rush into this thing; think it over for a week or so." Voices! My mouth opened for me to say to Tom, "Give me until next Sunday; I want to think." (What a stall! I'd been thinking about it for nigh onto twenty years!) Tom's eyes were filled with tears and pity. He turned away, without a word.

Roy was away on a trip, so he couldn't help me. I felt miserable and alone, as I drove home, ran upstairs to my bedroom, dropped to my knees beside the bed and cried as I had never cried in all my life. The dam broke, and it all poured out in a long, broken, stammering confession. When I had cried myself out, I started to pray quietly in a spirit of repentance. Never before had I talked with God in such a spirit, but I did now. My whole past stood up before my eyes, revealing all the lost years like an unrolling carpet. I shuddered at what I saw— sin, sin, sin—and all because I had refused to know and follow Christ. I had held Him only like an ace up my sleeve against the possibility of future punishment. I cried out in agony, "God, Lord God, forgive me! Just let me live until next Sunday, and I'll go down that aisle and make it a public confession."

He let me live. When the invitation was given the next Sunday evening, I bounced out of my pew and fairly flew down the aisle, grasped Dr. MacArthur's hand and was ushered into a

69

small prayer room for prayer and consultation with a counsellor. I came clean with God, not audibly shouting my misdeeds but remembering them before Him, asking Him to come into my heart and wash me clean by virtue of the blood He had shed for me on Calvary, to create a new clean heart and a right spirit within me, to break me if He had to but—please!—to take my life and use it for His glory.

An indescribable peace washed over my heart, washed out the dirt there, washed me clean and into a totally new creature. As I got up from my knees, I felt as though a crushing burden had fallen from my back and shoulders, and I felt as free as though I were walking on clouds with my feet not even touching the earth. I looked around me as I walked out of the church. The sky was brighter, the grass was greener, the flowers were bursting with a color I had never seen before. Every tree, every weed along the highway sang and waved to me. How great it was to be alive and free. How great Thou art!

Now I knew the meaning of the words of the Book: "If the Son therefore shall make you free, you shall be free indeed" (John 8:36).

Roy was home when I got there. I said to him, "Honey, I've just made the greatest decision of my life; I have dedicated my heart and my life to Jesus Christ." I was ecstatic, wild with joy. He looked at me with those penetrating, thoughtful eyes of his, and he said slowly, "I'm glad for you, Mama, if it makes you happy—and it sure seems to be doing something like that, right now. But be careful, won't you? Please don't go . . . overboard."

I suppose I might have been mad at that, or hurt, but I wasn't. That day, in my new frame of mind, I couldn't get mad at anybody or anything. Besides, I knew what he meant. He was thinking the same thing that my mother had been thinking when she said, "Dale rushes into things. . . ." Roy always looks before he jumps; he didn't want me to jump too far, too quickly, too impulsively.

Let me explain this business of going overboard for Christ. The more I look over my whole great spiritual experience, the more I am convinced that the newcomer to Christ *has* to go overboard for Him. That had been my trouble: I had always wanted to stay in my selfish little boat; but once the vision of Christ came clear, I was like Peter—I wanted to go overboard—wanted to go the limit in faith.

What does it mean to go overboard, anyway?

Not long ago I gave my personal testimony at a meeting held at the San Fernando Music Center to introduce an organization called Space Age Evangelism. This group is trying to create a religion-oriented park here in California—a public attraction reproducing the scenes of the Bible in a Holy Land setting. It will be informative, exciting, educational, faith-inspiring—and altogether beautiful. The enthusiasm of the group in this effort to bring the Bible alive to the visitors at this park is something to behold. They know their subject; they have done their home work—their research in the Bible. They are vibrant, concerned Christians who are willing to go out on a limb with this project, as a means of communicating God's boundless love to an unbelieving, heedless world. And sure as shooting, there will be those who will say they have gone overboard. They will have a lot of wisecracks and derogatory remarks about the project and the people backing it: "It's just another money-making scheme. . . . They're a lot of religious fanatics." But—*why?*

Why can't we think big about God? If we feel called by Him to be used in a big, unusual undertaking, if we want to go overboard in a new way, what's wrong with it? The enemies of God don't mind going overboard in their schemes to defeat Him. Peter went *really* overboard once, when he left his boat to walk on water toward Christ, and it was only when he took

71

his eyes off his Lord and began to be afraid that he began to sink. So it is with *our* faith! When we pay more attention to others than we do to our Christ, when we care more about what people will say and less about what God will say—then *we* begin to sink, in losing our witness. When the Holy Spirit fell upon the followers of Jesus at Pentecost, they went overboard with a vengeance—and they didn't care what the unbelievers said about them. They were accused of being drunk— and early in the morning, at that! Did they care? They did *not*. Some of the more timid ones may have backed off in the face of this slander, but most of them defied their slanderers. Certainly Peter did that; he won souls that day. He had a new power to save souls because He had seen his resurrected Lord and felt the surging power of the Holy Ghost within himself, and he *had* to transmit that power to others. He just couldn't help going overboard. He knew whom he had believed, and he was ready to lay down his life for his Master. *This* time he kept his eyes on Jesus, and he did *not* sink back into apathy and fear. It can happen to us today, if we are willing to get out of the boat and if we want to see big things happen for a big God.

No, I don't mind folks saying I have gone overboard for Christ. He has done tremendous things for me; He has revealed great truth to me, and I will not let anyone laugh or threaten me into silence about that. I think it's time that more Christians went overboard, got up and stepped out of their pitifully small denominational and cultural boats and got their feet wet in the great wide surging sea of struggling, suffering humanity. If we have experienced His love and forgiveness in our lives, if we have found healing in Him, if the Spirit has fallen upon us and empowered us, then let's speak up for Him; let's get going for Him. It isn't something we *might* do; it is an obligation.

I guarantee this: if you will keep your eyes on Him, He will never let you sink. Many, many mornings I wake up with thoughts of God, or how He is working in my life. I lie there and think, "I must write this down; I must pass it on to someone else before I lose it." But, often I neglect to write it down, and so I do lose it, and, losing it, lose another chance to witness. Paul said, *"Now* is the accepted time of salvation." We don't have yesterday and we don't have tomorrow; we have only the now. Speak—lest you forget!

Often, too, when I start thinking about my early failures in marriage, I want to go overboard more than ever in sheer gratitude to God for changing all that past error and guilt into present-sense joy. I was searching for the security of real love in those misadventures, and it never occurred to me to look to God for the only perfect love that exists for any of us. In my emotional and spiritual immaturity, I was looking for that Dream Prince to ride up in shining armor and sweep me away to endless love and contentment. I never quite realized that I was no prize lily, myself! I have a lot of compassion for those who are looking for perfection in others, jumping from one romance and marriage to another like so many restless, over-discriminating bees jumping from flower to flower, always tasting and never satisfied. I was like that. Not until I let go and let God take over my life and my love did I find satisfaction for the deep needs of my soul. There is no water to really slake the thirst of a questing heart except the Water of Life which is found in Jesus Christ, who is the Way, the Truth, and the Life. When we drink deeply of this Water we are satisfied beyond measure; we thirst no more; we are content where we are, *and we can offer the Water to those around us. We must offer it.*

If this is going overboard, then I'm overboard. I'm a good piece from the boat—and I love it with every fibre of my being.

But I remembered Roy's word of caution: "Please don't go overboard." He said it in the spirit of love, and I accepted it in love. He also said that day, "And don't start pushing me to make the same decision you have just made. Maybe I will, but

73

if I do, *I want it to be my own decision.*" I promised. But promise or no promise, everything seemed to work toward that moment of decision for him. He began to notice a change in me; the Christian life I was leading now was something new, and it was contagious. Example is always better than nagging, when one is near the gates of the Kingdom. I started taking the children regularly to church and Sunday school, reading the Bible at dinner and hearing their prayers at bedtime. The seeds were falling.

One day Frances Eilers came to see me. She was the wife of Leonard Eilers, the cowboy evangelist. She had met my son, Tom, at a youth meeting some years before at their ranch, and she and Tom had made a pact to pray me into the Kingdom of God. She gave me some things to read, among them a Bible in which she had written on the inside cover verses 10 to 31 of Proverbs. I sat there with her and read it, and the heavens opened. I was humbled, head to heels, by what I read. I asked her to have lunch with me at the Brown Derby, and in that playground of movie stars and show people she told me more about the Power of Christ than I had ever dreamed of before. God works in mysterious places His wonders to perform. She has been a lovely influence in my life ever since; so has Velma Spencer, the wife of Tim Spencer, one of the Sons of the Pioneers. Velma made me a member of a sorority called Lambda Theta Chi (Life Through Christ). That sorority for married women has helped me beyond words.

I never went to church without asking Roy to go along. When he declined, I made no issue of it. One Saturday night we had a huge party in our big den. It was a roaring roomful of show people who couldn't imagine any party without drinks and cigarettes. It got to me, and I said something to a friend about why I no longer cared about cocktail parties and why I no longer smoked or drank; that now I was interested not in whooping it up but in fulfilling my responsibilities to three small children. Roy misunderstood it, and we had a real to-do about it; it was one of the few arguments of our marriage, and it was a good one. I retreated to the bedroom in tears.

The next morning (Sunday) neither of us mentioned the incident, but when church time came I didn't have a chance to ask Roy to go with us. He announced that he was going with us. The party had broken up early in the morning, and during the sermon I noticed that Roy's eyes were closed. I thought to myself, "A lot of good this sermon will do him; he's sound asleep." To my amazement, when the sermon was over and the invitation was given, he sat up straight, squeezed my hand and said, "Maw, I'm going down there." And go he did. He had made his own decision with no pressure from me, and I was never happier in my life. He was baptized, with Cheryl, that same Easter Sunday night. There was now a spiritual bond between us that has never broken.

Not long after this, Danny Winkler (my agent) called to ask if I would like to do the leading role in the London company of the musical *Annie Get Your Gun*. A year or so earlier, I would have jumped at it; this was the big time toward which I had been shooting all my life. But not *now*. A little late, that offer! It was clear to me now that I would work with Roy if I worked at all. So it came about that Art Rush and I decided that we would buy back my contract from Danny Winkler. (It cost Art and me $2500 apiece, and it was several years before Roy knew that!) This meant Art would be agent for both of us. I felt a little foolish about it, since I had left Art so long ago because of his attachment to Roy Rogers.

Two more things happened that year that made us sing for joy. Tom and Barbara were married at Fountain Avenue Baptist Church, with Linda and Cheryl as junior bridesmaids. Most of our family came from Texas and Arkansas, and I wept a bucket of tears at the sight of Tom and Barbara standing there side by side. It was a marriage made in heaven; both were committed Christians. How grateful I was that Tom was not "unequally yoked" with a non-Christian! If I had handpicked a wife for my son, I could never have done better than Barbara Miller. God had blessed me in letting me see this marriage.

And in December I learned that I was to have a child. I accepted it as a miracle. My doctor had told me during a medical examination before obtaining a marriage license that it would be impossible for me to bear another child without extensive surgery. God, and not the doctors, always has the last word! When the gynecologist told me over the phone that a baby was on the way, I laughed long and loud. "Laugh or not," he said, "you're pregnant." He was right.

The second month of my pregnancy I came down with German measles. I didn't know what that meant, or that it spelled danger for my baby. I was given a shot of gamma globulin. Twice after that I had to take to my bed to prevent a miscarriage. I wanted this baby desperately; in my secret heart I wanted a girl this time, but I made up my mind to be content with either girl or boy—just so long as it was healthy.

During this time people would ask me, "Can you tell us something really *tangible* that the Lord has done for you since your conversion?" I never resented it; these folks were from Missouri, and they only wanted to be shown. And I had one good answer for them. Our church had a radio ministry every Sunday afternoon, with hymns and a dramatization of actual conversion experiences. Of course I was glad to go on the air for them. Up to the time of my conversion, I had always suffered acute attacks of stage fright when I performed before the public. When I felt "the fright" coming on the first time I sang and spoke on this church broadcast I stopped and prayed that God would work through me, that I would feel within myself that He was speaking and singing through me as His agent. The sense of relaxation and freedom that came over me is indescribable; I felt no fear, no nervousness whatever. In the modern idiom, "the heat was off me," and I breezed through it without a tremor or a tremble. We had little time to rehearse on that program, and some of the roles I played were far more difficult than anything I had done before. I was amazed at what came out of me when I listened to the rebroadcasts.

About the end of the second month of my pregnancy, I developed a severe case of laryngitis. I was hardly able to speak above a whisper. The slightest vocal effort would plunge me into hoarseness; but I stayed on the broadcasts, certain that God would help me through—somehow. I would go to the studio armed with cough drops, lemon and honey—and sounding like Louie Armstrong! When it came time for me to step up to the mike and sing or speak, I would bow my head and ask God please to "clear my vocal chords enough for me to do this broadcast for Your glory"—and believe it or not, my voice would come over clear as a bell for the entire taping. When it was over, I had no voice; I was whispering again. That happened every Sunday afternoon during my pregnancy!

Would you call that "something tangible"?

When I was five months pregnant and Roy was away one day filming a picture, a brush fire broke out in the hills behind our house. You've seen newspaper pictures of those California brush fires, and they frightened you. They really are terrifying. The Cass County Boys (a group I had once worked with in Dallas and who were now working with Gene Autry) were there, rehearsing with me for a TV short, and Roy's father was there. We called the fire department. The fire came closer and closer, and the men in the house used all the garden hose we had trying to stave off the flames. The fire raged on beyond their streams of water in a high wind and through dry grass, until the flames were within six feet of the house. Dusty was taking his afternoon nap. I stood beside him with my unborn baby writh-

77

ing within me, praying, wondering what to salvage, thankful that the other children were in school.

I prayed so hard for the fire department to come that my nails dug into the palms of my hands—but it never came. I was about ready to run for it when the wind shifted and the fire turned off in another direction. My doctor came to give me a sedative; Roy raced one hundred miles home to help, and he knew what I meant when I said that God had heard and helped me before he got there. Don't tell me that the day of miracles has passed!

At seven months the doctor took a blood count and gravely informed me that I had Rh-negative type blood factor and since Roy had the positive factor, our baby might have difficulties. My blood count had slipped dangerously; I was prone to anemia.

At 8 P.M. on August 25th, I knew my time had come. Roy drove me to Hollywood Presbyterian Hospital. Art Rush came to keep Roy company through what we all thought would be a very long night. But shortly after midnight Robin Elizabeth arrived. Groggy and weak, I turned my eyes to the glass-enclosed oxygen box and saw a pretty, delicate little girl kicking her legs. My first question was, "Is she all right?" To which someone answered, "She looks OK." I smiled as they wheeled me out past Roy, Art and my mother. Roy kissed me and said, "Honey, she's beautiful; she has little ears just like yours!"

Roy rode as grand marshal of the Sheriff's Rodeo the next day; he announced the arrival of Robin Elizabeth to ninety-odd thousand people in the stands. I was beside myself with happiness, laughing and resting in a roomful of flowers. Dr. Jack MacArthur dropped in on the third day and gave me a book to read. It was the strange story of John and Betty Stamm, two missionaries who had just been killed by Chinese Communists, leaving a six-month-old baby girl who was carried to the China Inland Mission by a Chinese Christian woman. I thought Dr.

78

MacArthur gave me a rather grave smile as he left, and I was uneasy for awhile.

The next day a nurse was giving me a bath. I complained that they didn't bring my baby to me as often as they brought other babies to their mothers, and that when they did bring her she was sleeping so soundly that I could hardly wake her up. Robin was pretty, all right—but I told that nurse that once while I was holding her up to the light, she looked faintly oriental. The nurse avoided my eyes, cleared her throat and asked, "Are they going to let you take her home?" She tried hard to be matter-of-fact about it, but it made me more uneasy than ever.

"Of course I'm taking her home. Is there any reason why I shouldn't?"

She looked at me and she said, "Tell your doctor to tell you the truth about her."

My heart began to pound; I demanded that *she* tell me if there was anything wrong, but of course there were restrictions which forbade her doing that.

I called my doctor and told him that he had better come to the hospital and tell me if there was anything wrong with my baby. He came, and he told me as gently as he could. Robin was not responding to certain routine tests; they couldn't tell how she would progress, but she had been in an oxygen tent ever since her birth, and that wasn't too good. He suggested that we take her home and love her and enjoy her, "Because, in cases like this, love does things that nothing else can do." My heart turned to cold stone. I was too numb to cry. I prayed, "Lord, I know you understand this. I don't, but I trust You."

Unbidden, the scene of yesteryear in the corridor of a Louisville, Kentucky, hospital flooded my mind. That was the day when I promised God that if He would save Tom from infantile paralysis, I would put my life in His hands. I flushed with remorse, and promised God that I would not question His wis-

79

dom in allowing Robin to come to us in this condition—that whatever He willed I would accept. I had already dedicated her to the Lord, and I felt that she would be used in some way to glorify Him, since it was miraculous that I could have her at all.

The pediatrician who was taking care of her told us that he suspected she was Mongoloid. He explained the characteristics of the Mongoloid child: the square little hands full of creases, the tiny ears, the undeveloped bridge of the nose, the slanting eyes. When he came to the description of the eyes I told him indignantly that she had Indian blood on her daddy's side of the family, and that would account for the slant in the eyes. I rationalized the whole prognosis and refused to accept their indictment of our baby.

We were advised to place her in an institution as quickly as possible, before we became too attached to her, because she needed special care which we couldn't give her at home. We refused to do that. We felt that God had sent her to us for a purpose, and we would never find that purpose if we were to put her away. Roy said, "We'll just take her home and love her and raise her as best we can, and trust God for the rest." Someone else said, "Of course, these children hardly ever live long, and that is a blessing." That was meant well, but it went into my heart like a knife. Putting my baby away was unthinkable.

The night Robin and I were brought home from the hospital, after she was tucked in her crib by her nurse and I was safely in bed, I heard her singing, the way babies often do just before they go to sleep. I thought, "How could anything be wrong with a little angel like that?" But in my heart I knew. I turned off the bed lamp and lay in the darkness, crying my heart out. In exhaustion, I finally fell asleep. Sometime around midnight I woke up with a start. There was a definite Presence in the room, so pronounced that I felt I could almost reach out and touch it. It was warm and bright, comforting, bringing peace to my heart. It was clear to me that the Holy Spirit of my loving

God was there to calm and strengthen me for what was ahead. I breathed a "Thank You, Lord. I know it is You. I'll be all right now," and went back to sleep until I heard Robin cry at about 6:30 in the morning. For a long time I never told a soul about this experience; they would not understand; they would think I had been out of my mind. But it was real—*very* real.

Two months later I left for New York to do a TV show with Gabby Hayes. When the Super Chief reached Chicago and we had to change trains, I searched the magazine counter for something to read, something to give me a lift. The current *Reader's Digest* had an article by Pearl Buck—"My Child Stopped Growing," and there was a book by Dr. Norman Vincent Peale, entitled *A Guide to Confident Living*. I bought them, and got on the train. The Pearl Buck article rang a bell of hope for my Robin; it described her so perfectly I started to cry, then opened Dr. Peale's book to the chapter entitled "How to Meet Sorrow." I devoured it—and it devoured my heartbreak. I promised myself that some day I would meet this man of God who had steadied me and given me courage and made me realize that God would meet every need as every need presented itself. I am still grateful to Norman Vincent Peale.

It was decided, after we returned to California, that Robin would be better off in the San Fernando Valley; Los Angeles and Hollywood were damp and smoggy, and the Valley air was invigorating. Until we found the place in the Valley we wanted, Robin was to live in the home of her nurse. We were busy taping a radio show for the Quaker Oats Company at that time; one night when I reached home after a hard day's work, I discovered that Robin and the nurse had moved out, lock, stock and barrel. They thought it would be easier for me if she was moved when I wasn't home. I walked into the deserted nursery and let out a bawl like a cow just deprived of her calf. I waited two days before going out to see her. I found her in a lovely sunny room and in a home of serenity and love—and I was glad.

Robin was difficult to feed, like most Mongoloid children; her tongue was thick, and she had trouble holding food in her mouth. We had to get a special bottle and nipple for her. She was controlling her eyes a little better now, but she still had difficulty holding her head up. These babies are helpless for a long, long time, in comparison with normal babies.

I would look at her and my heart would cry, "What shall we ever tell the press and the magazine interviewers when they want to photograph our baby?" How could we shield her from a curious world? Then an inner voice would say to me, "Trust Me, Trust Me!" And I would become steady again in my faith in One who cares what happens to us more than any other can care.

I would ask our minister, "Why did this happen to us? Is it because of sin, or sins in our past lives, or was it something I did when I was carrying her?" He replied in deep compassion, "These things happen because of cumulative sin over many generations. The Bible says that All have sinned, and come short of the glory of God. None of us knows exactly why these things are allowed to happen—only God, and if we trust Him some day we will understand. This experience will cut away the dross and the tinsel from your life and you will know, once and for all, what is really important in life."

He was right. It was a refining experience for both Roy and me. That refining, I believe, is necessary even if it is painful, if we are to be used of God. He had many different ways of refining people; usually the crucible is fashioned of whatever we hold most dear.

In November Roy and I went on a six-weeks' tour of one-nighters with a stage show company. It was pure agony to be separated from Robin, but I know now that it was best for me to go. In the middle of the tour I received word that Robin's

82

nurse was ill and would have to give up nursing our baby when we returned home. The Lord provided another, who took the baby to her home until we could move out to the Valley. At Christmas we had a little party for her; the whole family was there, including my mother and father. Her nurse had dressed her beautifully, and put a little bow in her hair, and she gave all of us a big smile. I took her little hands and tried to help her raise herself up, but to my dismay I watched her little face turning blue with the effort and I knew then that the doctor's prognosis of a congenital heart defect was true. She gasped for breath and broke out in perspiration. We stood there with tears in our eyes—all of us who had refused to believe that she was handicapped to that extent. It was a sad Christmas.

In February Tom's first child was born—my first natural grandchild. Melinda Christine Fox! I was a real grandmother; I held her in my arms and thanked God.

We moved out to the Valley—to a lovely rambling Spanish-type ranch house complete with swimming pool, cattle, horses, dogs—and a garden. Roy's father and uncle had built a little private apartment for Robin—one room and a bath—since she was nervous and required privacy. She seemed to be showing some improvement, and my heart sang with fresh new hope, for I knew that with God, all things are possible. Maybe . . . after all! Cheryl, Linda and Dusty had brand new quarters of their own in the children's wing, near Robin's, and Virginia, their nurse, and Emily, our housekeeper, were next door to them. I rejoiced in this big family now gathered under one roof. I rejoiced too in Gus, our green-thumbed gardener, who grew marvelous artichokes and Kentucky Wonder string beans in our vegetable garden. We also had orange trees, plum trees, and apricot trees. That summer I put up my first jams and jellies.

There was no Baptist church in Encino. I wished there were, and I wondered about the other churches. I wanted Virginia and Emily to take the children to *some* church while Roy and I

83

were on tour, and I wasn't sure which one. One morning I answered the phone and a kind voice said, "Dale, this is Father Smith, at St. Nicholas Episcopal Church. I'm calling to invite you and Roy to our family service next Sunday morning, at 9:45. I'm interested in you—and in that baby. I want you to know that I think you have done the right thing in bringing her home with you. God has a real purpose in this child's life; you will learn some wonderful lessons from her, and God will guide you." We went. We loved this church, and we loved its pastor, Harley Wright Smith. (Just for the record, he was the key inspiration for my book about Robin, *Angel Unaware,* and he was the first one outside the family to read the galley proofs when they came.)

We attended this church regularly, studied its Articles of Faith and the Book of Common Prayer, and had Robin dedicated and baptized there at sixteen months of age. Roy, Cheryl, Linda and I were confirmed there and joined the church.

I've sometimes been asked about that—about being first a Baptist, then an Episcopalian, then . . . something else. I am asked, "What is your church, anyway?" The question never bothers me. I just tell them the truth: "I am Baptist, Episcopalian, Methodist, Disciples of Christ, Presbyterian! I don't think of the Church as a building or as a denomination; it is a body of believers in Christ—in His birth and Person and ministry, in His Atonement, His Resurrection, His Coming Again to receive us unto Himself. Denominations are fellowships. The Church is His body, and it has many members—not all of which function in exactly the same way. Who is to say that one denomination (or function) is 100 percent right and another 100 percent wrong? God is the judge of all that. Our job is to serve wherever we are, with thankful hearts for the privilege of serving; and to love and serve a God who is a God of variety and not of monotony. As long as a church fellowship has the seal of the Cross, I am completely at home there."

84

For me, wherever the Christ is, in all His beauty and power, there is my church. I don't think we are going to be denied heaven if our faith is right—and I've come to believe that many people are going to be surprised at whom they will see in heaven—and whom they will *not* see. The Lamb's Book of Life isn't copied from denominational records!

That summer Tom and Barbara noticed that one of Mindy's legs seemed a trifle shorter than the other, and that it seemed to drag when she tried to crawl. I had a stab of pain in my heart as I watched the little girl and that leg. Was I to suffer *this,* too? We took her to a pediatrician, who told us that our first grandchild was minus one hip socket. Tom and Barbara seemed to have more faith than I did at that moment. They took it calmly, with such assurance that the child could and would be healed. Roy was a Shriner, and when he found that there was no orthopedic surgeon anywhere near Yreka, California (where Tom and Barbara now lived), he called the San Francisco Shrine Hospital for Crippled Children, and they accepted Mindy.

I went with them to San Francisco. With my heart pounding hard again, I watched them attach a steel brace to her shoes and slide her leg into it, forcing the leg into the hip to form its own socket. Today Mindy walks as easily and as normally as the rest of us. I saw that God had a purpose for this child, too, and I thanked Him.

The incident prompted me to search more and more to discover God's purpose for Robin, and I *really* searched. At the time we were shooting a series of half-hour Westerns with Pat Brady for NBC, and working from sunup to sundown, six days a week. I studied my Bible in my car on location more zealously than ever, and now and then a gleam of light broke through; but it was hard and exhausting. When I read in a medical magazine that there was a doctor in San Francisco who was doing things in group therapy for Mongoloid children, I left

85

location and took the train for San Francisco. The doctor was kind—and honest. He promised nothing, but he told us to try a powdered extract from the pituitary gland of a young calf; it might improve her muscle tone, and enable her to stand on her feet. He also suggested some orthopedic therapy for her legs. Her nurse and I took turns at that amateur therapy. Today I wonder why we tried her so with all that exercise, at a time when her little heart was in such poor condition. But we tried.

Roy and I attended the meetings of a new "Hollywood Christian Group" during these days. It was started in the home of the late beloved Henrietta Mears, Director of Christian Education at the Hollywood Presbyterian Church. She was deeply interested in the spiritual welfare of the people in show business. Tim and Velma Spencer, Jane Russell, Connie Haines, the late Porter Hall, Roy and I and several others knelt in meetings held in each other's homes and asked God to help us reach the entertainment industry for Christ. We had a different guest speaker each night, often someone in show business or in some related industry. It was, and is one of the great spiritual influences of my life.

Two movie magazines, learning of our church affiliation at St. Nicholas Church and of our interest in the Hollywood Christian Group, asked me to do a faith article on Robin. I declined, saying, "God hasn't yet shown me exactly what He is going to do about little Robin. But when the time is right, I'll give you an article." The magazine editors understood, and shelved the idea. I shall always be grateful to the press for the compassion and understanding they showed in not printing all the facts about Robin. They never did a home layout on us, without letting us edit her pictures. Although we never admitted that she was Mongoloid, they knew it, and they said nothing.

We took the baby back to the doctor in San Francisco two months later for a prearranged checkup, and this time it was really bad. He said that Robin's muscle tone was slightly better, but that her heart condition was worsening fast and that by September it would be critical. My heart was as heavy as lead all the way back to Los Angeles. Robin was upset by the trip, and suffered with violent diarrhea. In despair, I lay down beside her in the bedroom on the train, and began to pray. One of the overhead lights was on, and I noticed with a start that there was a bluish haze gathered around it that gradually filled the whole room. I threw open the door to see if it was something that had leaked in from outside. Everything was perfectly clear down the aisle of the car. All at once I knew: the Holy Spirit had come to comfort me; I felt His warmth, and was lifted up and strengthened.

Billy Graham asked Roy and me to fly to Houston to give our Christian witness at a huge rally in Rice Stadium. I declined, because it meant that I would have to fly, and I had promised myself that there would be no plane trips for me as long as Robin was alive. I just didn't want to leave her motherless. Then word came from Texas that my father had suffered a stroke, and I *had* to fly. I tossed on my bed all the night before taking off, praying, "Lord, you know I don't want to fly, to leave Robin. You don't really want me in Houston, do You?" And the Voice answered, "Who is first in your life? Robin?" I flew, stopping on my way to see my father, who seemed to be recovering. I think it was then that I really released Robin to her Heavenly Father.

When I reached Dallas, I went out to see Miss Carson, the matron of Hope Cottage, where Roy and Arlene Rogers had adopted Cheryl. Cheryl had asked me some difficult questions about her adoption, and I wanted to talk with the folks at Hope about her. My sister-in-law, Bennie Merle, was with me. Miss Carson took us on a personally conducted tour to see the new crop of babies.

There were about thirty of them, from a few days old to about three months of age. As I was going from crib to crib, loving every one of them, Bennie Merle called to me from the center of the room, "If you want to adopt a baby, just come and look at this one! This is the one I would want." The baby was a two-month-old girl with enormous deep brown eyes, a shock of straight black hair and lovely olive skin. At two months, she was holding her head and shoulders up on her elbows, and her eyes followed me around the room. I was fascinated at first sight; she was the exact opposite of Robin in every way—as vigorous as a jumping bean. Miss Carson said her name was Mary, and that she was of Choctaw Indian-Scottish-Irish descent. "That's a coincidence," I said. "Roy is part Choctaw, too." She said that Mary was to go to a home where there was Indian blood. I said I hoped it would be a *good* home where she would be appreciated, and went on to the next baby. Within the hour I was on my way to see my Dad in the Waxahachie Hospital, near our old home in Italy, Texas.

Dad had had a severe stroke, but he was not paralyzed. He was a Christian, and ready to meet his Master. I had a prayer with him at the hospital and in my heart silently committed him to God. He was to lie flat on that bed for six weeks, slowly recuperate—and die within the year. When I reached Houston and Rice Stadium I had a feeling of genuine relief for both my father and my baby. I was not overwhelmed with grief at the prospect of death—I had a new faith that conquered all that.

Later that same year I had a strange dream. I was in a houseboat on the muddy Mississippi River. Robin was in a tiny boat being towed by the larger one. There was a catwalk between them. All of a sudden there was a tremendous swell and in a panic I looked back to see her little craft almost submerged. I screamed as the water receded, flew across the catwalk and opened the door of her little house. She was lying peacefully in her crib with a slight smile on her face. I cried out her name, and she opened her eyes and laughed. It troubled me.

A week later I had a call from Texas telling me that my uncle had died of a heart attack. I thought, "This must be the end of my dream. This is what it was all about." Some folks put no stock in dreams and think they have no bearing on what is to happen. They feel the same way about dreams that they feel about miracles—the day for them is gone. I don't feel that way about it. There is too much evidence the other way.

5

*R*obin's nurse Claudia ("Cau-Cau" to Robin) left us; she had been with the baby day and night for a year, and she was near exhaustion. Her going was a wrenching experience for all of us, for she had been completely dedicated and devoted to our child. I wondered how we could possibly get along without her. But there is, as the Bible says, a time and a season for everything, and in my heart I knew that it was time for me to accept the responsibility of caring for the child.

Robin was restless and I think lonely for Cau-Cau; she became fretful and irritable. I was feeding her one day in the kitchen when she suddenly refused to eat and pushed her milk and crackers off the table. Tired and irritated, I gently tapped the little offending hand. She started to cry and then turned off the tears, turned around in her chair and pointed to a picture of Jesus hanging on the wall behind her. It took my breath; I had no idea that she had ever noticed the picture. There was the Christ surrounded by a group of children of all races and colors —and she seemed to see something there that I had missed. Often after that she would twist and turn until she could see it.

Virginia slept in Robin's quarters that night; in the morning she reported that Robin had been restless and crying most of the night. We didn't take it too seriously, for she had had nights like this before. Cheryl, Linda and Dusty heard it too; they had been awake most of the night fighting off the swelling and fever of an attack of mumps, but we had not taken Robin near them, so it must be just another one of those nights.

The restless nights continued, however. Robin refused her food, took only her milk and cried almost constantly. And after three days her face swelled and her fever soared; *she had caught the mumps!* A pediatrician came and gave her a shot, but she got steadily worse. I called the doctor who had examined her at the time of her birth—a fine Christian physician with a great sympathy for retarded children—and he levelled with me. He said that the infection had gone to her brain; she had encephalitis, and he doubted that she would make it. Even if she did, there would be severe brain damage. I asked him, "If a miracle should happen and she should make it, would it be possible to do open heart surgery on her, and close up that congenital defect—the hole in her heart? I will spend my last penny to help her." He smiled sadly, shook his head and said, "No. Don't do it. She would never survive the anesthetic. Keep her as comfortable as you can, and go on loving her, and learn from the experience. That is what I would do, if she were my child."

It was said kindly, but it was like the signing of a death warrant.

Near midnight I was awakened by a spine-chilling howling and wailing, coming from somewhere outside. I threw on a robe and rushed outdoors to find Lana, our German Weimaranar dog and Robin's special pet, at the door of her room. I remembered the stories I had heard of dogs wailing as death approached someone they loved, but Ruth, Robin's nurse, did her best to disabuse me of that idea—it was just a myth. Robin's fever was frighteningly high and her crying wracked my heart. Ruth's explanation that this was just a pain-reflex action from the headache did little to help. I stayed and prayed while Ruth got a little rest.

At six A.M. Virginia took over; she thought Robin had just had a convulsion. They put her in cool water and brought her out of it; we took turns walking her and bathing her face and giving her the prescribed coffee enema for inward stimulation. She slipped into a semi-coma. The doctor came, looked at her and shook his head; there was nothing more he could do.

At four in the afternoon I remembered with a pang of remorse that the other children had not had lunch and I went into the kitchen to fix something for them. They were very quiet. Standing by the sink I heard the words, "I am going to take Robin." I said, "All right, Lord. As You will." When the food was on the table I went back to find Robin breathing with an ominous rasping, rattling sound in her throat. I was dimly conscious of a bird singing in the eaves of her little house. It seemed to me that Robin and I were suspended between two worlds. Lana scratched wildly at the screen door in a last desperate effort to get inside, yelping the same bark she used whenever she stood between Robin and a stranger. Ruth and Virginia sent her away. I stumbled blindly out of the door for a breath of fresh air—and to pray. I walked with Roy, my face streaming with tears, asking God to take her quickly and not let her suffer any more. Virginia came out and said quietly, "She's gone." Never have I wept as I wept then.

Tom and Barbara couldn't come, for Barbara was about to have her baby. My father was still confined to his bed, so I asked Mother not to come. My brother Hillman came in her place. We sent the children out to their grandmother's home in Van Nuys. We thought it best that they were not subjected to the ordeal of the funeral.

I could not bear to look at Robin in death. Roy stayed with her until the doctor came to sign the death certificate, and the man from the Forest Lawn Mortuary came and took her little body away. Frances and Leonard Eilers came; Frances drove me around in her car for two hours while I cried it out and talked it out. Leonard stayed with Roy.

When Frances and I came back, the little house that was Robin's was closed and dark. I could not bear to look at it.

92

She was to be buried on her second birthday! Virginia put away her unwrapped birthday presents. Friends came, and a flood of phone calls and telegrams began.

Roy and Art made the arrangements for the services at Forest Lawn; they took Robin's little white christening dress, a blue ribbon for her hair and a photograph of her taken at the christening. On Monday evening Roy and I drove out to the airport to pick up my brother, and we stopped at Forest Lawn to see that everything was ready. Roy asked me to go in with him to look at her. I couldn't do it. I was afraid of breaking down in front of Roy and even of doing something foolish, like trying to pick her up. I could not trust myself.

When Roy came back to the car, there was a strange beauty of peace on his face. He said, "That's the hardest thing I ever did, but I'm glad I did it. I feel at peace about her now. The minute I looked at her, I knew she was with the Lord. She looks like . . . like a small-size sleeping angel." He had picked out a little child's blue casket and he said it looked very tiny among the flowers that had come from everywhere. We drove almost in silence to the airport. I was ashamed at having let him down. The last time he had been there was the day Arlene Rogers was buried. I knew how hard it was for him.

All morning, the day of the funeral, I prayed—and out of the prayers came strength to face the afternoon and the funeral. The limousine picked us up at three o'clock. I closed my eyes and prayed all along the freeway and I felt the comforting presence of the Holy Spirit. When we pulled up at the rear of the church, I asked that Robin be carried out of the other door at the close of the service so I wouldn't see the casket. What a coward I was! How much I had to learn about conquering the flesh! Roy had promised that the casket would be kept closed during the service, covered with flowers and opened only for the congregation after I was out of the room. Dr. Harley Wright Smith, who had baptized Robin, opened the service with a

93

prayer; Dr. Jack MacArthur delivered a short talk; Leonard Eilers made the closing prayer; our favorite Gospel hymns were played by the organist and from beginning to end a Voice whispered, "Let not your heart be troubled; you believe in Me."

Somehow, the little form under the blanket of pink roses had no real connection with Robin; what lay in the little blue casket was a shell, not my baby, and I couldn't bring myself to look at it. I was taken out to the limousine when they opened the casket. One of the attendants followed me out and did his best to make me go back and look at her: "She's beautiful. She looks like a big doll. You will never be sorry if you will only just look at her. Please! It will make you feel better." I still refused. How many, many times I was to regret that!

That night I realized that life goes on, however deep and searing the sorrow may be. I learned that there was a rehearsal with the Sons of the Pioneers, scheduled long ago and urgently necessary, since they had to leave the next morning for New York and Madison Square Garden. We had been booked for this engagement for more than a year. I thought it blasphemy, but it had to be. I had to get through it somehow, and I did, racked by the worst pain I had ever known. We do what we *must* do.

My brother came to me in the kitchen after the rehearsal was over, put his arms around me and said, "Sis, I'm proud of you. You're a real trouper. Where on earth did you get the strength to do it?" I knew that I hadn't gotten that strength from anything on earth; it was Someone in heaven who was holding me up.

Sedatives kept me quiet through the night, but I got up in the morning on the ragged edge of a nervous breakdown. I was sitting in the kitchen with Emily when the back door flew open and two strange women walked in. One of them said, "Mrs. Rogers, I know this is a bad time to come to your house right after your baby's death, but my aunt here is from the East and

94

she simply has to meet you and your husband and see your home before she goes back."

I stared at them. This *couldn't* be! Yes, we were celebrities, but must celebrities be gawked at like three-legged calves or baubles in a jeweler's window? I wanted to throw something at them, but I'm glad I didn't. I dabbed at my eyes with a napkin and said as quietly and civilly as I could, "You are right; this is not the time to see our home, and I'm not up to showing it to you. Roy is in the den, if you want to see him." With that they shoved past me and strode into the den. I don't know what Roy said to them, and I don't dare ask. I do know that they went out of the house in too much of a hurry to say good-bye.

Why do people think that show business folks are something other than human? That we are never tired, or sick, or in sorrow? I like to think that they are not inconsiderate, but that they just don't understand that we are subject to the same joys and sorrows and frustrations and problems that other people know. We live in a fishbowl, and it isn't all glamour.

I was thinking about all this the next day as I sat trying to make sense of all that had happened. Gazing up at a color etching of Robin, I recalled Roy's words: "She looks like a small-size sleeping angel"—and there flashed through my mind a verse from the thirteenth chapter of Hebrews: "Be not forgetful to entertain strangers, for thereby some have entertained angels unaware." Like the sun breaking through the clouds after many days of storm and darkness, it became clear: Robin had been a little ministering angel to our family, teaching us through her handicaps that the strength of the Lord is made perfect in weakness. She had taught us some badly needed lessons and true values in life. For two years she had been teaching us humility, patience, gratitude, too, and dependence upon God.

My hand flashed out to grab a pen and I started to write. For an hour I wrote so hard and so fast that my hand became cramped and I had to stop. Yes, I had to stop. I looked down

95

in unbelief at the little pile of paper on the desk covered with my handwriting, and I couldn't convince myself that it was *mine*. I wanted very much to write more, more, more, but I couldn't. A curtain had fallen over my mind. I wondered.

Some days later while Roy and I were doing a radio broadcast I had a few moments to rest, away from the mike. I closed my eyes and started to pray about Robin's message and the voice came again, saying, *"Let Robin write it!* You be the instrument. You will be given her message to help others. Get yourself out of the way. Let Robin speak for herself."

The compulsion of the voice, the great wisdom of it, did not pass; it dominated me completely for weeks. Robin's story flew from my pen; my hand was moved, *guided.* I kept a tablet and a pencil handy and jotted down notes and thoughts as they came to me. If no tablet was handy, I made notes on the backs of envelopes, script sheets, the margins of newspapers. It took three months to finish it. It was Robin's book—and God's— not mine. I was merely the hand He used.

Now all that remained was to get it published.

The night we left for New York by way of Dallas, we drove past the Forest Lawn mausoleum where Robin had been laid to rest. There was an illuminated cross on top of the building. As I looked up at it, the thought of her lying there and the memory of my refusal to look at her before the funeral swept over me, and a feeling of having let her down filled my eyes with tears again. I could not trust myself to speak. When we boarded the train I couldn't even manage a thank you to Art and Mary Jo Rush, who had driven us to the station. On the train, the minute the bedroom door closed the dam broke and I was near hysteria. I wanted to be strong and to help all the others, and most of all I wanted to witness to the strength of God in time of trouble. I had denied myself the therapy of weeping, as much as I was able, and it all piled up inside of me. Now I wept for nearly an hour.

Roy said, "Maybe we'd better adopt another baby, right now."

I shook my head. "No. I just want Robin." The thought of never holding her in my arms again, of never singing her to sleep again was a weight, crushing me.

Just as we pulled into the Dallas station Roy said, "When we come back to Dallas after we've seen your dad in the hospital, I want to run out and see Mrs. Carson at Hope Cottage. I think seeing the babies might help both of us."

I hardly heard him.

Dad was much improved after his stroke, and after a two-day visit we did drive out to Hope Cottage, just before taking the plane for New York. Halfway up the front steps of the home I remembered the little Choctaw Indian girl I had seen there two months earlier. I asked if she was still there, and a nurse said, "Yes, she's here, but she has just finished her tests and she is ready for adoption. There is a fine lady of Indian extraction here in Dallas who is interested in Mary, and she may adopt her."

The minute I saw little Mary I swept her up into my arms and hugged her fiercely. Her little arms locked themselves around my neck—or did God lock them there?

I cried out to Roy, "This is *our* child. I want her. May we have her?"

His eyes were wide with astonishment. "Are you sure?" he asked. I was sure—wildly, happily, brokenheartedly sure.

"Well," he said, "it's sure all right with me."

They promised to let us know by phone while we were in New York.

New York was hard for us this time. The press conferences were trying. I was still so emotionally upset that I couldn't make sense talking to anyone. I would pray every step of the way from our dressing rooms to the chutes, and during the show, asking God to steady me as Roy and I shook hands with the children in the stands, as we always did at the end of the show. I knew I would see Robin in the face of every little blonde, blue-eyed girl. God helped me; true to His words, He did not leave me comfortless. Each night I made it, dry-eyed, back to the hotel.

But the strain was telling on me. I got little sleep. There were nightmares in which I dreamed that I saw Robin in her casket, sitting up and looking at me with questioning eyes. I would wake up crying, trying to pray, knowing that my prayers never got higher than the ceiling. The Adversary was having a field day with me! I began to wonder if Robin was just a mistake of nature, if God really knew or cared, if her book was really His doing or simply my desire to get an affliction off my chest after hiding it from the public for two years.

There were ten days of that; on the tenth morning, hollow-eyed and shaking from shattered nerves, I said to Roy, "I'm going out in Central Park and sit there on a bench until God tells me something. I can't go on like this; I just have to have some rest and some assurance that He is directing me with Robin's book. He simply has to help me!"

I took my Bible and walked out into the lovely autumn sunshine to a stone bench near the Central Park Zoo. I bowed my head and prayed, "Thy will be done, Lord. Not my will, but Thine! But—*please* give me a word. Please give me peace about Robin and her book. Is it Your will that I seek a publisher for it? Will it help Your cause? Will it help children like Robin— and their parents? *Please.*

I looked up from that prayer and saw, walking toward me, a little Mongoloid girl about six years old, holding the hand of a middle-aged woman whose face was cut deeply with the scars of mental anguish. The child had all the characteristics of the full Mongoloid type: the slanted eyes weak and out of control, the tiny ears and little square hands, the thick tongue, the drooling, the unsteady, labored walk. There were hundreds of office workers there in the park, walking in the noon sunshine,

98

but I lost sight of them completely. I could see only that child walking *toward me*.

Then I saw it! I had asked God for a word, and He had sent it in this child. *He had spoken to me!* He was saying to me, "I have taken Robin so that you can speak of Me to children like this, and to mothers like this. Robin is safe in the Everlasting Arms. She is safe. Now tell others how she has blessed your life in giving you an awareness of Me, and how all the other little Mongoloids in the world can bless all these other mothers."

I fairly ran back through the park to the hotel, burst into our suite and shouted to Roy, "He did it! God did it! He *spoke* to me!" And as though God took my hand and led me, I picked up the phone and called Marble Collegiate Church and asked for an appointment with Dr. Norman Vincent Peale, the pastor at Collegiate who had written the book, *A Guide to Confident Living,* that had helped me so much. I vowed when I had read the chapter in that book on "How to Meet Sorrow" that some day I would find him and thank him. So I called Dr. Peale.

I got the answer from his secretary that I expected: Dr. Peale was a very, very busy man, working on a tight schedule; people often made appointments weeks ahead, and she rather doubted that I could see him, but she'd check and see. She checked. God opened the door for me, and fifteen minutes later I walked into his study.

"Dr. Peale, I have written a book about my baby. May I read just a little of it to you?"

"Of course; but first, we'll pray." We prayed, on our knees. I got a tight hold on my emotions, fought back the tears, and read what God had put on my pen. I looked up at him; he hadn't said a word all through the reading, and I was almost afraid that I was boring him. He looked at me with glistening eyes and said, "It's beautiful. I will help you get it published."

He sent me to his own publisher—Prentice-Hall. They declined the book because they were at that very moment launching a beautiful book written by Marie Killilea—a book called *Karen,* about a little girl who had cerebral palsy. They felt they couldn't do justice to another book of the same nature at the same time.

Then he sent me to Abingdon Press. These people were kind, but they were also wary of my "presumption that the soul of a two-year-old child should have such scope of spiritual understanding," and they doubted that "God could talk that way to a baby—or the baby to God." Two blows in a row! But somehow after that experience in Central Park I wasn't let down or discouraged.

The same afternoon I had a call from Dr. Frank S. Mead, Editor-in-Chief of the Fleming H. Revell Company. It just happened that he had been in the Abingdon office after I had left the building. He called to ask if he might read my manuscript on his way to Chicago, on a business trip. He called from Chicago and said, "We want it!"

I wept—this time in joy.

Later in the same week there was a call from Hope Cottage in Dallas. Miss Carson said, "Come and get Mary. She's yours! Could you stop and pick her up on your way home to California?" Could we! I sang, "My cup runneth over . . . He doeth all things well."

I wrote Virginia to send me Robin's little pink coat and hat. We finished our engagement at the Garden and played a few one-night engagements on the way home. The last show of the tour was in the big auditorium in Cincinnati, Ohio. Roy was idly leafing through a pile of mail on the desk in our hotel room when he came across a telegram from a woman in Covington, Kentucky, across the river from Cincinnati. She and her husband ran a welfare home for handicapped children—nineteen of them—on a farm. One of the children was her own daughter, Penny. Could she bring Penny to the show to meet Roy Rogers—*and* Trigger? Roy phoned her to bring Penny that

100

night. He also asked her, on a sudden impulse, "You don't happen to have an adoptable little boy about five years old, do you? I mean a boy I could take home as a companion for my son, Dusty." She allowed there was one. She'd bring him, too.

They came backstage during intermission: Mrs. Coleman, Penny and little Harry. Penny was in a wheelchair and Harry walked beside her, his hand on the arm of her chair. He was a towhead with great blue eyes just the color of Robin's. His head was too large for his body, but you should have seen that smile! He looked up at Roy, held out his hand and drawled, "Hiya, pahtnah!" We "was took" on the spot. Roy swept him up in his arms and held him tight.

Mrs. Coleman told us that he had been abandoned by his alcoholic parents and left in a terrible condition in a local motel. He had the worst case of rickets I have ever seen. He had spent eight months with his legs in braces. The doctors doubted that he would ever walk. She said he was all right mentally, but a bit slow in his reflexes. The youngsters at the home loved him; he fed the helpless ones at every meal. If we were serious about adopting him, she thought it might be arranged. We agreed to call her later in the evening.

Back in the hotel room after the performance, we talked about Harry for three hours. We wondered if we could really help him to become a normal little boy and if it would be fair to the other children to bring another "problem child" into the home after the experience with Robin. We had noticed that his walking and running were not quite free or normal.

Roy said, in a dreamy voice, "Look. Anybody will adopt a kid who has everything going for him, but what becomes of little guys like this one? Let's take him." I agreed. I remembered how tightly Roy had held him. In the middle of the night we called Mrs. Coleman. At nine the next morning we stood before a judge, signed the papers and walked out of the courtroom with a brand new son.

Don't let anyone tell me that the age of miracles is passed. God has taken one child—and given us *two*. Usually the machinery of adoption moves painfully slowly. There is a lot of red tape and it often takes months, and sometimes a year or two; it is not often that you can take a child from one state to another, as we were doing. It took us less than twenty-four hours! The Lord giveth and the Lord taketh away; blessed be the name of the Lord.

He had given us twofold.

6

$\mathcal{T}$he first thing Roy did with Harry was to give him a new name: Sandy. ("All we need now is another boy to name Filthy," said Roy, "to go along with Sandy and Dusty.") The second thing he did was to take him to a Dallas bootshop and buy him a pair of cowboy boots. Sandy put the boots on laughing like a banshee. We went out to Hope Cottage to pick up Mary (she was "Dodie," now). Sandy clung to Roy's hand and my skirt, afraid we would leave him there. The fear of a child with Sandy's background is a horrible thing to see.

With Sandy in his boots and Dodie in Robin's coat and hat, we got on the plane for Los Angeles. Dodie took to flying like the proverbial duck takes to water. She was as active as Sandy was passive. She ate as though food were going out of style. Sandy's clothes were drenched with perspiration. I charged it to too much excitement for such a little boy, never realizing that he had some really important physical problems.

Dusty had been told about the new baby girl but not about Sandy, because we wanted to surprise him with a new brother. We were the last passengers off the plane; our whole family was waiting at the bottom of the ramp and the place was crawling with press photographers. I saw Dusty take one quick incredulous look at the little boy holding his Daddy's hand and run to hide behind Virginia, his nurse. Cheryl and Linda were enchanted with Dodie, who took all the excitement in her stride. You'd have thought she had spent all her life before the cameras.

103

Roy got his hands on Dusty and introduced him to his new brother. Sandy grinned and stuck out his hand which Dusty ignored. He wasn't shaking hands with any stranger, thank you. And he was anything but sure about *this* stranger. Roy joined his hand with Sandy's, and Dusty did hold onto the strange new hand for some more press pictures.

Sandy talked a blue streak all the way home in the car while Dusty held his peace and his tongue. He was still wary of this new one and he took his time sizing him up. Dusty was six and Sandy was five. When we reached home the two new ones were shown their quarters and prepared for bed. Dodie screamed in protest when I put her in her new crib, letting out a war whoop that must have been heard in El Paso but which died a sudden death when I gave her a bottle. Sandy took it well; he was asleep before I had finished my prayer for him.

Life began again on the home lot. Emily, Virginia and the children adjusted nicely; Sandy and Dusty were soon playing together like old pals. We had both children examined by our pediatrician, who pronounced Dodie in fine condition but who had some doubts about Sandy. We found that Sandy had practically no bridge over his nose; one side of it was almost completely closed off either from a fall or a blow from a fist. From what we had been told about his parents, we were inclined to believe it was from a fist.

The pediatrician said, "All I can say is that you've got a lot of guts, adopting a child like this."

We said, "It's OK. Let us worry about that. We'll take our chances with him."

We had the nose operated on (a new bridge built), and his tonsils and adenoids removed. We kept him at home until February, and then sent him off to school with Dusty. There were problems with Sandy. He had a hard time trying to ride a tricycle. He was afraid to climb to any high place and he

104

had periodic spells of dizziness and vomiting. He also had enuresis, which was extremely trying for all of us. I tried everything, but he was quite unable to awaken during the night and each day fresh bed linen was required. Many times I have wept in shame over losing my temper with Sandy, especially when I remember his unfailing good humor and sweet disposition as we struggled with him. He was a lovable little boy. He and Dusty had great fun together. Conditioned by Robin to understanding handicaps, Dusty made allowances for him; he would tease him unmercifully at times, but just let anyone else try to tease him!

Thanksgiving Day I took the children out to Robin's crypt. We had talked so much about Robin that I felt it would be good for them to visit Forest Lawn. We stopped at a florist's shop and bought some beautiful bouquets of pink roses and lilies of the valley, which we placed at Robin's feet. I had been there only once—with Roy. That day wasn't too bad, but this day with the children was much more difficult than I had thought it would be. The thought of Robin in the casket behind the stone plaque burned like fire and I almost fainted. Cheryl steadied me, "Easy, Mama, easy!" and took the others off for hot dogs for lunch. I rushed home with Dodie, put her in her crib and then threw myself across my bed with one of Robin's little shoes clenched in my hand and cried most of the afternoon.

That was the last long cry. The other children demanded more and more of my attention, and I decided that they were entitled to it. Christmas came, and there was a little Christmas angel on top of the tree, representing Robin. By this time the children had adjusted to the situation even better than I had, so Robin's presence was a cheerful one, and not for tears. The wound was slowly healing.

What mental pictures I have of those days! Cheryl was becoming a young lady; Linda was attending Campbell Hall

105

School; the boys were learning to swim and going fishing with Daddy at Malibu. Dodie would sit quietly in her crib out on the lawn watching the birds, not making a sound but following every movement. I'll never forget the first Easter we had together with the egg hunt and real live rabbits (provided by Roy) hopping across the lawn. It seemed too good to be true, after all we had been through, but it was good. For every sorrow, God provides a joy.

Dodie was prone to croup. Remembering Robin, I watched her as an old mother hen watches her one chick. There was also a record of tuberculosis in her background, and I didn't intend to let *that* get started! She became somewhat solemn with strangers—when she first met them she would make them uncomfortable by just staring at them, unsmiling, until she decided that they were all right. A big grin was the signal that they were OK.

Dusty and Sandy were a handful. I would take them in the back seat of the car when I went shopping. I also took a switch to cool off their wrestling matches. Once I really caught Dusty with a good one; he howled more in humiliation than in pain.

"Mom, I'm leaving home!"

"That's a good idea. We'll pack your suitcase as soon as we get home." Silence—for two minutes. Then, "Well, maybe I'll wait a year or two."

The two of them went out one day and picked all the rubber off the dashboard of Roy's new outboard motorboat. Roy really blew his top on this one. There was an inquisition that went on for three days and which produced no evidence whatever as to which one was the culprit. They just didn't know *anything* about it. Sandy finally admitted his guilt when Roy promised he wouldn't spank whoever did it.

Then came the day when they went up and down our street opening the mailboxes of our neighbors. I looked out of my window and saw them—and took off after them with a belt.

It was a good chase, but I never got close enough to use the belt—and I never chased them again!

It was at a Hollywood Christian group meeting that we made an arrangement with Billy Graham that was to become one of the great experiences of our lives. The group was growing fast, and their activities widened. There were some spectacular life-changing conversions and wonderful weekend retreats at the Forest Home Christian Conference Grounds near San Bernardino. Tim and Velma Spencer were live-in host and hostess at HCG headquarters, a Hollywood home rented by the board. They kept the door open day and night for counselling and prayer. We had different guest speakers every Monday at meetings held in big homes with big living rooms or patios. Billy Graham came to a meeting held around the swimming pool in our backyard, and he lighted many a lamp in many a heart. Roy says, "Every time Billy comes into a room the whole place lights up." The Light is truly in this man of God.

Billy came back to visit us a day or so later and in the course of the conversation he told us that he had been invited to hold a Crusade for Christ in London. He was a bit awed at the prospect, and said that he was waiting upon God for the decision to go or not to go. I think Roy helped him go when he said, "I have a big fan club in the British Isles. We'll go over there—take Dale and Trigger and do some shows in advance of your Crusade, and then join you in London the first week you're there."

We went to England in February—the coldest month in the British year. We opened the tour in Glasgow and toured the Scottish highlands and the English countryside, driven by a most delightful cockney known as Griff. Griff was as warm as British toast. The weather was so cold, wet, snowy and miserable that I was sure the devil had planned it. We got some relief when we stopped for luncheon, dinner or tea at the country inns. Never had tea tasted so good. The coffee—

107

well, I pass! Coffee definitely isn't their cup of tea, but the welcome we got in Glasgow warmed our hearts. The street outside the theater was packed solidly with people who shouted, "We want Roy! We want Dale! Sing us a song!" We leaned out of a window and sang a chorus or two of western songs, and they roared for more. What a people!

Edinburgh was cold, too. We stayed at the old Caledonia Hotel, just below the royal castle, and we could hear the bagpipes playing up there in the clouds above us. Never have I been so physically cold—or numb. The maid kept a fire going for us in our room, banking it at night. When I slid into bed the first night, I thought I had opened the door to the North Pole. I gritted my teeth and stretched out—until my feet touched a hot water bottle. I wish I had bought that bottle, and brought it home and given it some years of retirement in sunny California before it went where all such bottles go!

I always read my Bible before going to sleep, wherever I am, and sometimes I read a newspaper as well. I read a newspaper one night in Edinburgh to see what was happening to Billy in London. Plenty was happening. The newspaper account was full of unfriendliness toward him—critical and often sarcastic to the point of insult. They complained, "He looked like a Madison Avenue TV salesman, with his bright tie." They wrote of "little old ladies singing Gospel songs," as his ship docked. They were quite dubious about "the big advertising campaign the American evangelist and his team were putting on." They doubted his sincerity—and that stung and disturbed and angered me. After all, he had been invited to come to England. There seemed to be some need for evangelism: one Sunday morning we went to an early Communion Service at the great cathedral in Carlisle and found a congregation of six.

We also sensed the pressure of opposition when we told the people of the press about our intention of giving our Christian witness during the first week of Billy's Crusade. Their eyebrows would go up and someone always asked, "What do you mean—your *witness?*" Some wanted to know why Billy had come to England when there were already plenty of churches in England. Didn't America need his preaching more than England needed it? On the whole, the press was friendly to Roy and to me, but we couldn't understand its harsh criticism of Billy.

One press lady, however, wasn't so friendly with me. When I told her that I had found the British people very kind and warm and friendly, and that we were enjoying the beautiful English countryside, she almost snarled, "Oh, don't be so trite! That's what the studios tell all you actresses to say when you come over here." I was startled at her impertinence and insulting language, but I told her bluntly that nobody had told me to say anything to anyone about England, that I spoke for myself and for no one else—and that I was not in the habit of lying. Pondering these things today, I think this underlying resentment against Americans is caused unwittingly by some of our rough riding and ill-advised visitors over there. I *loved* being there.

I prayed for Billy and I spoke for him, during our tour. How wise he was, all through those first hard days and weeks in England! He never replied to their insults. He simply ". . . set his face like a flint . . ." (Israel 50:7), to go to London and do what God and the outstanding clergymen and religious leaders of England had asked him to do. He was sincere and friendly—and he preached up a storm every night. The papers gradually changed their tune as the crowds at the Crusade grew larger and larger. What's that old saying? "Nothing succeeds like success."

In Edinburgh we met two most interesting people—a man and a little girl. The man was Chief Constable William Merilees, the Queen's personal guard in Scotland; the girl was Marion Fleming, a tiny girl with a haunting little voice, in an orphanage called Dunforth. She sang for us; I can still hear it. When we left, we invited Marion to have lunch with us at the hotel and then we invited her to visit us the following summer, in Hollywood. The matron at the orphanage thought it might be arranged.

We were both sick when we reached Liverpool. As Griff drove us through the shouting, jostling throng in the streets we were flushed with fever and aching from head to foot, having hardly enough strength to wave back at them. It was the European flu. A doctor put us to bed, stuffed us with sulfa and penicillin and started a medicated steam inhaler going full blast in our room. The newspaper people thought we were faking in order to cancel a news conference set for the afternoon, and they tried to trap us. They stuffed a bunch of daffodils in Trigger's mouth and had Glenn Randall, our trainer, walk the horse upstairs to our room to present them. When they saw our faces at the door of the room, they knew we were not faking, and the party was over.

Two days later we shuffled weakly onstage at the theater and somehow got through the performance. We had been threatened with a lawsuit if we didn't show after two days—sick or not sick. I remember clutching the curtains onstage to keep from falling.

Liverpool, Manchester, Belfast and then Dublin. Our bookers had suggested that we omit any reference to the Billy Graham Crusade—omit it there and anywhere else in Ireland. "You might get hit with vegetables." We ignored it. We don't frighten easily when witnessing is involved. We were concerned about it, yes, but our concern evaporated when we received the greatest response to our inspirational and Christian closing in Ireland that we had known anywhere—England, Scotland or even America. We got a standing ovation in Dublin. A delightful monk who was chaplain of the Abbey Players talked for a long time with us about Billy, and remarked that, "The man is doing a marvelous work." He gave us an entertainer's prayer book which was prefaced by the story of the Christian martyr

Genesius, the patron saint of the Abbey Players. We liked Dublin—and the Irish.

Two days later Roy galloped Trigger out into the centre of Harringay Arena in London to a deafening roar. It was as though there had never been a word of opposition to us, or to Billy Graham.

Billy preached well that day, to packed stands. The room was packed to the rafters for the evening indoor service. I looked at Billy and wondered how he was going to get through his sermon with cameras flashing all around him. What power flowed from him that night! I could feel it mounting when Roy and I spoke briefly and sang a duet; I felt it even more after Billy's sermon. He paused a moment before giving the invitation and in that moment a man in the balcony leaped to his feet, raised a clenched fist and shouted, "Mr. Graham, why don't you pray that the President of the United States stops this war?" Billy was quiet for a split second before he replied, "Too long have we looked to man. Let us look to God!" That answer just *had* to come from God. The response to the invitation was tremendous. One of those who came forward was a well-known young British actress who had been on the verge of suicide.

Another night, I saw young men with liquor bottles in the front row, drinking in front of Billy and the choir all through the service. A man yelled, "Mr. Graham, why don't you go out to the American air base and preach to your Americans and get them to quit getting our English girls pregnant?"

But on the whole, Billy was getting better and better notices, and it was working out well. The night he closed the Crusade, there were 90,000 at Wembley Stadium standing in the rain to hear him. The Archbishop of Canterbury held the umbrella while Billy preached! I was sure when I saw that, that Billy had overcome his opposition, and I was content to start for home.

Home! Home meant Cheryl, who was attending Corvalis High School, Linda, who was attending Campbell Hall and

111

Dusty and Sandy, who were enrolled at Northridge Military Academy—and Dodie, who had just celebrated her first birthday. I vowed I'd stay home with them from now on—and then discovered that we had a three-week tour through Ohio, Indiana, Michigan, Missouri, Tennessee and Texas. Show business! Just before going onstage at Columbus, Ohio, I was stopped by the same feeling that had come over me the day Robin died— nausea, stomach cramps and that odd feeling of being in another world and somehow apart from everything that was going on around me.

Roy was called away to the phone for a minute on a long distance call. He seemed preoccupied when he came back; when I asked him who it was, he said, "I'll tell you about it later; right now, we're on stage." Suddenly I felt release, and we went onstage.

We piled onto the bus after the show and I noticed immediately that everyone was unusually quiet. I overheard our road manager, Jack Lacey, say to Roy, "Have you told Dale anything yet?" I heard Roy answer, "Wait till we get to the hotel." In our room, he cleared his throat and started to tell me, "Dale, we've had word that . . . ."

I said, "My father is dead." He nodded.

"What time did he die?"

"He died just a short time before you had that sick spell, when we were going onstage." Call it telepathy, call it spiritual, call it anything you want—I have found that it is *there*—that voice between two suffering people in the great, deep moments of life.

I had to do this one on my own; Roy had to stay and finish the show in Columbus. I flew to Texas alone. My brother Hillman and his wife Bennie met me at the airfield and drove me to Italy. He must have been reading my mind during that trip, for he said, "Sis, you've got to look at Dad; he looks better in death than he has looked since he had that stroke."

I remembered Robin, and I started to beg off with the usual, "I want to remember Dad as I knew him in life," but it was a poor excuse, and I knew it. Hillman said, "Don't make that mistake again. You owe it to him and you owe it to yourself. If you don't, you'll have to go through the same agony that you went through after you refused to look at Robin. *Please. . . .*" The mention of Robin did it—that, and that awful feeling of cowardice in refusing to face up to the fact of death. Reluctantly, I went to the mortuary with my brother, his wife and my mother and saw my father.

Hillman was so right! God did a wonderful thing for me as I stood there and looked at Dad. *He removed all fear of death from me forever.* I looked and saw a Christian; I saw not a body but a soul united with Christ, and I never again allowed my human sorrow to blind me to that truth of reconciliation and redemption. And I knew that in the wisdom and the planning of God, we would all be reunited with him again in the perfect life—in the Everlasting.

Again there came unthinking fans and autograph seekers, as they had come after Robin died. A stranger from a nearby town heard that I was there, and she came with a car full of people *on the day of the funeral* to ask for autographs. My uncle was furious at their lack of respect and even ordinary decency, and he was all for telling them off, but I stopped him; most of those in the car were children. Besides, this autograph business was part of being a public figure. The mother of the children said they had literally goaded her into bringing them. They went off happy with their autographs—and I was happy for them. I was glad to have made someone else happy, while I was in the depths of sorrow. They will experience their sorrows, soon enough.

I tried to get my mother to come back to California with me for a rest—and learned another lesson. "No," she said, "not now. I have to face it alone, sooner or later, and I may as well start right now. Later, I'll come."

We cannot run from death, and its partings. We cannot run from anything. The sooner we accept the fact of death, and the sooner we resolve to work it out with the help of the Lord, the sooner we conquer it. Roy and I sometimes sing that old spiritual.

> You have to walk—that lonesome valley,
> You have to walk it by yourself—

The valley of the shadow—how we fear it, until we face it and travel it and find in it nothing of which we need to be afraid!

And there are other valleys we must travel. I went through one of the others the night Redd Harper, the singing evangelist, with his wife and adopted son came to have dinner with us. (It was shortly after my father died.) Just before dessert, the room started whirling around me, and I blacked out. Emily, our housekeeper, brought me to with the application of a cold wet towel and I dismissed it, thinking I was just overtired; but later it happened again—at the piano. This time I went to bed. The next morning I awoke with a loud buzzing in my ears, with bells ringing and the room spinning again. They got me to the hospital and the tests began. At first they said it might be a brain tumor, but later that was ruled out. It was labyrinthitis— a loss of balance due to an infection of the inner ear. For days I was so ill that I didn't care whether I lived or died. Everything inside me seemed to be out of whack: I had triple vision, my stomach would hold nothing, and my liver seemed to be bouncing around like a tennis ball. It took me two months before I could walk a straight line—and only then by pushing a straight-backed chair ahead of me.

Even after I got home, I was still deep in the valley of despondency. I thought that I had suffered just about everything,

114

and that nobody ever had to put up with such sickness and death as I had. The very weekend that I came home, the two-year-old son of one of our friends drowned in their swimming pool—and God gave me the strength to get up and go to them and to witness to them of how He had helped me through the valley of the shadow, not once, but many times. It helped them—*and* me.

I've had more than my share of illness and death, but I have discovered this: *you can always find someone whose troubles are worse than yours.* If you have gotten through yours, you owe it to those others and to God to *go!* Go to them, and help them with your witness.

Go! Share your comfort and your faith! As we use our own experiences of suffering constructively, we find our sorrows turning to blessings for ourselves and for others. I don't argue about this. I know. I have found that it works that way.

I was to have still another lesson in this business of sharing when on a bright Sunday morning Roy and I were leaving the house for a morning service at the church. On the front porch we found an old friend who had worked in some of Roy's pictures and who had a really bad alcohol problem. Reeking of liquor, he staggered up to me and grabbed my arm, demanding, "Dale, I've got to talk to you. You've got to help me. God has helped you and given you what I need. You remember me, Dale? I knew you *when.* You've found salvation. Help me find it. *Now!*"

Roy was impatient with the intrusion, and if I ever felt less like talking to anyone with a view to helping them, it was at that moment. I was swaying on my feet, worn-out—but I couldn't be mad with him because Jesus' words to the man possessed by evil spirits came to me: "Go home to thy friends, and tell them how great things the Lord has done for thee" (Mark 5:19). I had to stay with him.

115

He poured out his story—and what a story! I gave him prayer—and a cup of black coffee—and I took him to church! I needed the Communion Service that morning; he needed a talk with Father Smith, the rector—so we went. I've often wondered what the people in the church thought when we went reeling down the aisle to our pew, but I was too sick and distraught to think of it then. We made it to the pew—the weak leading the weak.

Father Smith asked him if he needed counselling—the understatement of the week! He needed it, and he got it after the service. It was a new start for Jack, and it lifted me, too. I marveled at the change in our old friend. As Stuart Hamblen says in his song, "It is no secret, what God can do."

It was a weird performance. I suppose some folks thought it was "out of place," but—I'd do it again. Church was the place for Jack that morning!

7

*M*other and Roy were worried about my periodic physical breakdowns. Mother cautioned me, "You had better slow down. God doesn't expect you to kill yourself. He gave you a mind to use in taking care of yourself. Use it! If you don't learn to say no, you will be getting down to where you can't say anything."

This is one of the reasons I am writing this witness. I am unable, *humanly unable,* to go with my testimony to all the places and to all the people I'd like to reach. I know I personally cannot go to all of them, but I also know that I *must* go to as many as I can. Neither I nor anyone else knows the date of departure from this earth—only God knows that. But Jesus said, "I must work the works of him that sent me, while it is day: the night cometh, when no man can work" (John 9:4). So I work—and get as much done as I can. While it is still day for me, I shall be used of Him to the limit, wherever, whenever, however it pleases Him. Sometimes He uses us when we are in perfect health— sometimes in our physical suffering. He can have me in either.

I am constantly aware that Satan is watching and hoping that I, as a Christian, will be rendered helpless in my work of proclaiming the Good News that Christ died to save sinners. I do not underestimate the old boy for a minute. The Apostle James tells me in the Bible, "Resist the devil, and he will flee from you" (4:7). Many times in the dead of night, I awaken with a sense of foreboding or in physical pain, intuitively aware that the Adversary is at work on me. He's wasting his time. All I have to do is to tell him (although he doesn't admit it) that he

117

has already been defeated at the Cross and that while he may some day claim my body, he will never take my spirit or my soul. Christ bought that at Calvary. I tell him that, and almost without exception, he leaves me. Satan cannot abide the name of Jesus Christ—and I intend to repeat it in his face so long as I have breath.

I found a way to say it in our little book, *Angel Unaware*. When I came home from the hospital, I found a mountain of mail from people who were reading the book. It had been published just before Easter and in a short time it was on the best seller list. God was doing everything possible to help me with *Angel*—but there was a lot I had to do for myself. I took a series of potent iron shots, to stimulate my very low hemoglobin, and went at the mountain of mail.

When I realized that this book was really going to click, I got to wondering about the royalties. (Doesn't every author think of that?) I had written the book to help little Mongolian Robins—and I came to see that my royalties, as well as my energies, should go to help handicapped and retarded children in the field of research, promotion and publicity, and to acquaint the public with this desperate need. Then I knew of no national organization specifically founded for such a purpose, and I was at a loss to know just *where* to allocate the funds. I prayed. God answered.

About a month after the release of the book, Roy and I were doing a radio broadcast at NBC when we were approached by a man and two women who wanted to take a publicity picture of us for use in a fund drive for the Exceptional Children's Foundation in Los Angeles. Exceptional Children! I liked that. I liked it even better when they explained that this foundation was a branch of the National Association for Retarded Children, headquartered in New York, which was started in 1950—the year Robin was born!

118

I was so overcome that I could hardly speak. This was it! I immediately wrote the Fleming H. Revell Company to send all my royalties to the National Association for Retarded Children, and the *Angel* was on her way!

More and more now, children took first place in my life—after God. God *and* our children—that was it! God and children everywhere. One day on location near Chatsworth, in the San Fernando Valley, I saw a little boy studying me intently, especially the western clothes I was wearing. His eyes were riveted on me, and I was a little uncomfortable about it until he casually strolled over to me and asked, "Dale Evans, how old are you?" The little rascal stunned me into silence. (Roy says any woman who will tell you her age will tell you anything!) But I don't mind telling my age. I'm proud that God has given me fifty-six years in which to help Him. The boy's curiosity amused me (when I got over the initial shock).

"Oh," I said, "I'm one hundred years old."

He gave me an icy stare and replied, "No, you are not one hundred, either."

"All right. How old do you think I am?"

"You're not a day over sixty-five."

That was fifteen years ago! I'm sure he thinks, by now, that I have joined my ancestors. But I still love him for his question —and his honesty!

(Every once in a while some woman asks me if I have had my face lifted, since my age is no secret. No, I haven't had my face lifted, but God has lifted my heart and made it eternally young. I tell them that. I tell them that it is the Spirit that quickens. I have met a lot of young old people whose countenances have been kept glowing only with the light which is spiritual.)

The children under our rooftree have kept me young, too. It hasn't been a chore to take care of them, in spite of all that has happened to them and to me. It has been a most rewarding *privilege*. I remember, for instance, the trip to Hawaii on which

119

we took Cheryl, Linda and Dodie. We had a booking in Honolulu that took a lot of time, but I have forgotten that and remembered the time we spent with *them*. Who could ever forget Hawaii, once he has seen it? The fantastic trade winds rippled through our hotel rooms on the first afternoon when we sat around eating the huge fresh pineapples brought up to us; nor can we forget the tour of the island of Maui, where we swam, idling in that incomparable Hawaiian sunshine. Cheryl and Linda took hula lessons with me so we could do a song-and-dance medley in the show. What memories! And the wee grass skirt we bought for Dodie! She ran to Roy at the end of the show, jumped into his arms and sang "Jesus Loves Me." We loved the Islands, loved the people—and loved the children more than ever.

Then there was the coming of Marion, the little Scottish girl from Edinburgh whom we had invited to come over to California for a little visit. We thought when we invited her, that our family was already large enough, but . . . ! Chief Constable Merilees told us that she was "unadoptable," since both her divorced parents were still living, but that she could visit for several weeks. He cleared the way with the authorities, and she came.

A tiny, pretty, slightly bewildered girl got off the plane in Los Angeles, looking as though she hadn't expected to come this far from bonnie Scotland, and wondering where the Indians were. No Indians, but the whole Rogers tribe was there to welcome her, and her face lit up like a Christmas tree when she saw us. Larry Kent, who worked for us in promotion, was there, too; he had met Marion in Edinburgh and the plan was for her to visit them first, and then come to our home. The kids loved her at first sight, and she loved them. Dusty, as we might have expected, was wary of her at first, and Dodie sat stock-still for a long time before she accepted the little Scot. But Sandy broke

120

into his broad grin and held out his hand in welcome, almost before she could get off the plane.

At her first dinner in our house, Marion said little and ate less. I wondered if she disliked both us and our food, and I wondered if we'd made a mistake bringing her over here. She explained it one day in an explosion that nearly knocked me flat. Staring at the table loaded with food, she said, "It isn't fair!"

"What isn't fair?"

"All this . . . all this food, and *everything*. It isn't fair that you have so much in America and that there's so little in other places. You've got too many cars, too many refrigerators and washing machines, too rich food and too much of it. In Scotland I got half of one egg on Sunday, once a week. We saved our pennies for days on end to buy an orange—and here you have them lying around under the trees on your lawn." (Never had I seen a child eat so many oranges!)

It slapped me awake to something I had missed in Scotland—and perhaps in other countries, too: I mean the *poverty*. I thanked God for sending Marion to make me aware of that—and I resolved not to miss it, the next time around.

A week before she was due to start for home, I found her crying in a corner of our breakfast room. Before I could say a word to her she sobbed, "Mama, I don't want to go home. I want to stay here with you."

"Why, child, I thought you didn't like it in America. You've acted as though you were homesick most of the time. What made you change your mind?"

"Because you are so *free* in America," she said.

That was hard for me to understand. I said that the people in Scotland had seemed quite free, to me.

"Mama, you don't understand. Over there, if your father is a plumber, you'll be a plumber. That's as high as you can go. That's all you can expect to be. But over here, you can be anything you want to be. I want to *stay*."

121

I explained that we couldn't keep her any longer because her visa had expired, but that didn't mean anything to *her*. She was sure we could arrange it.

We arranged. With the help of Mr. Merilees we got permission to keep her until February. She went to school. She went to church. She went everywhere, seeing everything with her great hungry eyes—and loving it. But . . . January came, and she begged to be allowed to finish the school year before going back. She was becoming an American, inside and out. Her delightful Scottish brogue was disappearing, and we noticed more and more American slang in her conversation. (I think I preferred the brogue!) She had settled down into the routine of our home as though she had been born there, and we were apprehensive about parting with her—with tears in our eyes. We got her visa extended to June.

You guessed it: she didn't go in June either. By June she was our ward. She stayed for keeps.

She and Linda became bosom pals, playing and swimming together; Dusty and Sandy were as close as blood brothers. Dodie was the loner of the crowd—except that she had adopted the family dog as *her* property, not to be touched or abused by anyone but her. Cheryl was having her first party dress and her first boy-and-girl party at the house. Tom and Barbara occasionally brought their two little ones to add to the confusion —and the joy—and to participate in our round table discussions, prayers and Bible readings. It was heaven! And it seemed that it *must* go on forever.

Now and then there was trouble, and when there was trouble we went looking for Sandy and Dusty. Sandy had become a sort of front man for Dusty—meaning that Dusty made the spit balls and got Sandy to throw them. One day Sandy just plain swiped some of Dusty's play money and fibbed about it; I had to chase him all over the backyard before justice was served with a peach tree switch.

122

Another day Dusty was the crook; we found his pockets loaded with coins that we knew represented unearned wealth. Roy and I were careless about leaving change lying on our dresser and on the office desk, and Pat O'Shea had a cash box in her desk that certainly *looked* looted, so we knew where Dusty got it. We decided that a little meditation and soul-searching in solitary confinement would be good for him, and so he was locked up in the men's dressing room near the swiming pool. At noon I took him a prisoner's lunch—bread and water. He didn't object; I thought he almost smiled at me! Something was wrong here! (I discovered later that Linda and Marion had climbed up on the roof of the building and handed down tasty little snacks to the criminal below.) I let him out in the middle of the afternoon—and he still didn't tell me where he got the money. But he never forgot that time in jail—and he still talks about it!

We had help with the children. A French bachelor friend, Joe Espetalier who was custodian of the Masonic Temple in Hollywood and who guided Roy through his Masonic activities, was sort of a big brother to the boys and took them on endless excursions on those long days when we were on location or off on a guest appearance tour. And there was Pat O'Shea, our marvelous secretary, who filled in for me many a time when the youngsters needed attention and guidance. My health was in a precarious state, and Pat just took over and did what had to be done. She had a degree in psychology and she was wonderful in her dealings with people—with business associates, friends, and the whole family. In a way she is my spiritual protégé; she accepted Christ, was baptized and confirmed at St. Nicholas' Church, and I was more than thrilled to be her sponsor. She was one of the big happy family.

Roy and I were to play the Canadian Exposition in Toronto, that summer—and suddenly Cheryl decided that she wanted to go with us. We took her; her boy problem was beginning

123

to get a bit out of hand, and we thought a change of scene might be good for her. She worked with us in the show, and she got a good share of whistles and applause from our enthusiastic audiences—so much so that she announced that she would go with us to do the show in New York's Madison Square Garden a month later. That would have meant missing almost four weeks of school at the beginning of the term, and we had to say no. She resented that. She was a teen-ager now, and she resented *all* authority. One night while we were in the middle of the New York engagement, she just packed up and went across the street to one of our neighbors, telling them that she was leaving home. The neighbors called Father Smith at the church. That was a good move, for Cheryl loved and respected him, and he could talk with her about her problem. He called us in New York and suggested that she be sent to an excellent girl's school—one like Kemper Hall, in Kenosha, Wisconsin. We were stunned, but we agreed; she was enrolled at Kemper Hall for the rest of the school year.

I rushed out to Kenosha when we finished in New York, and we talked it all over. I made Cheryl a promise: when she was twenty-one, if she felt so inclined, we would try to find her real mother—*provided* her record at Kemper was a good one. It was better than good. She made top grades in everything and when she came home in June it was as though nothing had happened. As promised we later found her mother and Cheryl spent a weekend in her home. Cheryl is a wonderful girl, the mother of two boys and two girls.

Now I have gone out of my way to talk about this problem with Cheryl, because I know that such problems with teen-agers occur in most families sooner or later. I'd like to say a little more about this generation gap that seems to be setting so many of us on our collective ears. What is it, anyway?

A gap is just a space between two points. That's how the dictionary might put it. Our gap is supposed to be between the point of view of our young people and the point of view of middle-aged or old people. Right? It is a *generation* gap. It's nothing new. It has been around for a long, long time. We are all born as babies; we all become children; we all become adults. That's been fact for thousands of years. It didn't just pop up in the last five or ten years—or since rock music was born! As a teen-ager I used to rock and roll mightily to the tune of "St. Louis Blues"; my mother would hold her ears and say, "Do you call *that* music?" I thought she didn't understand me—that she was an old fogey. When I got to be twenty-one, I wondered how she got so smart so quick!

She understood me, all right. Because she loved me, she made it her business to understand, even though many of my words and actions hurt her deeply. She knew I was groping for something in life—sometimes in anger, striking out, stumbling, getting up and running again. She was always there to help *because she remembered how she felt as a teen-ager.* She knew a lot of things had changed since then. She had her first date when she was sixteen in a horse-drawn buggy with her older brother as chaperon. Just try to find a horse and buggy now—or a chaperon on the first date! A lot has changed: the length of dresses, hair styles, shoes, means of transportation and communication. Things change every day, but the basic human problems haven't changed a bit since my mother was a girl, or since I was sixteen. *Neither has the answer changed!* Jesus Christ is still the answer—Jesus Christ, the Way, the Truth and the Life. Jesus Christ, and He alone!

Not long ago John Lennon of the Beatles made a facetious remark, in declaring, "Christianity will go. It will vanish and shrink. We [the Beatles] are more popular than Jesus now." He said it when the Beatles were at the top of their popularity. Even then they were not happy, nor even content. They were looking for answers, and the answers evaded them. They went all the way to India to see a guru, to learn from him how to

125

meditate and how to be happy; he didn't tell them anything they couldn't have heard at home. One by one, they were in trouble as they searched for answers—looking for them in drugs, in fancy cars and clothes, or barefooted, or in no clothes at all—and still they were not satisfied; still they did not find what they were seeking. Only Jesus Christ satisfies the deep need of the soul—only He who said, ". . . him that cometh to me, I will in no wise cast out" (John 6:37). ". . . we will come unto him and make our abode with him" (14:23). Only He!

Just the other day I read a booklet written by a brilliant American scientist. He is an expert in space physics, radio communication, radar and radio astronomy investigations, and a member of the Institute of Aeronautics and Astronautics, the American Association for the Advancement of Science, the Acoustical Society of America and the American Geophysical Union. It sounds like a page out of *Who's Who in Brains,* doesn't it? Yet, with all this, he is a man who was never satisfied (his personal life was a mess, he says) until he realized his need for a Saviour to forgive his sins and to give him assurance of everlasting life. I humbly suggest that this man is somewhat more intelligent than John Lennon. This man found the answer to the question of who made the universe, the constellations, the Milky Way, the atom—*when he found Jesus Christ.* Think that one over, you who are talking about science displacing God!

My generation doesn't have all the answers—and neither does the Now generation. But the Bible has them—the inspired word of God has *His* answers. It provides answers for the Establishment *and* for youth. (Speaking of the Establishment, let's keep it clear that the adolescent of today, the young people of today are the Establishment of tomorrow. That's why we should be sending them to the Bible *now* for the answers to the questions they're asking.)

It begins in the home—in parent-and-child relationships. The Bible says: "Children, obey your parents . . . Honour thy

126

father and mother . . ." (Ephesians 6:12). *Then* it says, "And ye fathers, provoke not your children to wrath: but bring them up in the nurture and admonition of the Lord" (v.4). In other words, children are to love and obey their parents *for God.* Parents are to love, serve, instruct and discipline their children *for God*—as caretakers of their children for God until they are ready to move out on their own.

That was the way we did it with Cheryl, and with all the children. We did it, or tried to do it, the Christian way, and it has paid off—handsomely. Every one of those children has found Christ—and all settle *their* problems the Christian way.

Dr. Bob Pierce, of World Vision, Inc., came out to our house one night to show us some films taken in Korea, depicting the plight of little Korean orphans who were the victims of racially mixed marriages. Most of them were the children of Korean mothers and soldier fathers in the United Nations troops occupying their country. I looked around the room at our little League-of-Nations family, and I wondered if we might find room for just one more—one of these Korean orphans, maybe one about Dodie's age, who could grow up with her. No, the house wasn't big enough, but . . . We gave Dr. Pierce a picture of Dodie, and he said he'd look around and see.

We couldn't get those Korean orphans out of our minds!

8

*W*e moved out to a 133-acre ranch in Chatsworth, near Canoga Park. There was an old brick and frame house that was large and comfortable but still not large enough; so we just built more house on each end. The children were excited about it, and no wonder. In view of what was to happen there, we should have named it Excitement Acres.

First, Dodie had a fierce attack of croup that we thought was going to kill her. She might have died if it hadn't been for a new nurse—a fine black woman named Leola. As the attack became worse and worse Dodie was actually turning blue as she fought for air. I screamed for Leola, who came paddling into the room, pushed me aside, held Dodie up by the heels, shook her, and ran her finger down her throat to release the blockage. She calmly put Dodie back in bed, turned to me and said, "What you so excited about? My old folks taught me how to help chillun like that. It ain't nuthin'." I just sat there and stared at her.

Excitement Number Two was Dodie again. We had purchased the ranch with an eye to shooting movies and TV specials there, and of renting the locations out to other companies. One of these companies came to do a "Brave Eagle" series, which was cowboy-and-Indian stuff, showing the better side of the Indians. One morning Dodie looked out of her window and saw a horde of screaming Indians come toward the house, complete with war paint and war whoops. She flew into my

Dale Evans, Queen of the West, age 5 months. *Below:* Dale (age 5) strikes a pose on Grandfather Wood's ranch, Uvalde, Texas.

1940—the young staff singer at CBS during the hard days in Chicago. *Below:* Concerned about his future, but ready for it—son Tom at 5 months.

Mother and Father Smith visit the rising young star at the old Republic Studios, between shots of an early Roy Rogers Western. *Below:* Roy and Dale—minutes after they said "I Do!"—at their wedding in Davis, Oklahoma, at the Flying L Ranch.

Mary Little Doe (Dodie) and John David (Sandy) Rogers leave the plane at Los Angeles International Airport, after their adoption from orphanages in Dallas, Texas, and Covington, Kentucky. (Get the cowboy boots on Sandy!) *Below:* Pardners! Dodie, at the age of 4, and Mother are on a tour of inspection of the ranch at Chatsworth.

The happy Rogers clan gets together for a picture at the ranch. Left to right — Roy, Linda Lou, Dusty, Sandy, Dale, Dodie; in the foreground, Debbie. *Below:* Every Sunday, come rain or shine, they worshiped at Fountain Avenue Baptist Church, in Hollywood — son Tom Fox, Roy Rogers, Jr. (Dusty), Dale, Linda Lou, Cheryl, Barbara (Mrs. Tom), and Roy.

Sandy and Dusty at Banff, Canada, during the Calgary Stampede appearance. *Below:* Little Dodie is little no more. She is 15 here, and in high school.

Eldest daughter, Cheryl Darlene, adjusts her veil for her wedding at Saint Nicholas' Episcopal Church in Encino, California. *Below:* A rare moment for the Rogers — just the two of them, having dinner at Apple Valley Inn in 1968.

Now, in 1970: life is abundantly rich and meaningful, in companionship with Christ.

arms, frightened out of her wits: "Mama! Mama! Those Indians are coming after me!"

Excitement Number Three: we began missing things around the house. Naturally, we asked Sandy and Dusty about it, but we got the whole truth from the principal of Northridge Military Academy where they were attending school. It seems that the two young men had set up a trading post at the academy, selling off a lot of things they didn't think we'd miss!

Excitement Number Four: the house caught fire. We had set up a large Christmas candle on the TV cabinet; Marion sat up late that night, and went to bed without blowing it out. Along about four in the morning Cheryl's voice came over the intercom in our bedroom: "Listen, Mom. Don't get excited, but get up quick. The house is on fire." I ran down the long hall to find the living room red with the ruddy reflection of the fire. Smoke was billowing out in all directions, the television set was a blazing ruin and the piano was beginning to burn. There was a huge hole burned out in the middle of the floor. Fortunately no windows were open. We got the children out, and I raced for a phone to call the fire department. Cheryl stopped me; she had already called them. What a manager she was! While the rest of us were flying around in all directions, she calmly took the jeep down to the gate of the ranch to show the firemen the way to the house.

Dodie wailed that Bimbo, her big stuffed monkey, was in the house and Mama ran back in to get him. We stood around on the lawn in our bathrobes, and waited—in a drizzling rain. We waited a terrible half hour before they got there; I was beside myself with fear that the flames would reach the heating unit under the living room and blow the whole place to smithereens. It didn't.

When it was all over, the living room, dining room and

129

kitchen were black, charred ruins. We set up for Christmas in the den—our first Christmas at Chatsworth.

We were filling an engagement at the Houston Fat Stock Show and Rodeo when a letter came from Dr. Bob Pierce of World Vision. Poor Bob! In all the excitement we had almost forgotten him, but he had not forgotten us. He sent us a picture of a little Korean orphan he thought might fit into our League-of-Nations home as a companion for Dodie. She was In Ai Lee, chosen from among 600 orphan "possibilities"—complete with a Dutch bob, soft brown eyes and a very, *very* solemn expression. Love at first sight! We all wanted her, and Bob Pierce went to work to clear her for our adoption. She was to arrive in June. Dodie couldn't wait.

Little In Ai Lee came off the plane at the Los Angeles airport in the arms of Bob Pierce. Roy reached for her, and she nestled into his arms without a struggle. Newsmen followed us out of the airport to our car, taking pictures. Debbie (we had already re-named her!) looked at them with an uninterested expression, which never changed. With that I began to have misgivings; was she all right? Everyone tried to make her smile. No luck. She and Dodie looked each other over in sullen silence, with inscrutable eyes.

Driving down to the Goldwyn Studios (we had to report for work that afternoon) I held her on my lap and tried to talk to her. I might as well have been talking to the Boulder Dam. She could speak a few words of English (*Mama, Daddy, milk, sleep*), but beyond that—nothing. When we reached the studio I asked one of the older girls to sit in my dressing room by Debbie while she took a nap. I was sure she was worn-out enough to sleep. One of the men on the set came into the room with a big red balloon. She reached out for it, grabbed it and held it close to her face, with a grin as wide as the Mississippi River.

Debbie, dear Debbie, was home!

130

Home, yes, but still in a strange, new environment. At the supper table her face suddenly took on a strained, painful expression, and, not speaking Korean myself, I couldn't determine what the trouble was. I tried to question her, but not speaking English, she couldn't tell me. Betty's husband (Betty was a new nurse who had come to us when Leola left to recuperate from illness) asked her a question in *his* language (he was Filipino), and Debbie nodded in relief. He picked her up and took her into the bathroom!

I tucked her into bed that night next to Dodie, pulled the covers up around her chin, and began to teach her a little bedtime prayer. She smiled, but didn't repeat; she couldn't, yet. I turned out the light, and left them with God.

Betty reported the next morning that Debbie had fallen out of bed three times during the night; when Betty tried to put her back in bed, she crawled under it for she was used to sleeping on the floor. That went on for about six months. She was determined to sleep Korean—and to *speak* Korean, too. One day she grabbed my hand and pulled me out to the driveway where our jeep was parked. She had something important on her little mind, and she jabbered away at me in Korean, pointing at the jeep. I couldn't understand a word of it, and I told her so—in English, which she didn't understand. She put her hands on her hips, shrugged her shoulders and sighed as if to say, "You dumbbell!"—and without another word turned and walked into the house.

That was the last word of Korean ever spoken by that child. Within a month she was speaking fluent English. I am still amazed at that—at the way children learn a new language so easily and so quickly. Perhaps it is because they have so little to unlearn. It had made me think that if children can pick up knowledge of a language like that, they can also pick up a knowledge of the love of God like that. They can accept and build faith quickly—hold it in the grooves of memory through childhood—and through all their lives, for that matter. Maybe this is what the psalmist meant when he admonished us, "Train up a child in the way he should go: and when he is old, he will not depart from it" (Proverbs 22:6). Intensive training in the early days goes deep and stays deep in the subconscious, and is held there for later need. My mother and I can witness to that!

With all the children in tow, we went off to do a show at the Columbus (Ohio) State Fair. They each had a part in the show, and they were an excited bunch of youngsters. Debbie experienced another form of excitement. When we got off the plane in Columbus the welcoming committee and a huge crowd of fans closed in around us, making such a racket that Debbie almost went into hysterics. She thought it was an air raid! She hadn't forgotten Korea, even yet. She didn't calm down until we got to the hotel.

The day we spent at Duck Run, where Roy had lived as a boy, was better. We saw the house Roy and his father had built, the well in the back of the house, the little schoolhouse, and we met the warm folks who lived in the holler beyond the house. It took me back to the time Roy had taken me there, just after our marriage. The tables and chairs had been moved out of the kitchen for a square dance, with Roy calling the dances. Some of the older fellows really tore up the place—and I nearly danced the shoes off my feet.

Sandy and Dusty got a bang out of Roy's ole swimmin' hole. They stared wide-eyed as he showed the boys the spot in the kitchen where he used to sit with a gun on his knees waiting for a shot at the rats that always came out at night. They hardly believed him, I think, when he told them that his mother would often tell him to go get meat for supper, and he would go out *with a slingshot* to hunt down a rabbit. I believed him. I think this is why he is such a dead shot with a gun today, even from the back of a horse.

132

His horse on that old farm was Babe; he rode her bareback. His father worked in a shoe factory in Portsmouth and got home only once every two weeks, which meant that Roy had to be the man of the family and do chores usually done by a grown man. He tells of plowing behind Babe and of hitting rocks and stumps that almost knocked him down. He says that one of the tests of mettle for the boys was to run barefoot over the short, hard stubble in the schoolyard without flinching. Rarely did he put on his shoes before the first frost. He finds it hard to have compassion for youngsters nowadays who feel put upon if they have to walk a block to catch a school bus. He has known the nitty-gritty of struggle for existence in his youth, and he has little sympathy for those young people of today who think the world owes them a living.

I'm with him. He believes in free enterprise—and in being enterprising. I'm with him there, too. When our children began to accept their Christmas gifts in a matter-of-fact way, as though they were something we *owed* them, he would tell them, almost in anger, of the one Christmas gift he remembered and cherished most—a Barlow pocket knife. One year he threatened to give the children nothing but a lot of pasteboard boxes so they could play with them and tear them up on Christmas Day. He told them the story of the pocket knife so often that they would put on that Here-we-go-again-kids look whenever he expressed his concern over their nonchalant attitude toward their gifts.

We had to think about other gifts, along about this time: two of our little flock left the roost. Cheryl and Marion were married. It was hard to believe that either one of them was of marriageable age—but they were—and each had decided on her one and only, so—what's a mother to do? Cheryl was married to Bill Rose on Valentine's day. She had just finished high school (which was more than I did!) and while I pleaded with her to wait a year or so—to get a little college—it was no use. She had a lovely red-and-white wedding in St. Nicholas' Church, with Dodie and Debbie as junior bridesmaids. Linda Lou was her sister's maid of honor and Marion was a bridesmaid.

Then Marion stepped off: a month later she married Dan Eaton, a Marine stationed at Camp Pendleton, California. Being Scottish (I think this was the reason) she wanted a quieter, less publicized wedding. (Cheryl had 750 at her wedding.) Marion chose to be married at home on the ranch.

So two were gone. Two from seven left five.

The weddings made me realize that the youngsters were growing up faster than I thought possible. In no time at all, they weren't youngsters any more, but teen-agers with a brand new set of interests and ideas. I looked at Linda Lou singing a song called "Seventeen," with her father. I heard the whistles of approval from the audience, and I knew she was no longer a child. Even Debbie and Dodie were growing like weeds. They sang on our shows like a couple of veterans. Debbie was the speaker and Dodie was the singer in a sister act that brought down the house. I knew they were changing, and as they grew, I began to look a little more closely at their backgrounds, to try to figure out their futures.

Dodie walked up to a wizened old Indian who was selling Indian trinkets in the street and asked him, "Are you a good Indian? I'm Indian, too, and I'm good!"

Indian! This probably started me thinking about blood and race and color as I had never thought of them before. Dodie was Indian; Roy had Indian blood in his veins. Marion was a Scot; Debbie was a Korean. The rest of us were white Americans—but that was a distinction we never seemed to notice in our house. We were a Christian family, and that was enough. We lived and worked and played and prayed together as though we had all been born in the same house. All that race and color stuff meant nothing to us.

134

Folks *outside* the family seemed more interested in drawing lines of race and color between us than we did. Often, someone would marvel at our League-of-Nations family, and occasionally the question would get through to us, "How do you manage to get along so well together?" I have never resented the question. I raise it here only because I want to explain how and *why* this experiment in racial togetherness has worked out so well—and so easily—in our home.

It worked out because of the attitude we all took toward it.

Dodie was Indian. Let's start with that. I've been interested in Indians for a long, long time—especially since I met Roy Rogers! Last year I went to Denver to give my testimony at a convention of the American Indian Crusade, and it was a great experience. Just to hear those Indians sing was a thrill. They sat there together and sang together and ate and talked together as though they had always been together—Indians, whites, missionaries, businessmen, show people, folks from all over and from every church in America—folks who were interested in taking the Gospel of Jesus Christ to the first Americans. As I sang and talked and prayed with them I was ashamed of the way we have treated the Indians in this country, and I resented almost bitterly that we had called them redskins and pictured them as savages. What *is* this skin color kick we seem to enjoy, anyway? How did it ever get started, and why do we keep at it? I saw just *people* in Denver.

The Indians themselves have a quaint little story in which they explain how skin color originated. It seems that the Great Spirit decided to make human beings to inhabit the earth. He took his dough from the dust of the earth and put it in His big oven to bake. The first batch came out undercooked—pale, white (these were the pale faces). The second batch came out overdone, black (the Negroes). The third batch came out a beautiful sun-kissed tan. Just right!—The Indians!

135

It's not a bad way of looking at it, when you think it through. It was God who made the races, not man. And nowhere do we hear God saying that He prefers any one race to another. Again it was man who developed that superiority complex, racially speaking. When you get right down to it, it is this *human pride* of race that causes all the trouble—those of one color looking down their noses at those of another color—that's *pride,* and pride is a sin and a stench in the nostrils of God. He knew what He was doing when he created the races.

That's the way we look at it in our house.

Someone said to me recently, "You don't see a crow mating with a canary, do you? All nature abides by God's laws in this area except humans, and they just have to *experiment.*" In other words, the races should be kept separate and recognized as basically separate and different from each other. I'll buy some of that, but not all of it. To our home in Chatsworth Roy once brought a beautiful little yellow bird in a cage. He said, "This bird is half-canary and half-wild linnet, and it sings the prettiest song you ever heard." He was right. This bird had the lilt of the wild meadow lark and the trill of the canary. There were two birds singing in one throat, and it was beautiful. What do you mean, keep them *apart?*

Or take our dog Bowser. Bowser is half coyote; the other half is made up of chow, boxer and bulldog (we think). He has the black tongue of a chow and a coat that is a mixture of coyote, yellowish-gray and bulldog brindle. His tail curls high on his back—the mark of the chow. A more lovable dog I have yet to see. His eyes are uncomfortably human. He's as steady as a rock—not flighty and high-strung, like so many pure-bred dogs. Bullet, our German shepherd, has a fine pedigree, and so has Bobo, our black French poodle. Our pure-bred Chihuahua has a pedigree as long as your arm, and so has Smokey, our big Persian tomcat. We love all of them, but I'll have to admit that Bowser is the number one favorite with the family, *because of*

136

his wonderful qualities and not because of any pedigree. The best of three breeds runs in his blood.

Every race has special and marvelous gifts. Why can't we look for those gifts, and learn to appreciate them? Why is it that we fear each other so? The Bible says, "He that feareth is not made perfect in love" (I John 4:18), and that "If a man saith I love God, and hateth his brother, he is a *liar*" (v.4:20). Love is not narrow, not restricted, certainly not racial! It is, as the song says, ". . . a many splendored thing." Read Paul's definition of love in the thirteenth chapter of First Corinthians; just try to put *that* in a racial straitjacket! Jesus said that men would know us as His followers when ". . . ye have love, one to another" (John 13:35). Love is *never* a respecter of persons—nor of any particular color or race of people. The Bible calls upon us to love *even our enemies.* Is that possible? Have you ever honestly tried it? Have you ever tried to go the second mile, to bless those who curse you, to pray for those who persecute you?

We talk about these things a lot in our house—about a love that knows no fences or barriers—yes, or races.

Love does it—Christian love. Think about that love, in terms of the children in your house. Is it an unselfish love you have for them? Do we love them for their own sakes, or for our own gratification? Are we hurt and bitter when they do not return our love—when they are thoughtless and thankless? If we become angry and resentful with them, we had better take a fresh look at our motives for self-sacrifice in their behalf. According to the Bible, we are supposed to do whatever we do as though we were doing it *unto the Lord*—never looking for reward, never counting the cost, never demanding a return. I admit to shortcomings in this department with our children once in a while, but always, after I have nursed my little hurt for awhile and then have taken a good look at myself, I am ashamed. *I know I have to go on loving, come what may.*

137

When Jesus healed the ten lepers and only one thanked Him for it, did He stop healing? No, he continued to heal for the glory of God—and not because He expected a word of thanks.

Let love, not appreciation, be your motive, and you *win*.

Let's get back to this business of race. We were sitting around the studio one afternoon, waiting between scenes, and we fell into one of those stimulating, thought-provoking conversations that we all enjoy. One of the men remarked that he loved Joy Eilers' song, "What Color Is Love" (I sing it often, on TV), and he said it was too bad that we couldn't put the philosophy of that song into wider practice. I said I believed that we *were* making real progress in the area of racial acceptance—and another man jumped all over me saying, "I'm sick of people who go around bragging about how tolerant they are and how some of their best friends are black people. But when it comes to issues like open housing, they renege in a hurry."

There was a moment of startled silence, and then someone else said, "Oh, it's better than it used to be. The kids today don't have the prejudices we had when we were their age." I told them I believed that love was the ultimate solution. We talked about our various backgrounds and prejudices, and I said I felt that we could overcome any and all of those differences if we loved one another as we should. For one thing, we had adopted two children of different racial ancestries and these children were as much our own as our natural children. If we care for others, we love them. That follows as the night the day.

Then we delved deeper and talked about intermarriage. I said I thought it would be a pity if all the different races melted into one, and we lost all the beauties of race and color. Who wanted a sky full of nothing but one species of birds? One of the fellows said, "I disagree with you. I think we should all be one color."

Then another chimed in, "That wouldn't solve our problems; we would still be prejudiced in some other way."

I think *he* really struck at the heart of the matter. Man's *heart* must be changed—supernaturally, by God and Christ—a new Spirit must be born in him before he can truly be one. All the social and political reforms we talk so much about will come to nothing until we are bathed in the Holy Spirit of God and see each other as creatures He made in His own image— creatures He loved enough to visit in the person of Jesus Christ and whom He loved enough to provide the great sacrifice for their redemption.

What is the color of such a love? It is beyond human comprehension.

A friend told me of being at the point of death while in a diabetic coma. He spoke of the sensation of being lifted into a cloud of indescribably beautiful color: "The aurora borealis was nothing, compared to this. I heard the Voice of Pure Love say, 'Come home, Son.' That voice I can never forget."

Now we all have conditioned reflexes which affect our thinking processes and of which we are not often aware. There are subjects buried deep in the subconscious mind which may reappear in some future situation or crisis, and we can't understand it. Afterward, we scold ourselves for the way we reacted, and vow that we will conquer and change that reflex.

For instance, when one of our daughters graduated from high school she asked permission to entertain the graduating class at a mid-morning swimming party on the ranch in Chatsworth. I was delighted. Being a very resourceful girl, she, along with some of her friends, did all the inviting and preparing of refreshments. They would take care of *everything;* they wanted it that way. The morning of the party I had some shopping to do; I got back home after they were through swimming and were playing records in the den and enjoying the refreshments. I walked in blithely and made the rounds, shaking hands —when suddenly I was hit by a brilliant smile from a very dark face. Fleeting, idiotic panic rose in me as I gripped the

139

hand of this black boy and moved on to the boy next to him, hoping he hadn't noticed my surprise. I knew I must have blushed—and I hated myself for the little scene.

You see, this is what I mean by conditioned reflex. I was of Mississippi-Texas parentage; I had spent all of my childhood in the South, and the old, familiar, deeply entrenched impressions and teachings of that childhood had surfaced in an unguarded moment. This is probably a very unscholarly way of relating it, but it's the only way I could explain it to myself afterward. I have not lived in the South for many years, but that early Southern training is still deep in my mind.

I told the man in the discussion at the studio that I tried always to be perfectly honest with myself and that with God's help I was doing my best to love and understand the Negro— and I prayed that he would try to love and understand me. I cannot help my color and he cannot help his, but we can both love the God who made us and God in turn will mold and teach us to love one another. The Bible says, "Shall the thing formed say to him that formed it, Why hast thou made me thus?" (Romans 9:20).

Whenever I visit an armed forces hospital (and I visit them as often as possible) I try never to see a disfigurement, a missing limb or eye—or a face a different color from my own. I always pray that the boy will look me straight in the eye—*for there we can communicate.* The eyes are the windows of the soul; we should understand that when we meet someone of another race. The common bond of humanity is great—forged with joy, suffering, expectation, despair. Basically, we are alike. Why can't we remember that? And each of us, of whatever color, has his contribution to make to the whole. It is a joy to me to see the entertainment world enriched more and more with the talents of different races and cultures, in every phase of entertainment. Each race has a magic of its own in the arts of expression, and they can all be justly proud—no, justly *grate-*

140

ful—for their gifts and attributes. The world is beautiful because of all of them.

I feel for the ministers of the churches in this day of racial crisis and confusion; they are in one of those spots where they will be wrong in someone's view no matter what they do or what position they take. I admire those who do not flinch from doing their Christian duty as they see it, according to the Light that is in them. I feel pity for them because I know the price so many of them have paid in loneliness and isolation and even persecution, when they take an unpopular stand. Let's not be overcritical about them or toward them. Let's be prayerful and self-searching and see if we ourselves are doing all we can to further God's Kingdom and the welfare of all His children, according to the Light which is within *us*.

I cannot agree with all their aims or with all their methods; I am only wishing that those who acknowledge Christ as Lord have the same spiritual stamina to stand up and be counted for our convictions. We shall never agree on every issue but we can admit that the other fellow has a right to his opinions, and even though we differ, we do not need to hate. We are all human. As Alexander Pope said, "To err is human; to forgive, divine." Disagreements can and often do turn into hatreds; they breed fights and fatal dissentions in the Church, and I hate *that*. What would happen if every marriage broke up over every disagreement of man and wife? What would happen to the children then? And what happens to the babes in Christ when older, more experienced Christians fall out in quarrel and disagreement? What's a babe to do—and what and whom is he to believe?

Again, love is the answer—Godly, unselfish love for one's neighbor. Love is of no one color; it's made up of all colors. Since we were all created in His image and in His love, can we do less than love all His creatures?

141

I realize that this is an explosive subject, but the love of God has a habit of surviving all explosions, and I will rest on that. If we are guilty of racial prejudice, we are not manifesting the love of God. The Bible says that God created the world and all therein and that when it was done He saw that it was *good,* all of it, every bit of it. He didn't say, "It's all good except for the black man, or the white man, or the red man or the yellow man." No, he said it was *all* good. He created man and He left man to show some appreciation for His creation—and I humbly suggest that according to His standards, our appreciation of Him isn't anything to brag about.

Jesus said that the greatest of the Commandments was this one: "Thou shalt love the Lord thy God with all thy heart, with all thy soul and with all thy mind . . . and that the second is like unto it, . . . *and thy neighbour as thyself"* (Matthew 22:37–39). And who *is* our neighbor? Must he be one of our own crowd or set, one who believes as we believe, one of our particular race? Jesus shouts an eloquent no to that in His story of the Good Samaritan. The Levite in that parable was a Jew; the Samaritan was—Samaritan, and there was bitter enmity and hatred between Jews and the people of Samaria. Neither saw anything good in the other; but notice that the Samaritan and not the Jew is the real hero of the parable. In showing his love and mercy for one in trouble, this despised Samaritan was the Levite's neighbor. There was no prejudice in him.

All my life, I have worried about racial prejudice, and all my life I have prayed God to take it out of me. It's a hard thing to get out; it is hard to put aside *all* prejudice and to love everyone we meet with the full love of Christ. We had a speaker at one of our Hollywood Christian group meetings who asked us this, "Suppose you were on Skid Row, and a drunken old wino came up to you and asked for help. Could you put your arms around him—dirt, liquor, breath, lice and all—and sincerely say to him,

142

'I love you, brother, in the name of the Christ who died for all of us'?" There was an embarrassed silence, and many an eye was riveted on the floor!

What color was Jesus when He was here on earth? Who cares? The important thing about Him has never been His color but the fact that He cared enough for this many-hued humanity to identify Himself with it. We might even say that He integrated with us; but it wasn't just the kind of integration we're talking about today. He became one with us in the flesh, but He stood high, high above and beyond us in the Spirit. The Bible says, ". . . saith the Lord. For as the heavens are higher than the earth, so are my ways higher than your ways . . ." (Isaiah 55:8, 9). It also says that God Himself is too pure to behold iniquity. We humans, *as* humans, were such an offense to Him, so unclean toward Him, that only the drastic sacrifice of His Son on the cross could cleanse us. Are you humbled by that?

I am. And I do not believe that the color of my skin, or my (supposed) Anglo-Saxon ancestry means anything whatever to God. He is interested only in the quality of the love in my heart for Him and for my fellow man. I say it again: *He made all of us and He loves all of us.*

I know that the Bible says the descendants of Ham (who are held to be Negroes by some Bible students) were condemned to serve the descendants of Shem and Japheth because Ham looked upon his father's (Noah's) nakedness, and that seems to smack of racial difference, of superiority and inferiority, of the punishment and degradation of one race and the elevation of another. But Ham's wasn't the only tribe to be punished for disobedience. Down through history, the descendants of every tribe you can think of have suffered at one time or another. Whatever our ancestry, there was a time when our forefathers were slaves! The entire Jewish nation has suffered terribly; the whips of prejudice have cut deeply into their backs, even right here in the land of the free and the home of the brave. Not only

143

have the Jews suffered in this country—remember the Irish, the Polish, the Orientals, the Puerto Ricans!

I doubt that we can blame it all on Ham. I think we need to remember that the more powerful white man has too often and too long thought of non-white races as races created to do his hard labor! We should remember, too, that Jesus Christ came as Redeemer to save all men from the bonds of slavery and prejudice: "If the Son therefore shall make you free, ye shall be free, indeed" (John 8:36).

I find myself resenting more and more this classification by color. As a child I resented the arrogance of some of the more favored and learned people in my town calling the poorer and less learned people who lived along the river "red necks." Their poor necks were red only because, as tenants, they had to work long hours in the blistering sun. Today I resent being called Whitey just as others resent being called Niggers. In the first place, I'm not even white. I'm beige, if you know what I mean. The only folks I've ever seen who are really white are the dead ones. Our blessed Leola said once of Dodie, "Her skin is so pretty. It's like real coffee with a lot of cream, so soft and so smooth, and her eyes are sparkly pretty. I had a daughter once with a skin kind o' like hers, 'ceptin it was a little darker tone. She was pretty, yes—but not as pretty as my boy Jesse. Now there's a *pretty* one. He's black, real black!" I can still hear her saying that.

Dodie watched me closely one day while I was combing her hair, and I knew something was coming. It came; she asked, "Why are you so white and why am I so tanned?" She held her little Indian-brown arm beside my white one, by way of emphasis. I reminded her that many men and women with white arms spent a lot of money and a lot of time in the sun trying to get a brown arm like hers, but that didn't satisfy her: "But you are out in the sun a lot. How come you're not as tan as me?"

144

I explained then that the world is God's garden and that in this garden He has many varieties of animals and plants—and people, and that it would be terribly dull in the garden if we were all exactly the same color and if we all had the same physical characteristics. She bought that.

To me, this is the best argument against wholesale intermarriage between the races. Basically I am opposed to such intermarriage, because I know that it seldom works, and that it can have a terrible effect upon the children of such a marriage. And basically I believe that each race has its own beauty and its particular value in God's creation. Would we like our pretty bouquets of many-colored flowers, if they were *all* red roses, or *all* yellow, or *all* white roses?

If one of my children should come to me and tell me, "I am in love with someone of a different race; we want to get married, and we want your blessing," I think my reply would be (and I would pray God to give me the grace to say it rationally and objectively) something like this.

> You know just as well as I do that you are in for trouble if you do this. People are confused about it, and there are many people who will just never accept it, or accept you, if you do it. There is a great, deep, bitter feeling against it all over the world. You will pay a high price for it— just as many other people, many of them in high places, have paid for it. You will face heartache and loneliness. So will your children. They will suffer even more than you will suffer. There has been some progress in racial tolerance in the last few years, some acceptance of interracial marriage—but not enough. There are still many who do not understand how a man and a woman of different races can possibly love each other. Is your beloved a Christian? And how strong a Christian are *you?* Do you love each other in Christ, and are you strong enough in the Lord to love those who will criticize you and perhaps persecute you *and* your children? Will you

145

teach your children to love those who will insult you and who will say fearful things to them? If you can do all this, take all this, if you sincerely feel that you are meant for each other and called of God to serve Him together and to serve your fellow man in love— then I must give you my blessing. But be *sure*.

A mixed marriage takes a lot of doing—a lot of being in the Lord. I know that many have tried it and failed. I know others who have made it work. To be absolutely honest, I know few black-white marriages that have made it; even among the best intentioned people, the pressures here have been just too much. But I have known missionaries who have come home with wives from another race—Orientals, Indians—who have found happiness and perfect understanding with each other; their radiant faces prove their love for God and for each other. At one Hollywood Christian group meeting I met a Christian missionary from India; a Caucasian woman, she was married to an East Indian Christian man. Their companionship was delightful, and it rejoiced my heart. I cannot quarrel with a marriage like that. They both had the mind which was in Christ; it was a union of two souls in their Redeemer—and it was beautiful.

Well, as the preacher said when he looked up at the clock, "This sermon has been longer than I thought it would be!" This discussion of the race problem has been longer than I planned— but I had to write it, had to get it down on paper, for I believe it to be the most crucial problem of our time. Albert Camus says, "We are all condemned to live together." I think we must all learn to live together in love and in peace, lest we all drown together in a holocaust of atomic dust.

9

*L*inda was going steady for some time before we realized it. She and Gary Johnson, a track star at school, were seeing no one else but each other and liking it. We came home late one night and heard her talking on the phone to Gary, long after she should have been in bed, and we realized then that things were really getting serious. Linda was too young for this. We wanted her to finish high school at least before thinking of marriage, so I took her to Kemper Hall in Wisconsin, where Cheryl had gone some years earlier. She didn't like it, but we believed it best for her and for Gary. She made excellent grades, and she was quite a young lady when she came home in June. We promised her that if she still wanted to marry Gary after she graduated, we would give our consent and any kind of wedding she wanted.

We planned it that way, but how often plans "Gang aft agley"! In October Linda and Gary announced that they had eloped to Las Vegas and been married, with Gary's parents as witnesses. Mad? I sure was—and then I remembered that I had done the same thing at an even earlier age. What could I say? I called Roy in New York with the news and he almost broke my eardrums as he shouted his objection. I knew he'd do that; I also knew that it would be better for him to get over his mad before he came home and faced the bride and groom.

Now our League was down to four—Dusty, Sandy, Dodie and Debbie—plus the dogs, cats, cows and horses.

When we moved to Chatsworth we found no Episcopal or Baptist churches, so we joined the Methodist Church. It was a good church. The pastor, Dr. Harold Hayward, baptized Debbie and Dusty, and we all went to work in the church school, choir, Vacation Bible School, M.Y.F. and in the adult organizations. There were some fine Christians in this church; the children adored Harold Johnson, the superintendent of the Sunday school. He had a gift for his job, and he knew his Bible and taught it well. The adult Bible class was stimulating and enjoyable, but the Sunday school lesson material sent to the church from national headquarters bothered me from the first; they seemed to lack any real Christian challenge. The great basic truths of Christianity—such as the atonement of the cross—were taken too much for granted, and were often ignored or treated too casually. I felt that the emphasis on social reform outweighed the emphasis on personal salvation through acceptance of Christ as Saviour, and that not nearly enough emphasis was put on personal, vital relationship with Christ.

We felt bad about another conflict in this church. Roy and I had participated in the Christian Anti-Communist Crusade at the Shrine Auditorium in Los Angeles, which was being conducted under the direction of Dr. Fred Schwartz, a man who was considered as something more than controversial by many church groups. Dr. Schwartz was a former Communist who had left the Party when he became aware of their plans for world domination and—principally, I think—because, following his conversion to Christ, he could not reconcile the faith of Christianity with the Godless, atheistic ideology of Communism. I despise godless Communism, and so does Roy. At the Shrine Auditorium we had given a brief Christian witness and we had commended the work of Dr. Schwartz. The very next day one of the leaders of the Methodist Conference in our area castigated Dr. Schwartz and his followers as rabble-rousers, and cautioned the congregation in our Chatsworth church to have nothing to do with anti-Communist movements of any kind. We thought this over carefully and prayerfully. When the Los Angeles Annual Conference almost tied in voting on whether the United Nations should admit Red China, we felt that we had had it, and we withdrew from the church.

That was then. As I think of it now, I think we might not do now what we did at that time. No church is perfect, no congregation is perfect and no two people in any congregation can agree perfectly on everything. And people *are* the church. Today, instead of running off to a new fellowship, I think I would stand my ground, as many of our friends in the Chatsworth Methodist Church wanted us to do. I have at last learned to keep my own counsel with God about many of the conflicts connected with Christian faith. I have also learned that Satan loves nothing better than a chance to split every Christian fellowship on the face of the earth; he loves to divide and conquer, and we should think twice before helping him do *that*.

Different churches stress different aspects of the truth. Some are sternly rock-bottom, insistent on obeying every commandment laid down in Scripture, in following every precept, in doing literally everything suggested in the Bible and by the Christ. That is necessary, they believe, if we are to make it to heaven. Others are not so strict or literal about this; the liberals among us are not so much concerned with letter-by-letter observance of the laws and ordinances and commandments of Scripture as they are with the application of Christian love in action to the problems that confront us all. To use a way-out illustration, the hippies (it might be hard to call *them* Christian at all!) in their determination never to conform in any way to the orthodox Christian Establishment or to have anything to do with a literal interpretation of the Bible, still put on sandals (they call them "Jesus' boots"), wear shawls and insist that all they want to do is to love—and to *be* just plain love, as Jesus was. I have my doubts about the hippies, generally, but I think Billy Graham is right when he says that the Jesus' boots and the shawls and the insistence upon love among them are all indications of their search for truth which ultimately may lead them to Christ. I don't agree with them in many areas, but I would like to talk with them about Christ and His love, if that is really what they want. I would not run from them, nor from any way-out seeker.

Jesus did not flout the old Jewish Law; he fulfilled it; He superseded it with acts of love and mercy. In His mercy He fulfilled the love-thy-neighbor commandment of the Jews, even though it appeared to some of the strict Law observers of His day that He was breaking the Law. He came not to add to the Law, but to give us a grace and a power to live in such love that we would not need the constraints of the Law. Let me illustrate this.

Our agent, Joe Rivkin, was with us one night at a personal appearance in Anaheim, California. It was the night of Rosh Hashanah, the Jewish New Year, and, being of that faith, he felt uncomfortable—guilty—at the thought of working with us on this, his High Holy Day. During the intermission a little boy with cerebral palsy was carried into our dressing room by his distraught parents. Joe met them at the door where he was standing guard. He was supposed to keep people out, but he brought them in, with tears streaming down his face. I have never seen a deeper compassion on any human face. He saw to it that the whole family had choice seats for the rest of the show and he opened the gates of Disneyland for them to see everything there, *free!*

Now Joe is Jewish and I am Christian. When the little family had gone I said to him, "Joe, you have kept the highest law of God this day, loving and serving your neighbor as yourself. *Our* God will love that!" See what I mean? Different as we are in our various faiths and creeds and ideologies and theologies, we have this in common: we are all under orders to Go! Heal! Love!

And we are to understand each other in love, as the Good Samaritan understood his Jewish sufferer on the road to Jericho.

We had intended to visit several churches before placing our membership but we visited only one. We found The Chapel in the Canyon in Canoga Park—an independent church with a Disciples of Christ background. One visit was enough; we knew that this was a church in which we could give a bold, vital witness for Christ. Its pastor, Larry White, had a passion for young people, and I liked that. He invited me to help with the choir— and I liked that. It wasn't long before we had choirs of children, teen-agers and adults singing the old, familiar hymns with new, lively arrangements. I was happy there.

I was more than happy when Billy Graham came to Los Angeles on a Crusade and the buses began to roll from the Chapel to the Coliseum. The Chapel went all-out in cooperation with Billy. It was in the Coliseum on Youth Night that Dusty, Sandy, Dodie and Debbie went down the aisle and gave their hearts to Christ. In that one moment, the memories of years of pain and hurt and sorrow were washed out of my heart. All four of them had been baptized previously, but Dusty and Sandy asked for immersion at the Chapel. (Dusty has *really* been baptized with water: he was christened at six months of age, sprinkled at seven in the Methodist Church, and immersed at the Chapel as a teen-ager!)

A lot of things happened in the summer of 1963. Our family was growing by leaps and bounds; I had always wanted a large family—and believe me, I got it! Grandchildren made their appearances so fast that I had trouble keeping track of them. One grandchild was born with trouble. Tom and Barbara had three girls—Mindy, Julie and Candy who became a diabetic at the age of sixteen months. That was hard for all of us to take— after all we had been through. Tom inspired and helped us, with a really Christian approach to the problem. He gave up his teaching job in Yreka, California, at the beginning of the school year,

151

and brought his family back to Los Angeles where Candy could get good diabetic treatment at Children's Hospital. As I watched him I saw a dramatic Christian faith demonstrated right before my eyes.

"I don't know where I'll find a teaching job in October that will pay enough to support my family," said Tom, "but God does, and He will take care of it." And take care of it God did. Shortly after Candy entered the hospital, Tom received a call to apply for an excellent teaching post in the Glendale School District. He got it—a far better job than the one he had left. I have seen it with this little family time after time. They never ask questions when adversity strikes; they simply trust God and do whatever has to be done without a murmur. God has come through for them every time. They are faithful—and He rewards that faithfulness. Many a time they have not had money enough to meet current expenses, but when their salary checks come in they give God a tenth of it, in tithe—and from somewhere, or from Someone, they find help to make a little more, or they get an extension of credit. It has always worked that way with them.

If I sound like a doting mother, forgive me. I reckon I am a doter, for God has given me much to dote on. He has given me Tom and Barbara and their three children—a family beautifully Christian. This has been a wondrous revelation and assurance that the promises of God are valid. He has given me thirteen grandchildren and one foster grandchild. Cheryl has two girls, Lisa and Kim, and two boys, Brian and Mark. Marion has a girl, Laurie, and two boys, Danny and David. Linda has a girl, Sherry, a boy, Robbie, and a foster-son, Victor. Dusty and his Linda have a girl, Shawna.

All of the children are now married. Dodie was married last fall to a staff sergeant in the United States Air Force, and will be residing on the East Coast until his duty is over, when they plan to return to California to live. Who knows how big our family will be by this time next year! Am I happy!

152

Late that summer we decided to take our four young children on a camper trip. Have you ever taken a camper trip with four young ones? If you haven't, you haven't lived! It is exciting, exhausting—and fun. We had a custom-built camper complete with tents, folding cots, a little picnic table with seats attached, a good cookstove and a kerosene lantern. You might call that trip a "roar," for it was the noisiest and most exciting trip this family of ours ever took. We roared down the Snake River, from Jackson Hole, Wyoming, in two big rubber rafts—the girls, a guide and I in one, Roy and the boys and another guide in the other. This was white water (rapids) and believe it or not Roy and the boys fished all the way downstream! What's more, they caught trout—and I had to fry them. They fished, too, in Yellowstone Lake, surrounded by bears and geysers and the most enchanting scenery in the world.

Roy did all the driving, and he drove like Jehu. We took turns sitting in the big double-bed bunk overhanging the truck cab; the kids fought for a place up there because it was a beautiful observation deck. I spent a lot of time up there, too, marveling at the landscape in the park that defies description. I found myself repeating Psalm 104. How in Yellowstone Park could anyone doubt the existence of God? I can't imagine anyone with enough arrogance to do that! Driving through the breathtaking Shoshone Canyon to Cody, the words of Habakkuk 3:19 raced through my mind as we wound along a road cut out of the side of the mountain, along high, sheer cliffs with no outside rails and with drops of hundreds of feet to the bottom: "The Lord God is my strength, and he will make my feet like hinds' feet, and he will make me to walk upon mine high places. . . ." It was like walking a tightrope—like the often narrow, perilous way of the Christian, when the eyes must look straight ahead and not *down,* if he is to see the unexpected obstacles that may be just around the bend. Yes, we had a roaring time of it in that canyon!

153

But I spent most of my time below—watching the pots and pans on the rattling stove. Every time Roy put on the brakes I made a dash to keep everything from sliding off the stove onto the floor. I sat there and thought of those pioneer women traveling through the same country in their covered wagons, and I did *not* envy them. But how I respected them! What Americans they were!

We ran into roaring storms in the Grand Canyon country. One storm ripped a hole as big as your washtub in the boys' tent (they were sleeping out that night), and they came into the camper soaked to the skin and covered with thick, red mud. Some of it was still with us when we got home.

The kids went along with us when we played the Seattle Exposition later that year. They got wet all over, all of them, all over again, when we had to play in the rain. It was all very uncomfortable—and it was all good for all of us. The family that goes through such experiences as these can go through *anything*—and I mean anything!

I got a phone call one morning at the motel in Seattle from a Reverend Harold Bredesen, a Dutch Reformed Minister from New York City. He invited me to have breakfast with him and Reverend Dennis Bennett, the rector of an Episcopal Church in Van Nuys, California. I didn't know quite what it was all about, but I had enjoyed breakfasts and luncheons with other clergymen who were interested in our witness, so I had breakfast with them the next morning. When the usual informal chitchat was over, they got down to business. They asked me if I had received "the in-filling of the Holy Spirit." A little surprised, I told them that I had been baptized by immersion at ten, had definitely been born again at thirty-five, and that I had experienced the Presence of the Holy Spirit twice during Robin's life. They accepted that, but they explained that there was a "second blessing"—a baptism "as by fire"—available to the seeking Christian. The hair on the back of my neck started to rise, and a warning whistle

154

blew; this, I suspected, was "speaking in tongues" experience, and I had shied away from such way-out experiences, for I had been taught that the gift of tongues and speaking in tongues was not vital to salvation. These gifts, I believed, did not belong to this dispensation, but only to that of the disciples in the early Church, and then for a very special reason. Sitting at the breakfast table, I recalled the days—and nights—when I went with my parents and relatives to sit outside a Holy Roller church in Arkansas to listen to the strange goings-on inside. People in there, we were told, in their frenzy would grasp hot oil lamps in their bare hands; the shouting that came through those windows was deafening—and, I thought, a bit too much.

I told the two clergymen that I wanted no part of this second baptism and in-filling of the Spirit. I tried to explain my position to these obviously sincere, intelligent and completely dedicated men of God. I felt that God had called me to be simply a witness as an entertainer to all entertainers and churches and religious persuasions, and that since this charisma business had become such a controversial issue, my involvement in it might curtail the influence of my witness.

They asked then if they might pray with me. Inside I thought, "Here? In this restaurant?" Audibly I agreed. We bowed our heads and they started to pray for me and for my witness. Immediately, I felt the thrust of a great power behind their words, and it stirred me deeply. I felt strangely moved by it— when suddenly one of the men began to talk beautifully in a strange, foreign language which I could not understand. I pulled back, putting on the brakes.

When they finished, I thanked them and promised that I would try to attend one of their Full Gospel meetings. Roy and I had witnessed at a Full Gospel meeting at Disneyland, some years before this, and we had attended a similar Assembly of God meeting at Tulsa, Oklahoma, while on tour. We had both agreed then that we must respect these people who felt their

155

religion so warmly and deeply, but that somehow, it was not for us, or within the frame of our religious thinking.

When I got back to my room, I wanted to pray. I dropped to my knees by my bed and told the Lord that if He wanted me to have this strange gift of tongues, I was ready to accept it. Immediately I felt a great, burning joy, and a sense of being lifted. I wanted to speak to God of what I felt, but I could not find the right words. I said, "Father, if it is Your will, let the Holy Spirit use my tongue to praise You."

A strange sound came from my throat—a sound completely foreign to me—then more—and more—jumbled, but after a few seconds coming more smoothly in a pattern of flowing speech. There was a great sense of power in it, an elation, a thanksgiving, and it was almost as though I would burst with it. I heard footsteps in the hall outside.

I stopped it, quenched it, cut it off. Perhaps I was fearful of Roy's reaction and I was sure this was Roy coming down the hall. It wasn't. The footsteps were not his, and I felt a little foolish, being so afraid in the midst of such an overwhelming experience. I was also thinking, "This is too much. This is dangerous business—and it is not for me. Neither Roy nor the rest of my family will understand; they will think I have lost my mind, *and they will not listen any more to my witness.*"

I thanked God for the experience, and decided not to pursue it further.

We had another experience at the Seattle Exposition that shook us up—and strengthened us. Roy and I, the Sons of the Pioneers and Cliff Arquette had signed for thirteen hour-long shows for ABC Television, the first of which was to be filmed at Seattle. Our closing number was "How Great Thou Art," that wonderful song sung by Bev Shea at Billy Graham's meetings. Roy and I sang it standing under one of the beautiful arches of the Science Building, with great fleecy clouds as a backdrop. Just before we started to do the first take on the

156

number, Art Rush got a call from the powers-that-be on the network, ordering us to delete the word "Christ" from the third verse of the song. We refused, just as we had refused to take out the cross on light thrown on the turf in Madison Square Garden when Roy sang "Peace in the Valley" some years before. The pressure was really put on us, but we were adamant about it. Later we found that our refusal to delete His name was one of the factors that cancelled out our show at the first option.

What does Christ say about such things? He says, ". . . let him . . . take up his cross daily and follow me" (Luke 9:23). He also says that those who follow Him may be persecuted for their loyalty to Him. So? Think of what He went through to give us eternal life. How paltry is a television contract in comparison with *that!* He said that with every temptation to waver in doing right He would give us a way of escape. Though Roy and I have lost out more than once in secular work and opportunities, we have never gone hungry. When one door has been slammed in our faces, another has always opened. We have found Him completely honest in His promise. ". . . I will never leave thee, nor forsake thee" (Hebrews 13:5). He will be with us, whatever happens. He has said so, and I believe Him.

There are those who say, "Well, why does God give so many breaks to the disgusting, wicked people who ignore or hate Him? Why does He let them get away with theft, lying, murder—everything? Why does He let everything go so great for them, when some Christian like you gets the book thrown at him when he tried to do right?" I have found the answer to that question in the Seventy-third Psalm. Read it, and you will have the answer, too. In London, Billy Graham advised Roy to read this psalm when Roy asked him the same question. *Read it!* "When I thought to know this, it was too painful for me, Until I went into the Sanctuary of God; then understood

157

I their end" (vs. 16, 17). The end of the wicked, that is—the wicked, who are cut off at last with no hope. Read of the assurance held out to the faithful Christian: "Nevertheless, I am continually with thee: thou hast holden me by my right hand. Thou shalt guide me with thy counsel, and afterward receive me to glory" (vs. 23, 24).

That's good enough for me.

By the time we got back to Los Angeles it was time for the children to start school and for the adults to start taping a series for ABC. Two blows hit us in quick succession. The smog of L.A. hit me in the throat, and I had the same old trouble making myself speak above a whisper—and again God brought me through it. Then the Cuban crisis came. It looked like war, and none of us liked that. Poor Debbie was frightened almost out of her wits. She had memories of the war in Korea, memories planted in her mind as a baby—many memories. She came running to Roy one day.

"Daddy, are we going to have a war?"

"Honey, we hope not, but if we do, we must be ready for it."

She burst into tears: "Please, Daddy, I don't want a war. Please—*please!*"

She listened to us discuss the building of a bomb shelter on the ranch, and it terrified her.

I have seen much of war and its disastrous consequences in my lifetime. I hate it. War is hell on earth—the devil's business, not God's. I worry often over the words of Jesus, "And ye shall hear of wars and rumors of wars . . ." (Matthew 24:6). He said that because He knew the heart of man, and the ways of Satan with the heart of man. My Bible tells me that "the heart . . . is desperately wicked; who can know it?" (Jeremiah 17:9). I know this: the heart of unregenerate men is capable of *anything*. Only the grace of God can tame the human heart. When man refuses to acknowledge the only One who can bring peace to the human heart, then war *is* inevitable. God in the

158

heart is the Author of peace; Satan is the author of confusion.

I have wrestled with war much as a Christian. I wrestled with it in that moment with Debbie, and I was to wrestle with it even more horribly in the days that lay just ahead, though I did not know it then. I am torn by the thought that all of us must ". . . Go ye into all the world, and preach the Gospel to every creature" (Mark 16:15)—and by the thought that war is terribly anti-God and anti-Christian. Yet, when war comes with those who would impose godlessness and atheism on the world—then what are we who believe in God and Christ to do? Are we to stand by and see the great commission torn to shreds?

What can we do, as Christian individuals, to bring peace on earth? We can, as the old song says, "Let peace begin with me." We can live like Christians in our everyday walk, in every small thing and matter. We can let our light so shine in the little crises of life that it will penetrate into the bigger places— so infuse men and this world with the light of Christ, the Prince of Peace, that war will be impossible.

Only He and His Light can bring the peace we pray for.

10

*M*aybe I have mis-titled this book; perhaps it should be called "Trouble, Testing and Triumph," for that is the story of my life, after all—and it may be the story of your life, too. The year 1964, especially, was like that.

In 1964 the Religious Heritage of America chose me for their Churchwoman of the Year Award. That was good! I was invited to speak at the World's Fair in New York; that was good, too, and a prominent lay evangelist came to The Chapel in the Canyon and led a speaking-in-tongues service. In spite of my resolve to stay clear of such meetings, this one really gave me a joy I had never experienced before. It is impossible to explain it, but it was there. I was left more puzzled than ever about this form of worship.

This was the year Roy had a bad time of it in the hospital— and that was bad. He had been complaining of severe neck pains for some time, and the doctors found that three vertebrae were jammed together because of worn discs, and only an operation could correct it. His almost furious physical activity over the years—riding, racing speedboats in the ocean (that is really tough!), motorcycling, mountain climbing, hunting bobcats and bear—well, what could we expect? To the hospital he must go.

Just before he went, he insisted that I go to Hawaii with the children. We had promised them this a long time ago, and we felt that it would be good to go before Roy's confinement in the hospital. I'm glad we went, for I learned two very important things in Hawaii.

One was that Sandy was fascinated with every sailor, soldier and marine he met—and he met a lot of them. He spent most of his days with them on the beach, and I saw for the first time one of the major interests of his life. A burning desire to enlist took hold of Sandy on that beach.

Dusty liked the shops, the curios, the flowers—and the hula dancers! Dodie got sick again, and had to rest a lot. Debbie . . . ah, Debbie! She seemed a part of Hawaii, from the first day. I can still see her standing in the bow of a sailboat, her hair blowing in the breeze, her eyes closed in ecstacy. She loved everything and everybody in Hawaii; the music of this lovely land answered the music in her heart. Debbie was barely twelve, that year, but as I looked at her I realized that she was no longer a child.

Roy's operation went well; he was on the operating table for five hours, and a week after the operation a staph infection frightened us, but he slowly started to mend. We brought him to the convalescent home in Bel Air August 14th, the day after Debbie's birthday. When Debbie went to see her daddy, she was all dressed up in clothes she had picked out herself. (She had begun to question Mama's taste in clothes!) She was almost as tall as I was—exuberant, tireless, a frolicking filly who gave promise of tremendous energy and speed. I was not at all sure that I was going to keep up with her and I worried about her easy familiarity with strangers. I thought with a pang, "It won't be long before she leaves us; she looks more like eighteen than twelve right now." She was no longer interested in twelve-year-old children—or twelve-year-old ideas; she loved to sit and talk with adults.

Debbie sang in the church choir that Sunday morning, and her face was radiant. How *alive* she was! The radiance could have been due, in part, to the fact that she was going on a bus ride with her friends from the church to an orphanage in Tijuana, to take a load of gifts to the children out there; but I think it was mostly the radiance that comes to every girl when she realizes that she is becoming a young lady. Either way, her face was pure joy.

Halfway through the service she caught my eye and motioned toward Dodie, who sat across the aisle from me. Dodie's face was as white as chalk; she looked at me and whispered, "Mama, I'm sick." When we got her home after the service, we told Debbie that the bus trip was off. That hurt; she pleaded tearfully, and she told us that her two young friends, Kathy and Joanne Russell, couldn't go if she didn't go. We relented. Come Monday morning, she and the Russells climbed into the bus and waved good-bye. Good-bye!

I spent most of that day with Roy at the Bel Air Convalescent Home. Driving home over the San Diego Freeway at about 3:30, I was deep in thought about many things—about our family, our health problems, about the house and the growing children. For once I hadn't turned on the car radio—thank the Lord! If it had been on, I would have gone berserk. As I turned into the driveway at the ranch, I saw Ruth Miner ("Granny," to the children) looking at me strangely. I parked the car and walked toward the house. The wind was swift and hot, blowing leaves into the dining room behind me.

"Ruth!" I exploded, "It's stifling in here. Why haven't you turned on the air conditioner?"

She walked over to me, took my arm and led me into the living room.

"Dale," she said, "Get hold of yourself. Something has happened. The bus had an accident after it left San Diego. Debbie and Joanne Russell are with the Lord."

I looked at her blankly. "With . . . the *Lord?*"

162

Then like the blow of a hammer, it struck into my brain. She was telling me that Debbie had been killed.

I screamed, "No! No! Not my baby, again!" I pounded the door with my fists. "Jesus! Jesus! *Help* me!"

Dusty walked in at that moment from the Chapel. He grabbed me and shook me violently. "Mom! You've told me to trust Jesus, as long as I can remember. If you meant that, you'd better start trusting Him right now. Debbie is OK. She's with Him!"

Thank you for that, Dusty. I needed it, in that moment.

The doctor came and gave me a sedative. I looked around for Dodie; she was nowhere to be seen. They found her huddled in a knot with her dogs in the rocks back of the house, sobbing her heart out. Through her tears she asked me, "Mom, are the angels jealous?" I suspected that she was remorsefully remembering the times when Debbie bested her in different situations and Dodie had been resentful of her—which was natural. Somehow I managed to tell her that the angels were never jealous, that in heaven there is nothing to make anyone unhappy and Debbie was in a place far better than the place *we* were in.

Asked Dodie, "Could you . . . get me another sister?" I said it was too early to even think about that.

All of a sudden I thought of Roy—and of the little portable TV set in his room. He watched it all day long! I dragged myself to the telephone to call the nurse, and Art Rush answered. He said that the news media had promised not to release anything on Debbie's death until I had been told. Bless them, forever!

The phone began ringing. The press, friends. . . .

The phone at the Chapel was going crazy, too. Dusty and Sandy were helping there, as the frantic fathers and mothers who had children on the bus called and came in person. It was a nightmare. I clung to hope, like the drowning man clinging to a straw. I refused to accept her death. Maybe there was some mistake . . . maybe. . . . There was no mistake. The

163

coroner in San Diego called and told me that Ernestine White (our minister's wife) had identified Debbie and Joanne. It was then that I called my mother in Texas and told her. She came by the next plane.

Friends poured into the house—Pat O'Shea, Judy Whisenant, so many others! They helped: I slowly regained control, and "got a new seat in the saddle."

Roy's surgeon told him. He told Art Rush later that the news sent Roy into a complete tailspin, and they had to rush him back to the hospital in Los Angeles. No wonder! Debbie was the one who had always met him at the door with a kiss and a smile; she was the one who took off his boots, rubbed his aching neck and brought him coffee. She and Dodie often took turns combing Daddy's hair, trying different hair styles while he watched TV. I think, perhaps, that Debbie was closest to her Daddy. One of the women at the church who had charge of Debbie's team that day said that just before the tire blew, hurling Debbie and Joanne into eternity, she had complimented Debbie on her new short summer haircut. Debbie said, "Mommy likes it short for the summer, but Daddy likes it long, and I'm going to let it grow out right away for him." Debbie had also asked special prayers for her Daddy that day.

In the middle of the night I was awakened by a loud, anguished moaning. It sounded like Debbie, until I remembered. Then I thought it might be Ruth Miner. I stumbled down the hall to her room and found her wide awake, too. She thought it was I who was moaning. We went to investigate and found Bowser, our dog, in a big chair in the living room, his head hanging over the seat, sobbing like a stricken human being. Ruth went back to bed and I went to the altar in our living room.

I lighted the candles and looked down at the huge family Bible which was open. My eyes fell on the words of Paul to the Hebrews, in Chapter Twelve: "If ye endure chastening, God

164

dealeth with you as with sons; for what son is he whom the father chasteneth not? But if ye be without chastisement whereof all are partakers, then are ye bastards and not sons. Furthermore, we have had fathers of our flesh which corrected us, and we gave them reverence; shall we not much rather be in subjection unto the Father of spirits and live? For they verily for a few days chastened us after their own pleasure; but he for our profit, that we might be partakers of his holiness. Now no chastening for the present seemeth to be joyous but grievous; nevertheless afterward it yieldeth the peaceable fruit of righteousness unto them which are exercised thereby. Wherefore, lift up the hands which hang down and the feeble knees; and make straight paths for your feet, lest that which is lame be turned out of the way; but let it rather be healed" (Hebrews 12:7–13).

What does this mean: "lest that which is lame be turned out of the way"? I believe it refers to those Christians who are watching the professing Christians in time of deep trouble, who might be attracted to the Way—and watching to see if it really works in life. If the Christian fails to demonstrate the power and grace of God in extremity, that person might be turned from the Way, thinking that the Way is not adequate to meet the vicissitudes we are all called upon to meet.

I read it, and I was strengthened; I was aware of the Presence of God within and around me. The psalmist said, "Examine me, O Lord, and prove me" (Psalm 26:2). He is the Word; He was in Paul, talking to those Hebrews, and He was talking straight to me now. I knew it; I felt it, and I heeded His words. I went back to bed, confident that He would "perfect that which concerneth me" (Psalm 138:8). I knew He was going to be with me all through what was ahead. He had promised: "Lo, I am with you *always* . . ." (Matthew 28:20).

And He was with me—all through it. If he had not been with me, I could never have gotten through it. He was with me when I went to see Roy in the UCLA Medical Center, and from

165

there to Forest Lawn to make the funeral arrangements. I had to make arrangements all by myself; the Russells were with their other daughter, Kathy, who had been hurt in the accident. The rest was up to me. When I tried to get up from my chair in Roy's room at the hospital, I hardly made it. I felt wooden.

And He was with me at Forest Lawn, as I picked out the two caskets, and the flowers, and made arrangements for the services. Mrs. White, our pastor's wife, would give the eulogy, since her husband (who had been on the bus) was still in the hospital in Oceanside. The attendant at Forest Lawn explained that the coroner had advised that under no circumstances were the caskets to be opened.

The next day Mother, Art Rush, my friend Judy Whisenant and I drove out there again. Art talked briefly with the man in charge, and came back to me shaken and agitated. "Dale," he said, "I have been asked to make a decision here that I simply cannot make. They tell me that they think you can and should see Debbie, but it has to be your decision. They have worked very hard to make her presentable, and . . . ."

I made the decision immediately. I would not make the mistake again I had made in refusing to look at Robin and I went in with the Russell family—and with God—to look at my baby. I saw a pretty, sleeping young girl dressed in the white dress she had worn at her sixth-grade commencement, with a pink bow in her lustrous black hair, her long slender fingers clasping a little blue stuffed animal she had won at Pacific Ocean Park on Saturday. She looked about eighteen. I stood there with her, knowing that my real Debbie was in eternity—*and in that moment I was with her in eternity, out of the body, in the Spirit*. There are no words to describe this experience; one has to go through it himself to understand it.

I fell to my knees and thanked God for the nine years He had let us have Debbie. I told Him that I trusted Him with

166

her, and I committed her into His hands. I got up and walked out of that place. God walked with me. He had not left me desolate. He had come to me and taken my heartbreak into His own heart. When I reached the house in Chatsworth a friend said to me, "Dale, your face is positively *glowing;* it is . . . radiant. How . . . ?" Only God could do it. He kept the radiance there all through the services that followed. He had removed from me forever all fear of death.

The following Sunday He gave me the strength to speak briefly at the Chapel about the great truth of His everlasting arms, about His being ". . . a very present help in time of trouble" (Psalm 46:1).

Of course there were painful moments after that. That is to be expected, for death always means the loss of the presence of the loved one who leaves us. It is the end of a personal, physical relationship that is hard to bear. A week after the funeral I went into Debbie's closet—too soon!—to see what I could do about her clothes. Staring at those clothes, I realized that the little laughing Debbie would never wear them again, and momentarily I went to pieces. I ran into the kitchen, reached for a cup of coffee and turned to see my mother. She saw my pale face, my trembling hands. She heard me say, "It isn't right! It isn't fair! Why did it have to happen? She had a brilliant future before her, and it was all snapped off, just like *that! Why?"*

She looked me in the eye and let me have it. "I'm surprised and disappointed in you. You know better than to give way to this. *What's happened to your faith?"*

I deserved it; I had asked for this. I was humbled and ashamed, and I asked the forgiveness of God. He seemed to be standing there, waiting to forgive. In perfect peace I went first to our family altar and then to my desk. No, He *led* me to my desk. I picked up my pen and asked Him to guide it as I wrote about Debbie—as I had written about Robin. I had to

167

get this down on paper, for the benefit of other mothers who might lose other Debbies.

It poured from my pen for hours, for days. I could not stop writing; I could do nothing else, think of nothing else, until it was a finished book. We called it, *Dearest Debbie,* and we dedicated it and donated its royalties to World Vision, Inc.— Bob Pierce's organization, through which Debbie had come to us from Korea.

Roy came home, his neck in a big steel brace. When Christmas came, we sang a song together, "Happy Birthday, Gentle Saviour," at the Music Center in Los Angeles for Teen World Opportunity. I was never prouder of him.

God was with us there, too!

11

*E*arly in January Sandy told us he wanted to enlist in the army. He had asked us for our consent to enlist a year previously, when the Viet Nam affair was developing so quickly. We had refused then, for we wanted him to finish high school. Now he said, "I want to serve my country. I want to prove myself a man. I promise you that I will get my high-school diploma in the service." He was engaged to a lovely girl who attended the Chapel services with him, and we asked him about that, and about her. He said she had promised to wait for him.

We gave our consent. This time his courage and determination were too much for us. Off he went to Fort Polk in Louisiana. I went to see him graduate at Polk and watched him march in review with his company, and I was proud—proud of this boy who was making such a gallant fight against his handicaps, proud of his love of the flag and of his desire to keep that flag flying. He volunteered to go to Viet Nam—and was turned down. Instead he was assigned to the tank corps and sent to Germany. As a matter of fact, he volunteered twice for Viet Nam, but they wouldn't let him go. His officers said to him, "Your family has suffered enough; we are sending you to Germany." Later they told us that his reflex actions were just too slow for hand to hand combat.

So our Sandy went off to Germany, and we went out to a new home in Apple Valley, where Roy had leased the Apple Valley Inn. Apple Valley is in desert country, and that was good for me, with my bronchitis and touch of asthma. I took

169

to desert life with ease; the glorious early mornings and late afternoons were balm from heaven! We joined the (Presbyterian) Church of the Valley, where Dodie began taking instruction for membership. Dusty had a number of friends in nearby Victorville High School who attended the High Desert Baptist Church, so he went there. He was in his senior year of high school; Dodie was in the eighth grade.

We bought an old adobe house near the Inn, a house shaped like a horseshoe with a big backyard that was perfect for our menagerie: Bullet, Bowser, Bobo, Bambi (our Chihuahau), Sugar (half bobcat and half just plain cat) and Smokey (proud Persian cat). It is a happy house and we have found great happiness in it. It isn't fancy, but it is adequate—and a constant challenge to experiment. I was born an experimenter with houses. Roy says I'm a natural furniture mover, forever changing things around—so much so that he never knows where to sit down! We painted it a forest green with white trim, and it stands there in a desert devoid of any other green, like an oasis. We love it.

Let me tell you about Smokey. While Debbie was still with us, she begged for a kitten. We said no, because we knew what could and probably would happen to a kitten in a house full of cat-hating dogs. I am still haunted and hurt by the memory of Debbie's tears when we told her she couldn't keep a kitten given her by one of our neighbors. We already had a big black tomcat we called "Knight," a pitiful rack of bones who had to be thrown bits of food up on the roof of the house because our cat-despising dogs wouldn't let him come down. We finally coaxed him down and took him away to a dairy, where he got plenty of milk for the rest of his life. After that, we vowed there would be no more cats.

But two weeks after Debbie's death this big Persian cat ambled into the kitchen door (left open in a moment of carelessness) and Dodie promptly gave him a saucer of nice

170

fresh milk. I scolded her, for I knew what would happen. It happened. The Persian refused to leave the House of Rogers. I set myself for war between cat and dogs, and it came—but it didn't end as I expected. This cat was no amateur in battle. When a dog took just one step in his direction, he made a flying leap to the back, head or neck of the startled dog, dug his claws in and rode the dog until he yelped "Uncle." Smokey did that to every dog in the place in turn. Soon all was peace and love and understanding. Even Roy, who had never liked cats, became a Smokey fan. If Debbie could only have seen *that!*

Late in October I went to Texas to spend my birthday with my mother. On the thirty-first of the month, I had a dream that shook me badly. I dreamed that I saw a rider galloping full speed across a wide plain, heading straight for me. Suddenly his horse stumbled and fell and they rolled over and over in the sand. The horse got up, but the man didn't; he lay there motionless, and I knew that he was dead. I woke up with a scream.

I was terribly depressed all the next morning, even as I sang in church and gave a brief testimony. Late in the afternoon the whole family had dinner with me at Waxahachie, in celebration of my birthday, but I didn't feel like celebrating. I had that feeling of detachment and suspension again—that other-world feeling. I felt that something had happened, or was about to happen, that would change my life. I wondered, uneasily, if one of us around that table was in danger—perhaps in danger of death.

On Monday I flew back to Los Angeles. Marion was to meet me at the Los Angeles airport for coffee. Marion was there—and Cheryl was with her, and there was an odd look on their faces. Sensing some kind of undercurrent, I sang out, "Do we have a problem, kids?"

Cheryl replied, soberly and carefully, "Sort of, Mom."

171

The panic signal went up. In rising fear I asked, "Who is it?" Cheryl said, "Mom, it's Sandy. He's gone."

My voice started to rise, uncontrollably, and I shouted, "What do you mean—gone? Sandy isn't in Viet Nam. He's in Germany!"

Dusty and Roy came and took me by the arms and Dusty said gently, "I know, Mom. Sandy was at a party Saturday night," (the man on horseback in my dream!) "and some guys got him to drink a lot of hard liquor, and it killed him."

I almost fell to the floor. In the airport office Cheryl gave me a tranquilizer, and I heard the rest of the story. Sandy's body was to be flown home immediately after the military funeral in Germany, accompanied by an officer.

Once more—Forest Lawn. We arranged for a military funeral. Sandy was to be laid to rest in a crypt beside Robin and Debbie. When I went in to look at the boy who wanted so much to be a part of our country's action in Viet Nam, I almost cracked. There he lay in his beloved uniform—a private, first class, felled not by a bullet but by a bottle! In my heart raged bitter denunciation of the lack of regulations that would allow an eighteen-year-old private to be served enough liquor to kill him. I was beside myself with sorrow and anger for this boy who had tried so hard to measure up—to prove himself a man even in a drinking bout!

The officer who had brought Sandy's body all the way from Germany sat down with me and told me how it had happened.

He told me how hard Sandy had worked on a three-week maneuver in Germany to earn his first-class stripe, and how overjoyed he was the day he got it. He was tired out that night, too tired for the wetting-down-the-stripes party in which his buddies participated. That sort of party wasn't meant for Sandy; he was no drinker, but this was a custom in the service, and he went along with it. Spurred on by his pals, and not wishing to be a wet blanket—and to prove himself a man—he drank

172

with the rest of them. He strangled from this overdose of liquor to which his body was not accustomed. The boys in the service use all sorts of tricks to get liquor, and the officers were almost powerless to stop it, much as they disliked it. Sandy wasn't the first victim of this sort of thing, and he probably will not be the last.

After a while, I calmed down. I remembered the last letter Sandy had written, telling us how grateful he was for the Christian home he had enjoyed, how he believed in God and his country and his flag, and how anxious he was to get to Viet Nam. It hurt me that he didn't get there, because I was sure he would have preferred death there to death with that bottle. I apologized for my outburst and went back to touch his hand and to thank God that Sandy was a Christian. As I stood there I saw that God had led Sandy to prove himself as a first-class private, that he had known the love of a fine girl whom he planned to marry, and that in his death he might be spared future frustration and heartache as he struggled with his handicaps. The fact that he had died in such an ignominious manner in no way nullified what he had accomplished. We had been surprised that he passed the army physical and made it through boot camp; now we were proud of him. I did not want to let him go. I almost broke when the flag was lifted from his casket, folded and presented to me. On the way out, I hardly saw anyone for my tears.

Just before Christmas we received a small package from his commanding officer in Germany; it was the wedding and engagement ring he had purchased for his beloved Sharon. She arranged to have a cross made of them. Sandy would have liked that.

That summer the USO asked us to do an entertainment tour in Viet Nam. We promised to go for two reasons: we wanted to go to Viet Nam as sort of substitutes for Sandy, who couldn't go; and we wanted to satisfy ourselves as to why the United States was engaged in this conflict. We almost didn't make it;

my world started spinning again. The inner-ear infection was back. I couldn't keep my balance when I tried to walk, I vomited endlessly and was so ill that I was rushed off to the hospital. The Adversary whispered to me, "You don't want to go to Viet Nam. *You can't go!*" I gritted my teeth and said to God, "Lord, I am not trying to tempt You by demanding some sort of sign about this trip, but You know I can't go while I'm as sick as this. Do You want us to go? If You do, let my vision and my equilibrium and my stomach be normal in the morning." I went to sleep, and slept like a baby. In the morning I opened my eyes upon a hospital room and a world that was steady as a rock. The dizziness and the pain were gone.

We took our shots, and flew to Viet Nam.

The story of what happened to us in Viet Nam is written in detail in my little book, *Salute to Sandy,* and I will not repeat it all here. It is enough to say that it was one of the great strengthening experiences of our lives. We saw American youth at its best, its noblest; our hearts broke at the sight of their suffering, but our hearts sang a new song as we saw how they took it. There was no whimpering, no complaining; there was only a sense of duty and consecration in getting a mean and deadly job done. They knew it *had* to be done, whatever it cost. They were there to give everything they had, including their lives, to get it done. All the doubts I ever had about American youth disappeared as we entertained them, and talked with them, and visited them in the hospitals. We worked unbelievably long hours, doing what we could to help them, but what we did, compared with what they were doing, seemed so little! I would do it all over again, for Sandy, for the boys—and for the cause for which they were fighting and dying. I came home believing in that cause, and believing in them, and loving them.

It was exhausting, though: We came home dead tired to Apple Valley. I finished off the *Salute to Sandy,* which I had

174

worked on in Viet Nam and in airplanes going there and coming back. I finished it, sent it off to the publishers and arranged with them to pay its royalties to the Campus Crusade for Christ, International. The book was published on Sandy's birthday; Campus Crusade is still benefitting from its sale.

It was hard, settling down after those days at the heart of the hurricane of war, but we had one blessed day that helped a lot. That was the day Dusty got married. Dusty had been working in a big supermarket in Middlefield, Ohio, with his close friend George White, whose family owned the business. Here he had fallen in love with Linda Yoder, a Middlefield girl. Roy wanted him to stay closer to home, and to find his lifework somewhere near us, or with us, but Dusty wanted to make it on his own, and we respected his decision. We went to his wedding.

I wept at the wedding—but for joy. I wept at the thought of another child leaving the Rogers' roost. It was not easy to let him go, nor was it, I think, easy for him to go. Nothing is ever easy for the children of people in public life. Somehow, there is always some pressure upon them, demanding that they measure up to what other people expect of them as the children of so-called celebrities. It is difficult for them to be individuals, to be human beings in their own right, to do what they want to do and to be what they want to be. We would miss our Dusty, but he deserved his chance to spread his wings in new territory.

There they stood—Dusty tall, broad-shouldered, and Linda, so tiny! She was radiant. Dodie was a bridesmaid—a vision in her long red empire velvet dress. Dusty's eyes widened in surprise as he watched her come down the aisle of the church— the scrawny little girl with the long dark pigtails who had played with him and wrestled with him and Sandy and Debbie. Even when he was wrong, she took his side! Memories soared in the hearts and ears and eyes of all of us.

175

So the last boy was married. He works today with the Yoder Construction Company in Middlefield, and does an occasional personal appearance with Roy at the openings of the Roy Rogers Chuckwagons (beef sandwiches) across the country. At home he idolizes his baby—Shawna Marie.

We came home then to Apple Valley—just we three.

12

*W*e had moved to Apple Valley to "retire"—to take it a bit easier, to slow down, to think and rest and to do a lot of things we had never had time to do in the busy past. Alas for all that! We found ourselves as busy as ever. We were still doing TV appearances; I was away on speaking engagements much of the time; Roy had his restaurant openings and his activity with horse breeding—and the management of the Inn was a heavy, heavy load.

It was just too much. We changed our relationship with the Inn, turning over the lease and all managerial duties to the owners, but we bought—outright—a big bowling alley across the street, and started converting it into our personal museum. Into it we put row upon row of photographs and scrapbook materials; Robin, Debbie, Sandy and Roy's mother each have a separate display, and there is an exhibit which we call "The Religious Heritage of Our Country." Good old Trigger, beautifully mounted, has a room of his own. When Roy had suggested, at the time of Trigger's death, that he would have him mounted "for posterity," I hooted and objected, but he had his way about it. Trigger was mounted and set up, and now I'm glad he was. The rapt expressions of the kids and grown-ups who visit the museum and look at him convince me that it was the thing to do. When Bullet and Buttermilk leave us, I have no doubt that they will also be readied for posterity by a taxidermist. Right now, they are not concerned about it. Buttermilk and Bullet are enjoying retirement, and they act as though they owned the whole place!

With the slowing of the pace I found time to think and evaluate much that has happened in our lives. I had time now to "sum up," to estimate our failures and our successes, to decide what had been good about it, and what had been bad. I have come to several conclusions about it all.

I have come to believe that *everything* in our lives which we had entrusted to God was good, and that those parts of it in which we tried to go it alone were (frequently) not so good. Like the woman at the well, we were happy when we let down our buckets into the Living Waters of God and Christ; when we did not, we were *not* happy. Yet even those years in which we tried to live without God were not wasted; He used them to work out His purpose in our lives. I am more than grateful for that. God runs a good school here on earth, and we who are His pupils get good marks only when we listen to Teacher!

And I have become more and more optimistic and hopeful about the future. Our past is prologue; we can and must build on it for tomorrow. I am confident that the future will be better than the past. "He holds the whole world in His hands." I rest on that.

I sum up with this: *I believe in the younger generation; I believe in our country; I believe in God.*

I love our young people. On the whole I think they are courageous, brave, honest and intelligent—and too often frustrated by too much permissiveness at the hands of overmaterialistic parents. Even though we do not always agree with them, the least we can do is to *listen* to them. Wisdom does not begin and end with parents; it is something that is passed down from generation to generation. Sometimes the kids are right and we are wrong. "Out of the mouth of babes and sucklings," says the psalmist, "hast thou ordained strength . . ." (Psalm 8:2)— and wisdom. Their world is hurtling into change after change— fast, too fast, and our young people are trying desperately to

178

meet the changes at their level of understanding. Beneath their rock-and-roll flamboyance they have a surprising depth of understanding.

I realized this one day last spring, when Dodie bounced into the kitchen, threw a sheet of paper at me and said, in an off-hand way, "Wanna read something crazy?" and bounced out again. I read it. Here it is:

TO WHOM IT MAY CONCERN: I was at my type-writer wondering what to do next, when all of a sudden my fingers started running over the keys. . . . Please bear with me and my mistakes, because it's been so long. I am also getting senile! My grandchildren seem to think so, though I don't believe it for an instant. Rather, with the end so near, I see things in a different perspective. I still see a future, and not a materialistic one—but a future that I will not have to struggle through, as I have struggled in the past. I am quick to point out peoples' faults, but this is only because they take life as if it were going to last forever. There are times when my memory fails me, but I can still remember so much more! My eyesight is nearly gone, but I see more things now than I've ever seen before, and though I can't hear well I have heard what I should have heard—and when I could have done something about it. My fingers are not as nimble now, and only through other hands can my thoughts be conveyed.

Yes, I am what you call old and aged, but soon I will once again be romping around. I may look like a dried-up old prune, and these wrinkles may tell a story, but I am so beautiful. It is too bad you do not understand. You feel sorry for me when I hobble across the street or when your young men bump into me and spill my packages. You have even laughed at me in my good dress with that crooked little hat, but I feel no sorrow. If only you could have what I have! This young girl beside me knows noth-ing of what she will be or even what she wants to be when age permits her. Oh, yes, she may outrun me, but unless she awakens, as so many others ought to, she will

179

never outlive me, nor outgo me. I have more energy to see the truth and have it revealed to me forever—but my body is decaying, as it must. All I have said is nothing, and yet it is everything. Look at me. You see an old woman. Look again. You see a young heart. A young soul! I have known sorrow, but comfort has always followed. No, I really have not much to say; how I do ramble on about nothing! I am growing weaker with each word that pours from my mouth, and soon I will be gone—but I will keep watch and know that I must not interfere. I will be rooting for the blind to see!

I say *that* is filled with wisdom. Here was a seventeen-year-old girl looking ahead to the day when she will be old. She has depth of perception; she stumbles a bit (don't we all?); she is reaching for something she can't quite understand or describe, but she is *reaching*. She is looking ahead, not back. She has no past, only a future—and she is deeply, spiritually concerned about it. I love her for that, as I love all youth.

Roy and I attended the high-school graduation exercises of our first grandchild, Melinda Christine Fox. Mindy was an honor student and student-council officer, and she plans to continue her education at the Bible Institute of Los Angeles. Earlier she and another fine Christian girl had debated two atheistic boys on the subject, "Is God Dead, or Not?"—and the girls won, hands down.

At the commencement, however, Roy and I were distressed and saddened as we listened to two addresses by an obviously rebellious boy and girl. There was not a hint of gratitude to home, church, school or God for their accomplishments, not a shred of hope for the future—only condemnation and bitterness. They delivered their sour apples with a sure hand—brilliant and cutting, and it nearly ruined the whole commencement as far as we were concerned. One wonders, who in good conscience could have approved those addresses, free speech notwithstanding! It was obvious that the Adversary had had a field

180

day with these two young people. The young lady was accurate when she said that they were leaving school totally unprepared to meet the challenges of this confusing world. I was sure that *they* were unprepared to meet any problem, if their words meant anything at all.

Someone had failed to give these intellectually gifted young people the undergirding of that vital relationship to God through Christ—wherein lies our hope of the future. Someone must *not* have shown them the real love of God, the true wisdom that is of God—that every good gift of life is the gift of God. The young man deplored the expenditure of money on arms and on space flights; in his opinion, our government was inexcusably responsible for the deaths of three astronauts in their flaming capsule. He will learn, as we all learn, that man is fallible and that sometimes his failures result in tragedy to himself and to others—but that is not the question! The question, in my mind, is why he did not spend some time discussing the dedication of the astronauts and of all the others involved in the tragedy. He missed that completely.

I could not help comparing the attitudes of these two young people with that of Mindy, Candy and Julie. At Christmastime they had a beautiful group photograph made in color of themselves holding their violins; they presented this to their parents, with a letter of appreciation, and a scrapbook of their lives together as a Christian family. The letter was a masterpiece of gratitude for the home and the hope they had been given by their parents. I am certain that the Christian character of all three of them is the result of their training in a home where Christ is an ever-present guest, where there is peace, purpose and challenge—and love. Tom found the Better Way years ago; it is transplanted in his children.

Yes, they and their parents, I am sure, will be called squares by some people, but I'll take their kind of square deal every time. The square young people will be the ones to survive and to conquer this jungle. I know that there are more squares in the ranks of youth than there are atheists. In them lies our hope—and God tells me that we will not be disappointed.

I believe in the squares among youth. I believe that their quiet faith in all that is good will outlast the ravings of our loud-mouthed, sophisticated rebels, unwashed and unresponsible hippies, draft-card burners and sexual deviates. The squares are the majority; the others are the lunatic fringe. They will pass, and be forgotten.

I believe in my country. I *cannot* believe that God went to all the trouble of bringing the Pilgrims and other settlers to these shores and of guiding the building of the greatest democracy the world has ever seen, only to let it be destroyed. Just as He created man for eternal life, He created America for a purpose still to be worked out in a long, if distant, future. His one increasing purpose for this country must be and will be worked out in the dedicated lives of God-oriented Americans.

One morning in Houston a tall, handsome young man knocked on the door of our hotel room. He had heard our "Salute to God and Country," at the rodeo the night before. He had a clipping in his hand (he had walked across the city to bring it to us), which contained an article protesting the efforts of an atheistic group of people who were trying to eliminate the words "In God We Trust" from our coins. He was a marine just back from Viet Nam, with three bullet wounds in his body (a tough Texan!). I told him that we had just done a tour in Viet Nam in memory of a boy who could not go to the battlefront, and to satisfy our questions as to why we were fighting there. I asked him if he knew why we were there. He answered, "I thought I did, but a lot of folks here at home—even preachers—are saying we should not be there at all, and that we shouldn't even talk of God for fear of offending the Communists! I have told them that I would rather offend the Communists than the God who made them." Amen, soldier! He said that he was going back to Viet

Nam as soon as he could. I thank God for that boy and for all others like him, who salute the flag instead of desecrating it, who love their country and are ready to die for it.

This nation's greatness depends upon her faith in the purposes of God. The whole world is watching and waiting to see if we shall keep that faith, or lose it. The Bible describes the only faith upon which we can continue to be strong and great when it says that "Righteousness exalteth a nation" (Proverbs 14: 34); it also says, "Blessed is that nation whose God is the Lord" (Psalm 33:12). I think we *must* keep this awareness of God and His righteousness as our national foundation, if we are to endure.

Just after our three great astronauts, Anders, Borman and Lovell, circuited the moon and read from up there a part of the creation story in Genesis we took time out to salute and honor them during a show at the Astrodome. It was one of the great moments in the march of man and history—and the Bible was the only Book big enough to be read in that moment! God bless them for doing that—and God help us to do something more than just honor them for doing it! May we have the courage to stand by Him as the creator of our Republic, the courage and strength to work for it, fight for it, live for it and if necessary to die for it! That is the least we can do for God and country.

A good friend, Hal Southern (a country and western composer and musician), gets down to brass tacks on this question, and he says well what I would like to say to all America. Here is his declaration of faith in his country:

Some day in the not too distant future, historians and scientists will look at the physical and written remains of our present-day civilization and shake their heads in total disbelief, unable to comprehend how an advanced culture such as ours could totally disintegrate in a mass of crime, social strife, wars, welfarism and total lack of involvement of the people in their own destiny.

183

You would think, that in our present state of confusion, both national and international, we would take heed of the lessons of history. History does repeat itself and we are going through a phase of permissiveness, self-gratification, racial disintegration, violence and moral destruction that can only lead to self-destruction on a scale unparalleled in history.

Isn't it about time we stand up and be counted? Do we want the kind of a country where it is considered square to be patriotic, stupid to be honest, insane to follow the Golden Rule, where you are considered Establishment if you work hard, raise a family and pay your bills? Is it wrong to be clean, literate, thrifty and have a short haircut? Is it wrong to like country music, tunes that have a melody, lyrics that say "I love you," rhythms that want to make you dance with a partner, or are we square because we don't like ear-shattering, wild, psychedelic sounds with obscene lyrics and clothes to match?

This nation wasn't made great by unwashed lazy hippies, crybaby welfarism or racial minorities begging for a handout. This nation was built on the honest hard work, thrift, guts, desires and needs of Irish, Jew, Negro, Mexican, Chinese and endless other people. Common people who had the guts to be uncommon, people of all races, creeds and nationalities, people with one common bond—*freedom*. In their hearts they must have known that America was the last stand for the individual, the last chance to justify man's existence on earth.

Is it wrong to ask that our communications media be a little more impartial in its treatment of things patriotic? All too often, it seems that some radio stations, for instance, will not play anything they label as patriotic or controversial, but will turn around and play protest and anti-Establishment records all day long. Is it controversial to say on record that you like being an American, are proud to be an American and that you will fight to the death for the chance to continue being an American?

Why should Capitalism, Free Enterprise and Conservatism be dirty words? Is it so wrong to want to make a profit on honest endeavors? What is wrong with making money

184

and reinvesting it in a strong America? This great nation wasn't built on a cradle-to-the-grave philosophy, nor will it survive with the government always acting as a big brother. Remember, Uncle Sam is your uncle—not your Dad!

Well, I insist on being counted. I'm four-square for Mom, Apple Pie, the Bible and the Flag. I'm for free enterprise, capitalism, do-it-yourself guts, less government in private enterprise and, last, but never least, I'm for freedom, a kind of freedom the whole world envies, a freedom that makes people all over the world risk their lives to achieve, a freedom that allows us the strength to have inscribed on the Statue of Liberty:

> Give me your tired, your poor,
> Your huddled masses yearning to breathe free,
> The wretched refuse of your teeming shore.
> Send these, the homeless, tempest-tossed to me.
> I lift my lamp beside the golden door!

That says it, for me!

I believe in God, and in God in Christ. I believe in Them not only because I want to, but because I *have* to! Their power in my life and experience has been so overwhelming that, without Them, I would feel like an astronaut lost and wandering helplessly, forever in space. When a famous astronomer was asked why he believed in God, he replied, "How can anyone go out at night and look up at the stars and *not* believe in God?" He says it for me.

You know, I used to fly into a rage when I heard someone say, "God is dead." But I don't, any more. That crazy idea didn't last very long, did it? *It* seems to be dead now! Why did I ever worry about it? Why did I let myself get so mad? When God wearied of such chatter, He took care of it in His own way.

No, God isn't dead; neither is He obsolete. His laws are as certain and as eternal as His presence in the stars, in the universe around us—and as contemporary as the sun, the stars, the moon

185

or the common winds that brush the cheeks of all of us. He is here, and He cares.

We deceive ourselves when we think of Him *only* as a God of love and forgiveness—great as all that is; and that He doesn't really care very much if and when we ignore His teachings; yes, and that we can go about committing every sin in the catalog and still be sure that, like a doting father with a spoiled child, He will forget and forgive us as though we had lived like saints. He is a God of *justice* as well as a God of mercy.

I believe what my Bible tells me—that we are made in the image of God. I do *not* believe that God is made in the image of man. Man cannot whittle Him down to man's size, much as man would like to do just that. You cannot test or analyze God; you cannot put Him in a test tube. He is *omnipotent* (all-power-ful), *omniscient* (all-knowing), *omnipresent* (present every-where, all the time). I read this about Him, in Psalm 139, "Whither shall I go from thy spirit? or whither shall I flee from thy presence? If I ascend up into heaven, thou art there; if I make my bed in hell, behold thou art there; if I take the wings of the morning and dwell in the uttermost parts of the sea, Even there shall thy hand lead me, and thy right hand shall hold me" (vs. 7–10). This isn't poetry, to me; it is truth and reality, *and it has been proved in my life's experience*. He has been with me when I passed through the hell of sorrow and suffering, many, many times; He was with me then, and He is with me now that I walk in a heaven-on-earth that is heaven because He is here with me, *now*.

In February of 1969 Roy and I faced a press conference in Houston. Press conferences are always ordeals; you never know what questions the reporters are going to throw at you. At this conference, one of them said to us, "You two people seem almost unreal, as though you had suddenly appeared out of a cloud in the West. Tell me: is it hard to be thought of as 'goody two-shoes'?" That set me back a bit, because never since

186

God revealed my unworthiness to me in 1948 have I thought of myself as "good." I am certainly not good (even Jesus asked, in Matthew 19:17, "Why callest thou me good?"); and if there is anything about me that is at all acceptable in that sense, it is strictly due to my faith in Jesus Christ. Whatever good I do, He does through me.

Roy and I have those moments which every married man and woman have, when we are less Christian and less good than we should be. I would be less than honest if I said there had never been any squalls in my Christian walk or in our marriage. There have been tempests—but our house is built on the Rock, and it has stood firm through every squall and storm. We have grown together in our faith, and growing is sometimes a painful process. But with it comes—has come to us—a quiet, inner joy in knowing that by the grace of God we have learned to accept ourselves and each other as God's children and creation. As human creatures, we still make mistakes, but our God makes no mistakes. He makes no two of us alike, but He breathes His spirit into all of us.

I told all this to the interviewer at that press conference. I told him that we were like all the rest of men and women—two humans struggling, and looking hopefully toward heaven.

How I pity those Christians who put on the false face of the spiritual snob! How I pity those who fall into the trap of believing that they are good, that they have it made, and that sin is forever behind them. This is just the moment when the Adversary gets a good hold on our souls and shakes the foundations of our faith in shattering experiences. Then it is that we realize (or *should* realize) that we are not saints at all but *still* blundering sinners very much in need of instruction in the Way —that actually we are still dragging our spiritual feet. Beware of thinking that you have heard everything and read everything regarding your faith and that you have no need of further instruction—*and continuing humility*. Beware of sitting smugly

187

back and waiting to be translated into heaven! That is just plain stupid. Every day we live is a priceless gift of God, loaded with possibilities to learn something new, to gain fresh insights into His great truths. To close our minds and hearts is to reject the inner promptings of the Spirit—to discover new dimensions of His truth.

In this autobiography, I am sure that I have said some things with which some may not agree; perhaps I should expect that. But I have not written to please anybody or everybody—that usually ends up in pleasing nobody! I have, to the best of my ability, tried to set down here an account of my personal experience before and after Christ came into my life. I have studied many religions, many different persuasions of thought in Christian belief, and I have come, in this experience, to this: *the most important question in anyone's life is the question asked by poor Pilate in Matthew 27:22:* "What shall I do then with Jesus which is called Christ?" No other question in the whole sweep of human experience is as important as this. It is the choice between life and death, between meaningless existence and life abundant. What will *you* do with Christ? Accept Him and live, or reject Him and die? *What else is there?*

His gifts are beyond reckoning, and He has bestowed them upon us with a generous hand. They are the fruits (benefits) of the Spirit. He is the Tree; we are the branches, and as the branches of an oak draw life from the trunk of the tree, so when we draw upon His strength, we find and produce rich fruits in our lives. God is good in His benefits. I know, for He has cushioned the hardest moments of my life, and given me strength to go on. However hard the way has been, I am at peace, forgetting that which is behind, I press forward to the mark of the high calling in Christ Jesus. I know I can trust Him.

I have been the woman at the well—and He has given me Living Water that has made fertile and meaningful the desert spots of my life.

Epilogue

*I*n one way or another, in the past (that's in the "B.C.," or "Before Christ" came into my life), I think I tried to break nearly every one of the Ten Commandments in thought, word or deed.

I broke them to my sorrow. I have found that those Commandments *stand,* that they are irrevocable, and that those who attempt to break them break only themselves. We are wrong when we flatter ourselves in arrogance that we can break them. The reverse is true.

Jesus said, "Think not that I am come to destroy the law . . . , but to fulfil" (Matthew 5:17). He died to give us eternal life, by allowing Himself in His perfection, to be crucified as ransom for our failures to keep the Law—which includes the Commandments. I have no question whatever about this. I know in my heart, firsthand, that this is true, because it has worked out as plain gospel truth in my life.

Galatians 6:7–10 says, "Be not deceived; God is not mocked; for whatsoever a man soweth, that shall he also reap. For he that soweth to his flesh shall of the flesh reap corruption; but he that soweth to the Spirit shall of the Spirit reap life everlasting. And let us not be weary in well doing: for in due season we shall reap, if we faint not. As we have therefore opportunity, let us do good unto all men, especially unto them who are of the household of faith."

The illnesses, the tragedies of my life and the disillusionments have served as spiritual correction to my soul. They have shown

189

me, beyond the shadow of a doubt, that in the flesh dwelleth no good thing, and that it is "the spirit that quickeneth; the flesh profiteth nothing" (John 6:63).

I am not bitter, nor questioning, toward God. I know better than to fall into that trap. Had I taken that attitude toward the semblance of tragedy that He has allowed in my Christian walk since the day He came into my heart and changed my life, I would not have learned a thing.

I do not say that God gave me German measles just before Robin was born, or that He led me to do something that would interrupt my pregnancy with her, causing her to be born congenitally imperfect. I do not say that God blew the tire on the church bus in the accident that took Debbie's life. I do not say that God inspired Sandy to drink that hard liquor in his attempt to prove himself a man, and which ended in his death. But I do believe that God knew these things would happen, for He knows our end, from the beginning of our lives. He allowed those things to happen, knowing that ". . . all things work together for good to them that love God and who are called according to his purpose" (Romans 8:28). I am His child, and He cares what happens to me and to those all about me; His Word tells me that "The Lord will perfect that which concerneth me" (Psalm 138:8). Robin, Debbie and Sandy are His children. He cared what happened to them.

Praise His Holy Name! He gave me heart assurance that these three children of mine were eternally safe in His keeping. Robin was an infant when He took her, but she had been committed to His care. Debbie and Sandy had given their lives to Christ. God gave me the blessed assurance that Debbie was prayed up the day I saw her walk to the altar (it was the day before her death), rededicating her life to the Lord only forty-eight hours after her twelfth birthday. She was radiant that day. Now, looking back, I know that the light of God's smile was already on Debbie's brow, and that He was preparing her for the journey.

Sandy was known to the men of his army company as "the guy who always bowed his head and said grace at chow-time, no matter who was looking." The letter he wrote us one week before his death was eloquent witness to his faith in his Saviour and in his country.

God is a good God! The indescribable joy He has let me experience in the Spirit far transcends any trials He has let me experience. The joy He has given me in allowing me to work out my own salvation in fear and trembling—well, I wouldn't trade that for anything the world has to offer. The fact that He has permitted me to see each one of the children, and Roy, accept Jesus Christ means that He has been far more than fair with me. The tears He has allowed to dim the eyes of my flesh have cleared the eyes of my soul, bringing each time a new depth of spiritual understanding and vision—because I trust Him.

Yes, this woman at the well loves Him with her whole heart, and she is not ashamed to tell the world what He has done for her.

> For I am not ashamed of the Gospel of Jesus Christ: for it is the power of God unto salvation to everyone that believeth (Romans 1:16).

LOVE
IS THE
ANSWER

Robert V. Ozment

GUIDEPOSTS ASSOCIATES, INC.

Carmel, New York

Scripture passages identified as PHILLIPS are from J. B. Phillips, *The New Testament in Modern English,* The Macmillan Company, 1965.

Scripture passages identified as MOFFATT are from James Moffatt, *The Bible: A New Translation,* Harper & Row, Publishers, Incorporated.

All other Scripture passages are from *The King James Version of the Bible.*

The poem by Ella Wheeler Wilcox is used by permission of Rand Mc-Nally & Company, Book Manufacturing Division.

The verse from "Just When I Need Him Most" is by Wm. Poole. Words and Music Copyright 1936 Renewal (Extended) The Rodeheaver Co., Owner. Used by permission.

"Tragedy of a Hunchback" and "There is Grief" are from the book *From My Window* by Frances Shumate, published by Vantage Press, New York. Used by permission.

*Dedicated to the loyal and faithful
members of Atlanta's First United Methodist
Church whom it is
my privilege to serve*

Preface

One of the greatest needs of our generation is to learn to practice the love we see so clearly expressed in the life of our Lord. Love is the subject of the first and greatest commandment. Paul gives priority to love in his First Letter to the Corinthians: "In this life we have three great lasting qualities —faith, hope and love. But the greatest of them is love" (I CORINTHIANS 13:13, PHILLIPS). The gospel is saturated with God's love, and the cross is undeniable evidence of His unfathomable compassion.

Love is the answer to most of the baffling and perplexing problems that plague humanity. When we learn to apply in our daily lives the principle of love as taught *by*, and lived *in*, the life of Jesus, the clouds of bitterness and war will disappear from the horizon. Then we will see the sun of "peace on earth and good will toward men" sending its rays across our troubled world.

When the storms come, when we stand in the valley of despair and self-pity, when the future looks blurred, we need to direct our thoughts to the fact that God loves us. Such a startling truth will pierce any darkness that begins to descend upon us.

The Psalmist, while meditating on the greatness of God, exclaimed, "Thou hast beset me behind and before, and laid thine hand upon me" (PSALM 139:5, KJV). We do not use this little word "beset" very often. Actually, it means to "hem in," or "to surround." It is amazing to realize that we are "surrounded" or "hemmed in" by the love of God.

As the minister of a large urban church, I see a lot of people whose lives are tangled and whose problems are legion. I am fully convinced that most of their problems could be solved if they were only willing to practice the commandment of love. Love is the long, steep road God traveled from heaven to earth, and it is the same road we must travel from earth to heaven. Christian compassion is the bridge that spans the chasms of prejudice, envy, jealousy, and hate.

May this little volume help each one of us to live in the sunshine of God's love each passing day.

R.V.O.

Contents

PREFACE   7

1 *When the Storms Come*   13
2 *Take the Lantern of Hope*   19
3 *Lonely, But Not Alone*   32
4 *Somebody Loves You*   41
5 *Things We Do Not Deserve*   48
6 *Patch Up the Past*   57
7 *But What Can I Do About My Problems?*   70
8 *Five Steps to a Better Life*   76
9 *How to Get Rid of Self-Pity*   87
10 *Things I Know About God*   95
11 *You Can Be Forgiven*   104
12 *When the Lamps of Faith Flicker*   111
13 *Life Is a Million Little Things*   119
14 *All Things Are Possible With God*   125
15 *Take a Look at Yourself*   131
16 *Life Can Be Better*   139
17 *Don't Be Afraid of Tomorrow*   148
18 *Discovering God's Will Through Prayer*   159

1

When the Storms Come

There are several theological cloaks under which we may take cover when the storms of life descend, and there are many philosophical systems which have emerged; but basically man lives by one of two philosophies. Jesus expressed them in a parable in His Sermon on the Mount.

Some live by the philosophy that "today is all that matters," and they proceed to "make hay while the sun shines." I saw that philosophy expressed on the window of an automobile establishment a few months ago. A sign, painted in big colorful letters, stated: THERE AIN'T NO TOMORROW—THIS IS ALL THERE IS! Little wonder that we lose our perspective and sense of brotherhood. The man who believes only in today pushes God aside.

The other philosophy is based on faith. It can be expressed in this fashion: The man who gives life his best today will find the hand of God to guide him through each tomorrow. Such a man sees a silver thread running through the tapestry of life. It makes its way through each tomorrow, and doesn't end until it returns to the hand of God.

In the parable Jesus told, there are two men, and one does not recognize a great difference between them. Apparently, both were respectable. They lived in the same neighborhood and may have worked in the same office. They belonged to the same clubs and rode similar camels. To a casual observer, their houses were similar; it would be difficult, by observing, to determine which had the good foundation. (Once an electrician called to his assistant, "Put your hand on one of those

13

wires—feel anything?" "No," replied the assistant. "Good, I wasn't sure which was which—don't touch the other one or you'll drop dead," answered the electrician.)

On the surface, the men in the parable appeared the same, but actually there was a tremendous difference between them. One was a very wise man who had built his house on a good foundation. He was very careful in choosing his material; every piece of material was set with care. When the storms came and the wind blew, that house stood the test.

The other man was foolish; he thought only of today. His only wish was to satisfy his every desire. He nailed the decaying boards of greed with the fragile nails of lust to the sagging timbers of selfishness. Such a house will never stand the high winds of adversity and the floods of sorrow that rage in every life. Jesus gives us an account of the end of such a life: "And the rain descended, and the floods came, and the winds blew, and beat upon that house; and it fell: and great was the fall of it" (MATTHEW 7:27).

Four thrilling truths can be grasped in this little parable. They are not speculative truths; they are as certain as night and day. They may be ignored, but they cannot be evaded:

(1) The first truth we discover is that God does not always pay off on Saturday night. That is to say, we are neither rewarded for our virtues nor punished for our sins at the end of each week or month.

Life is like a visit to the supermarket. You walk through aisles which are well stocked with many good things to eat. You are free to choose what you wish. You can take as little or as much as you want. You must keep in mind that before the visit is over, you must face the cashier. Before you pack your bags to leave, you must pay for what you have taken. You face the cashier alone, with what you have chosen. In many respects, life is like that. You must face the Great Cashier before the journey is over, and pay for the things you have taken from God's great store of goods.

Very often a person will point out someone they know who

lives life as he pleases, taking what he wants and rarely ever tipping his hat to God. "He is ruthless, vain and sinful. Yet, he seems to be getting along about as well as, if not better than, I," the conversation continues. "Yet, I try to be a Christian, and my troubles are more than I can number."

Almost every week I need to remind people that God neither rewards virtue with easy living, nor good deeds with an immunity from cruel blows or heavy loads. The Christian life is, in part, its own reward. We do not walk with God because He plucks from our hearts burdens we wish to discharge; we walk with God because He gives us strength to bear our burdens.

I am writing these lines on a beautiful day in October. I can see trees waving gently in the breeze. The landscape has been touched by the hand of God, and Mother Nature offers a magnificent scene that defies description. Every now and then I can see a leaf floating gently toward the ground. I am reminded of the law of gravitation. This law is constant, and without it man could not build skyscrapers or walk across a lawn. This is a natural law, and we never doubt its dependability.

God has a spiritual law which Moses expressed to Israel a long time ago: ". . . be sure your sin will find you out" (NUMBERS 32:23). Someday the real you will be revealed in the presence of God. Such a thought makes you shudder with the knowledge that the garments of pretense and pride will be removed. We all will stand in the presence of God, away from the false lights of flattery and compliments which are not applicable to our lives.

Jesus pointed out, in His parable of the two men building their houses, that the results of life will be revealed. The man who builds his house on a strong foundation will stand, and the man who builds his house on sand will fall.

(2) We may as well look for the storms, because they come to all of us. We are told that the Buddhists have a story about a mother who brings the lifeless body of her dead child to

15

Buddha, requesting that he perform the miracle of resurrection and bring the child back to life. Buddha does not deny the request. First he asks the woman to find one family in which there is no sorrow. After a long and weary search, the woman returns; she has come back to withdraw her request. Sorrow, tragedy, pain, and suffering are universal. They come to men of every generation.

Bishop Gerald Kennedy tells a story about a professor who had finished his dinner at a campus cafeteria and was walking across the parking lot toward his home. He was overtaken by a student who appeared frightened. "I want to talk to you!" the student blurted out. "I can't eat, I can't sleep. I've just realized that one day I have to die!"

We cannot escape the conflicts of life. Edwin Lewis reminds us, in his little book *Christian Truth for Christian Living,* that "our world is much more a battleground than a playground. We are wise to remember that." When one enters through the door of birth and makes his way down the winding trail that finally brings him to the gate of death, he will encounter some of life's difficulties. All the roads of life wind through the valleys of sorrow and the Garden of Gethsemane.

Jesus never tried to obscure the risks involved in life. His invitation to discipleship was: ". . . take up the cross, and follow me" (MARK 10:21). In the parable Jesus told, He did not say, "*If* the storms come," or "The storms *may* come." He said, "And the rain descended, and the floods came, and the winds blew, and beat upon that house. . . ."

Some storms are sudden. They come without any warning. A few years ago, I lived in Lynn, Massachusetts, when a tornado struck about seventy miles away. It swept down into a sleeping town and killed dozens of people. There had been no warning. We have made great strides in forecasting weather conditions in this country. In spite of our scientific equipment, however, we cannot always tell with absolute precision what will happen.

Any religion that promises smooth sailing is deceptive and

16

false. Bishop Gerald Kennedy suggests, in his book *The Parables*, "If the storm does not strike in one place, it will overtake us in another." Jesus never taught that to follow Him would offer us insurance against the hardships of life. He taught that to follow Him would give us assurance during the hardships.

(3) When the storms come, we must look within for our defense against them. I am not talking about human strength, but about divine strength. We have almost forgotten that our strength must be found in the spiritual realm if we are to face life confidently. We need to build braces of faith and trust within ourselves. We must develop a faith that believes in the goodness of God even when the shadows lengthen and the clouds of sorrow hide the bright stars that remind us of God's watchful care. We must trust God when the road is steep, our burdens are heavy, and the way is blurred.

In George Watts' famous picture "Hope," many people see only despair. They point to the bent figure, the lyre with all but one of the strings missing, and the poor woman who sits blindfolded in her defeat and misery. Some have suggested that the title might well be "Despair." What you see in the picture, however, represents the circumstances that surround the poor woman. The thing that makes her play the one remaining string is the hope in her heart. She does not draw strength from the pitiful conditions that surround her, but from the hope within her.

(4) The storms can be endured. God never gives us a task for which He does not provide the strength we need. He never permits life to place upon us an impossible burden. Jesus reminded us that ". . . with God all things are possible" (MARK 10:27).

When the storms come your way, what you do will be determined by what you believe. If, for example, you believe that God has been unfair to you, then you will likely become bitter toward God and move into a little room of self-pity. On the other hand, if you believe that God is behind life, and that Jesus Christ revealed unto us the true nature of God, then you will take your disappointments and sorrows and commit them to Him. This commitment may not stop the tears that flow from your eyes, but you will walk with a steady step and an unflinching confidence that when life on earth is finished, you will look into the face of a heavenly Father whose loving arms have supported you every step of the way.

Paul knew adversity. He was acquainted with the dingy prison cells of his day. Yet we hear him say, ". . . I know whom I have believed, and am persuaded that he is able to keep that which I have committed unto him . . ." (II TIMOTHY 1:12).

Now, the big question! What must we do in order to ride out and conquer the storms of life? Jesus gave us the answer to this question in His little parable: ". . . whosoever heareth these sayings of mine, and doeth them . . ." (MATTHEW 7:24). Whosoever heareth and doeth will be able to stand when the rains of sorrow descend, when the floods of trouble come, and when the winds of adversity blow.

But what did Jesus mean by ". . . these sayings of mine . . ."? He was just finishing the Sermon on the Mount. I find three golden threads winding through this sermon: (1) *love:* love God, and then love our neighbors as we love ourselves; (2) *forgiveness:* forgive others as well as receive the forgiveness of God; (3) *seeking first the Kingdom of God:* put God first in our lives, and other things will begin to fall into place.

If we can keep these sayings of our Lord, we can be triumphant in all of life. That is quite an order, but with His help we can do it.

18

2

Take the Lantern of Hope

A man drove a great distance to see me. He talked at length about the despair and futility that had settled in his soul. He outlined, in an articulate fashion, his intellectual doubts and skepticism. "You have related your doubts to me," I replied; "Now tell me about your faith and hope." He shook his head and answered, "I have no faith in God, and no hope for to-morrow." I did my best to push back the clouds of skepticism and show him God as revealed in the Gentle Galilean. Before my visitor left, I offered a prayer. I prayed that God would make him sensitive to the constant knock on the door of his heart, and give him the assurance of His presence.

I wanted the man to catch a glimpse of the truth expressed by the psalmist when he said, "Whither shall I go from thy spirit? or whither shall I flee from thy presence? If I ascend up into heaven, thou art there: if I make my bed in hell, be-hold thou art there. If I take the wings of the morning, and dwell in the uttermost parts of the sea; Even there shall thy hand lead me, and thy right hand shall hold me" (PSALM 139: 7-10).

I assured my visitor of my prayers and urged him to listen for the voice of God to speak to his empty soul. I felt the sting of defeat in my heart as I watched him walk away. I sat down and wrote this sentence on a little card: "A man ceases to live when the lights of hope are extinguished in his soul."

If I could give to a man only one thing, I would give him hope. I am talking about the hope the psalmist wrote about when he said, "For in thee, O Lord, do I hope . . ." (PSALM 38:15). Hope in God is the only basis that exists for any worthwhile aspirations.

When hope is gone, a man quits trying. As long as he can see a flickering light from the lamp of hope, he is never completely defeated. Little wonder Samuel T. Coleridge wrote, "He is the best physician who is the most ingenious inspirer of hope." A woman will find the courage to keep her family together in spite of a drinking husband, as long as she can see a spark of hope. A man can tolerate the many faults of his wife, if he has hope in his heart. A salesman can live with many negative responses to his product, if the light of hope burns in his soul. The minister will return to his place of prayer and study to give his best to preparing sermons, as long as he keeps hope alive.

"What is the difference between faith and hope?" is a question many people have asked me. I submit to you that the two are somewhat alike. Faith is the power to believe. Ralph Waldo Emerson wrote, "All I have seen teaches me to trust the Creator for all I have not seen." Faith in God is the power to trust Him when reason and logic fail us. Hope, on the other hand, is the power that sustains us when we must wait during some dark night in life. One might say that hope is the extension of our faith when we bear heavy loads and walk through lonely valleys. Oliver Goldsmith wrote:

> Hope, like the gleaming taper's light
> Adorns and cheers our way;
> And still, as darker grows the night,
> Emits a brighter ray.

The Captivity, on Oratorio

Robert Louis Stevenson spent most of his life trying to

escape the ravages of tuberculosis. One of his poems, "The Lamplighter," reflects a delightful boyhood dream. On winter evenings, Stevenson loved to watch the lamplighter make his way up and down the streets, lighting the lamps. The humble workman would move through the shadows of evening, climbing his ladder at every lamp post and leaving a glow that pierced the darkness. It was an indescribable thrill when the lamplighter would pause and give Stevenson a friendly smile. The poet wrote:

> But I, when I am stronger and can choose what I'm to do,
> O Leerie, I'll go round at night and light the lamps with you!

There is a lot of darkness in our world, some of it caused by hate and ignorance. Some of it grows out of our selfishness and stupidity. Still, some of the darkness has its source in our greed and complacency. Disappointment, trouble, and sorrow bring darkness to many hearts. It is up to us to light the darkness of hate and ignorance with lanterns of love and knowledge. Giving ourselves to God and living according to the teachings of the Master will dispel the darkness that has settled over our society.

Ask yourself these questions: What am I doing to help bring light to the dark places in the world? Have I offered a word of hope to the discouraged? Have I prayed for those who walk through the valley of grief? Have I offered to share the burden of one who bears a heavy load? The Christian church is dedicated to drive away the shadows of darkness caused by sin and injustice. We must point a frustrated world, which bears the stains of many sins, toward the Saviour who redeems and restores. We must show a weary humanity the way to the Christ who invites us to come into His presence and rest. Ours is the mountainous task of bringing a wounded society to the Great Physician who can heal its ugly sores.

As long as men have hope, they can reach their destiny.

Most of us could say, with the ancient poet, "My hopes are not always realized." We know what it is like to hold a heart full of crushed dreams. Actually, the poet did not end his statement on such a negative note. He went on to say: ". . . but I always have hope." Such a philosophy will keep us from despair when the clouds of disappointment descend upon us.

That wise poet knew something about the realities of life. He was saying, "I do not always get my way in life, but in spite of that, I believe God will sustain me, and through His strength I can be triumphant." He was saying, "Regardless of the circumstances of life, I will trust in the goodness and wisdom of God." Is this not the same philosophy Jesus expressed in the Garden of Gethsemane? Calvary looked cruel and was only a few days away. Jesus prayed, "Father, all things are possible unto thee; take away this cup from me: nevertheless not what I will, but what thou wilt" (MARK 14:36). Jesus never intended to abandon His faith in God, even though He had to drink from the cup. He was not spared the cross, but He was filled with divine hope.

When I was preaching a series of services in a small town recently, a house burned to the ground. The newspaper printed the story of the disaster, and in the opening sentence the reporter wrote, ". . . nothing saved." I am sure most people knew what the reporter meant. He meant that all the household furniture was destroyed by the fire. Actually, he could have emphasized the things the fire did not destroy. For example, the story might have begun with this line: "Everything of importance was saved."

I happen to know that the three children were rescued, and the wife was unharmed. The good name of the family was not even scorched. They still had their health, and the husband still had his job. They kept their friends, and the compassion of their good neighbors was expressed in their offer to let the family stay in their homes until another house could be built. In the final analysis, the most important things were saved. Many valuable possessions were lost, but the family still had hope. They were already talking about rebuilding their home.

Before you allow the lights of hope to be extinguished in your life, take another look at the life of Christ. Let Him be your example in suffering and sorrow. Follow Christ when the way is hard and the opposition fierce. One could never conclude that Jesus was victorious because His life was easy. On the contrary, it was Christ who met and mastered the hard experiences of life.

Jesus walked away from the carpenter's shop at the age of thirty, with a burning passion to save the entire suffering human race. He wanted to make, out of a divided humanity, a brotherhood of love where human lives and deeds would be a tribute to God. His dreams were noble and His purpose was pure.

During His early ministry, He drew large crowds and was accepted by many people. Then hostility against Him grew into open opposition. The crowds dwindled and the voices against Him spoke louder and more often. His own family failed to understand Him. His friends deserted Him, and about three years after He launched His public ministry with so much compassion, He faced the dark shadows of death. Humanity was far from a brotherhood, and Jesus' dreams seemed to crumble into dust. What then? Most of us would have abandoned our hopes, but not Christ. He walked to the cross with a steady step that expressed His undaunted faith and hope in God. James S. Stewart wrote, "He was quite sure that someday, in God's good time, it would all come gloriously true." He had a hope that did not fade in the face of so much suffering and so many trials. That is the hope we must have if we are to meet the trials of life successfully.

I have heard people say that Christ is a good example, but that it is impossible for us to follow His example. Let us not forget that, very often, when Jesus gave the invitation to discipleship, He would say, ". . . take up the cross, and follow me" (MARK 10:21). Read the Master's words to His frustrated disciples, "In the world ye shall have tribulation: but be of good cheer; I have overcome the world" (JOHN 16:33). What did Jesus mean? Perhaps He did not mean that you and I would be able to meet all the difficulties of life with the assurance and courage that were His. On the other hand, not even a pessimist could read defeat in His words. Whatever else Jesus may have meant, He was offering a word of hope to His disciples. He was saying, "Life may look impossible and hopeless at times, but I tell you, with God's help all things are possible."

Let us trust Him when the way is dark and the load is heavy. When we face the dark shadows of Gethsemane, or the rugged slopes of Calvary, or the burning fires of criticism, let us remember that the same divine power that was our Lord's is available to us. When we stumble through deserts of sorrow or walk on the brink of temptation, we must look for the footprints of the Master and walk in them.

Almost two hundred years ago, a young man worked at his cobbler's bench, repairing shoes. More than anything else, he wanted his life to count for God. Mending shoes was an honorable job, but the cobbler felt that God had greater work for him to do. He became a Baptist minister, and on May 31, 1792, William Cary, the former cobbler, preached a sermon that has become famous for these words: "Expect great things from God. Attempt great things for God." Then, in 1793, he sailed to India and gave his life as a missionary. No person can expect great things from God or attempt great things for God unless he keeps the light of hope burning in his heart.

A man must believe three things if he is to walk through life with the lantern of hope in his hand:

(1) He must believe that God is the creative force behind this marvelous universe. This universe, with its precision and order, did not emerge from a sea of chaos and nothingness. It is the work of a power that defies description, and a mind that is unfathomable. The person who is so blind that he is unable to see God's intelligence in the orderliness of the universe will never know the hope that leaps in the heart of one who is more sensitive to the mind of God.

24

(2) Not only must a person believe that God is the Creator, but he must also believe that God is the sustaining force in His creation. Unless we are able to feel the gentle touch of God's hand upon us, we are headed toward the valley of hopelessness where defeat and misery are the order of the day. You and I are neither wise nor strong enough to face life victoriously with mere human wisdom and strength.

(3) A man must believe that God waits in each tomorrow. He can face tomorrow with an unwavering hope if he believes that God stands in the shadows, guarding His own. A man cannot march with a steady step unless he expects to find love, joy, and goodness in tomorrow. No one can walk triumphantly into a sea of nothingness.

When you feel alone, remember that you are still in the presence of the King. When you see God revealed in Jesus Christ, you find fresh hope and new courage. Jesus gave us a verbal picture of God as a Good Shepherd. In Jesus' day, a good shepherd would not turn his sheep out of the fold and let them hunt green pastures while he engaged himself with other work. The shepherd never said to the sheep, "Now you are on your own. Go out and find tender grass and fresh water. You'll have to watch out for yourself, because I have other duties that demand my attention." Not at all! The good shepherd would find the green pastures and guard the sheep from any impending danger.

After the resurrection, Jesus gave His disciples the Great Commission, their greatest challenge: "Go ye therefore, and teach all nations, baptizing them in the name of the Father, and of the Son, and of the Holy Ghost: Teaching them to observe all things whatsoever I have commanded you . . ." (MATTHEW 28:19-20). That was a challenge because Jesus had just struggled up Golgotha to the cross for preaching the gospel He was asking them to preach. There was still bitterness and hostility toward those who were close to Jesus. Only a few days before, the disciples had hidden behind locked doors.

Not only did Jesus give them a great challenge, but He also gave them a great hope. Like the Good Commander, He did not send them alone into the battlefields of evil. ". . . lo, I am with you alway . . ." (MATTHEW 28:20). That is a different picture.

When my son Randall was about six years old, we were walking from my study to the house. It was a dark night and we walked hand in hand. On the way, I noticed the door to the toolhouse had been left open. It was not more than fifty feet away, but the tall pines cast black shadows all around. "Go close the door to the toolhouse," I suggested; "I will wait here." Randall took two steps toward the toolhouse, and a dog down the street let out an awful yell. Randall jumped back and said, "I don't want to go." "There isn't any reason to be afraid," I urged him; "Anyway, I can see you all the way." As quick as a flash, he answered, "If you'll go with me, I won't be afraid." It must have been a great source of comfort and courage when the disciples heard that last phrase, "I am with you alway."

I am positive God did not intend for me to be a poet. I just don't have the ability to make the lines come out right. But I did write a few lines after talking to a lovely lady who had known many disappointments. Her shoulders were stooped and her heart had borne many burdens, but her faith was inspiring. I went back to my desk, and wrote:

Sometimes the road is rough and the way is steep,
   But no matter how stony the path, or how dark the night,
Let us always remember we're the Good Shepherd's sheep
   And we move and live in the Good Shepherd's sight.

So the disciples went out into a hostile world with the hope that came from the knowledge that God walked with them. Let us move out with that same hope.

When life becomes a burdensome task instead of a thrilling adventure, there is hope. Some months ago, I visited a man in a hospital. He had endured great pain, and the marks of sleepless nights and excruciating pain were evident in his face. "I didn't know I would come this way," he said. He expressed a universal truth. None of us ever expect to lift the heavy burdens of life, but all of us will.

I walked through a lovely rose garden last summer. Stately roses of every color and variety waved gently in the summer breeze. The rose has been lavishly blessed with sweet perfume as well as beauty, which cannot be adequately described with all the flowing adjectives at our command. Then, one cold, blustery day in January, I took a hurried walk through the same rose garden. What a transition! A rose garden in January is a pretty horrible sight. You see ugly stalks wearing their garments of unsightly thorns. They stand like little soldiers waiting for a command to march out of winter into spring.

For many of us, life is like that. We face the hard days of winter when we see only the thorns and feel the sharp edges of the gardener's shears. Life becomes more of a strain and less of an adventure. But remember, God's help is available, and spring always follows winter.

Take the advice of the psalmist: "Cast thy burden upon the Lord, and he shall sustain thee: he shall never suffer the righteous to be moved" (PSALM 55:22). The first thing the psalmist suggests, when our burdens are heavy, is to cast them upon the Lord. He knew the foolishness of struggling up the path of life alone. Paul advised us to let our requests be made known to God. Jesus encouraged men to ask, seek, and knock. He assured us that our asking would get results, and our seeking would lead to fulfillment, and our knocking would open doors that were closed.

Then the psalmist said, ". . . he shall sustain thee. . . ." He did not indicate that God would lift our burdens. He did not say that God would wipe away all our tears and relieve our pain. He promised only that God would sustain us.

Look up that word *sustain*. Find out what it means. It means "to provide for," or "to give support." When we cast our burdens upon the Lord, we find a fresh supply of strength. He supports us with His strength and presence.

27

Finally, the psalmist wrote, ". . . he shall never suffer the righteous to be moved." God does not always take His wounded soldiers out of the battle, but He will never suffer them to be defeated. Those who are faithful to His commands shall win the victory. When the battle is raging, do not think for one moment that God has forsaken you. Do not become fearful and desert your post. God is near, and His grace is adequate.

God never sends us into a valley from which there is no escape. He never sends us up a mountain that cannot be climbed. He never places a chasm before us which we cannot span. Life is never impossible, because God refuses to deceive us.

The man who feels the touch of God's hand today will not be afraid of tomorrow. Tomorrow may bring its disappointments, but God will be near to steady him. There may be some unexpected sorrows in tomorrow, but once a man walks with God, he knows that His presence is all he needs to face tomorrow unafraid.

When God called Moses to lead the children of Israel out of Egypt, Moses made a number of excuses. He reminded God that he had many handicaps. Moses told God that he could not speak very well; he was certain that the Hebrews would not listen to him. "Who am I, that I should go unto Pharaoh, and that I should bring forth the children of Israel out of Egypt?" (EXODUS 3:11). Had it been left up to Moses, he would have preferred to live a shepherd's life.

God assured Moses that He would walk with him and that his efforts would not fail. Finally, Moses consented to go. He faced many trials and tribulations, but they neither made him afraid nor dimmed his faith. Near the end of his earthly journey, he turned his place of leadership over to Joshua. It had been a long, hard journey, but Moses' words were full of courage and his heart was steadfast. He said, "Be strong and of a good courage, fear not, nor be afraid: . . . for the Lord thy God, he it is that doth go with thee; he will not fail thee, nor forsake thee" (DEUTERONOMY 31:6). What made the difference in Moses? It was his walk with God.

Even in death, the Christian can hear the bells of hope ringing clear and loud. Death is always a time of sorrow, but it is also a time of hope. If the resurrection is not true, then Jesus Christ has deceived us. I, for one, will trust the Master, and my daily song will always be, "I am the resurrection, and the life: he that believeth in me, though he were dead, yet shall he live" (JOHN 11:25).

Just recently, in one of our church papers, I was reading a memorial service for some of God's faithful servants. At the end of the service, the author had written a prayer. The typesetter had made a mistake. The prayer began: "Our dead Heavenly Father. . . ." It should have read, "Our *dear* Heavenly Father. . . ." That one little letter makes the difference between despair and hope.

Charles Warner ended a poem with these words:

And death's not the end 'neath the cold, black sod—
'Tis the inn by the road on the way to God.

The tears of sorrow are less stinging when one comes to realize the great truth of the resurrection. The cross could not stop our Master; the grave could not hold Him. He lives, and because He lives, the bells of hope ring out sweet music to sorrowing hearts.

The Christian is never without hope. Read the words of Paul, the spiritual giant, expressing his magnanimous faith: "We are troubled on every side, yet not distressed; we are perplexed, but not in despair; Persecuted, but not forsaken; cast down, but not destroyed" (II CORINTHIANS 4:8-9). Paul was reminding us that God never sends us down a dead-end street. In spite of the hardships Paul endured, none of them ever brought him to defeat, because the power of God sustained him. Paul was saying, "I have known trouble, but I have never given up. I have been perplexed, but I have always had hope. I have been persecuted, but through all of it, I have felt the hand of God. I have been cast down, but never defeated." When our human eyes fail to see the light of hope, God's long arm of love surrounds us. Paul knew what it meant to be forsaken by his friends, but he never had the experience of being forsaken by his Father. ". . . the Lord stood with me," he wrote (II TIMOTHY 4:17).

Recently I called on a man who had suffered a severe heart attack. For almost two weeks, he had been flat on his back. It looked as if he would be there for several more weeks. It is might easy to get discouraged while one is sick. I sat in the man's room for a few minutes and offered a prayer. As I left, I remarked, "Keep your chin up!" He replied, "I am helpless— but not without hope." There may be times when you and I shall feel helpless, but if we walk with God we shall never be without hope.

There is a story about an old man who lived in a desert wasteland of Arizona. He had the only good well of water in the entire area. Each evening, he would light his lantern and hang it high on a post outside his cabin. Some thought the old man was crazy to waste his precious oil. Nevertheless, night after night, the little lantern sent its ray of light out into the darkness.

Late one night, in the terrible heat of summer, the friendly old man heard a faint knock at the cabin door. He opened the door to find a traveler almost dead for want of water. The exhausted man had seen the glimmer of light from a distance and, with his last ounce of energy, had made his way toward it in the hope of finding water. A man's life was saved because an old man cared enough to light a lantern every night so that one who might be lost could find his way.

Almost two thousand years ago, God lit His lantern. It shines across the centuries, offering hope to all who will come and rest in its light. The cross is God's lantern and it shines along the path you are traveling. Do you have a sorrow that you cannot bear alone? Take it to the Christ of Calvary. Do you have some stains of sin that need cleansing? Take them to the Christ of Calvary. Do you have dreams that lie crushed, and hopes that are shattered? Take them to the Christ of Calvary. God's lantern will guide you safely through life, and it never, never goes out.

3

Lonely, But Not Alone

The streets of every large city in the world are crowded with lonely people. Atlanta, the city in which I live, is a city of beautiful homes, fine hospitals, expanding industry, stately churches, as well as honored universities and colleges. One might think that such a place would insure bliss and happiness. There are unnumbered thousands who know the folly of such a conclusion. A parade of the lonely and frustrated people of any great city would include marching feet from every social status. You would see the rich and poor, the ignorant and educated, the young and old in such a parade.

Why are people lonely? Many people become lonely and unhappy because of a distorted sense of values. Are we not guilty of thinking that inner happiness comes from the glitter of material things? A man said to me recently, "I'm about as miserable as a man can get, and yet I can find no reason for my unhappiness." Then he told me about his lovely wife and fine children. He talked about his success in the business world and his host of friends. He owns a summer home and travels extensively. "I've been everywhere," he said, "and done everything, and still life is empty." I told him that he had placed the emphasis on the wrong things in life. It is not enough to make money and be successful in the business world. Life is too big to be satisfied with superficial things. Then I said, "You may not like what I'm going to say, but I believe it ought to be said. You have been everywhere except to visit God, and you've done everything except to give your heart to Him. You must do this before you will ever be genuinely happy."

Human beings are never happy because of that which surrounds them, but because of that which lives within them. Paul said, "For to me to live is Christ . . ." (PHILIPPIANS 1:21). Paul was saying two very important things in that phrase: (1) he had completely dedicated his life to Christ; and (2) in his dedication he had found the purpose of life, and with Christ he could reach the destiny for which he was created.

Our business is to follow God, and if we are faithful He will eventually bring us to that Eternal City where the sorrows and frustrations of life are lost in the sea of yesterday. It is true that God may lead us down some strange paths, but let us have no fear, because His Way is always the best. Joshua Liebman, in his book *Peace of Mind,* wrote: "When we enter the tunnel of darkness, we forget that there is an exit as well as an entrance, and that we can come out into the light again. . . . It is a brief tunnel of darkness carved into the mountain of light."

Some months ago, I preached the funeral of a very gracious woman. She had loved the church and was devoted to her husband. The couple had been married many years, and parting was difficult. "I just can't give her up. I just can't go on without her!" the husband kept saying over and over. He was having a hard time adjusting to life without his wife, but he knew that he must try. I visited with him for a few minutes some months after the funeral. Before I left, he said, "This has been a long, dark night, but I believe I see the dawn breaking. Two things have sustained me," he continued; "first, my faith in a good God who always works for the best interest of His children. I know my wife is waiting for me on the shores of eternity. Then, I cannot help but remember that while life here will never be the same again, it never would have been what it is without the many wonderful years we spent together."

Keep in mind that no depression is a permanent state of life.

The night may be dark and long, but the dawn is sure to come. I like that little story about the man who asked the wise old man to quote his favorite passage in the Bible. The old man replied, "My favorite passage is this: 'And it came to pass . . .'" (LUKE 18:35). The man waited patiently for the rest of the verse, and then asked, "Tell me the rest of it." The wise old man replied, "That is all of it." He went on to explain, "You see, I have had many troubles during my life, but none of them ever stayed for long. That is the reason I say my favorite passage, is 'And it came to pass.' Troubles will come, but they will also pass away." When the clouds of despair descend upon us, we must keep in mind that they are only temporarily present. We need not entertain them for very long.

Some people permit their circumstances to determine their attitude toward life. That is a very dangerous guide. Instead of permitting your outward circumstances to determine your whole attitude toward life, let your faith in God help you to meet and master your circumstances. You will never be utterly defeated if you develop a strong faith in God. I am not talking about simply believing that God exists; your faith must be deeper and stronger than that. You must believe in a God of perfect love and wisdom. You must trust God completely. It is mighty important that you believe in a God who loves you and whose actions reflect His perfect wisdom.

Katharine Hathaway's father was a professor at Boston University. When Katharine was five years of age, she was stricken with a spinal disease that took her off the playground and placed her in a bed of pain. For the next ten years of her life she lay on her back. She was strapped on a sloping board and her head was kept from sinking onto her chest by means of a leather halter. As a little girl, she had often watched a hunchbacked locksmith who came to her house to repair locks. He seemed to live in a world of his own, seldom looking up from his work.

34

After ten years of living in her strange world, Katharine was able to get up, and painfully she learned to walk again. Finally, when alone, she got up enough courage to look at herself in the mirror. She was a hunchback, not very attractive. As she looked in the mirror, she said, "That person in the mirror couldn't be me." Adjusting to a new life was not easy. She was often depressed and unhappy. Determined that misfortune would not defeat her, she grasped one truth that all of us need to know. She knew that her mind could grow independently of the size and shape of her body. She thought of the body much as she thought of a house. The body is the place where the real person lives, much as a house is a place where people live. The body is not really important. The person who lives in the body is important.

Katharine Hathaway may not shake the foundations of society, but she has learned to face life honestly and to believe in a God who can be trusted. Somehow, I believe she satisfied God by the way she faced the hard circumstances of her life.

Helen Keller wrote, "Dark as my path may seem to others, I carry a magic light in my heart. Faith, the spiritual strong searchlight, illumines the way and, although doubts lurk in the shadows, I walk unafraid toward the Enchanted Wood where the foliage is always green, where joy abides, where nightingales nest and sing, and where life and earth are one in the presence of the Lord."

The secret of dealing with the trials of life is the little magic light of faith we carry in our hearts. Carry faith with you and, while the clouds of despair may descend upon you, the way will never be so dark that you cannot see how to take the next step. The next step is really the most important step that any of us needs to take now. Let us not brood about tomorrow; rather let us make the most of the opportunities and challenges of today.

In the closing paragraph of Pierre van Passen's book *Days of Our Years*, he writes, "However dark the immediate future,

all is not lost. Humanity will live by the faith and the hope
. . . of the men who say: 'Nevertheless and in spite of everything, and whatever may come, I believe.'"

What you believe about God and life will mean the difference between defeat and victory. If, in spite of everything,
you believe that God stands behind life and is the Sovereign
Ruler of the universe, you will be triumphant. If you feel that
life is a mere accident and that there is no compassion at the
heart of this world, you will be crushed by both the circumstances that surround you and your lack of faith within.

When the lights of faith grow dim and the soul is burdened
with heavy loads, you would do well to remember some of the
lessons that history teaches us. Often, you may begin to think
that God has singled you out, and that you walk the stony
path alone. When you are lonely and frustrated, remember
these four things:

(1) Never say, "God doesn't love me." When you were
born, God showered His love upon you, and nothing can
change that love. Paul wrote, "For I am persuaded, that . . .
[nothing] shall be able to separate us from the love of God,
which is in Christ Jesus our Lord" (ROMANS 8:38-39).

I have read a lot of clever phrases and clichés that may
soothe some troubled souls, but they offer little comfort to me.
For example, some say, "God gives the heaviest load to those
He loves the most." I cannot accept that. I remember when I
was a lad helping my father cut wood. He always said, "Now,
son, let me take the heavier end." That is very much like God:
He takes the heavier end. Oscar Wilde wrote, "Where there
is sorrow, there is holy ground." Sorrow does not necessarily
draw us closer to God; it sometimes causes us to turn our
backs on God. I am inclined to agree with Plato when he
said, "Of our troubles we must seek some other cause than
God."

You do not love your children less when they are sick or in
trouble. Actually, you draw close to them and stand ready to
do anything possible to help them. God is like that. When we

are in trouble, He stands near us to do what He can to help us. Rev. William Poole expressed this in his song, "Just When I Need Him Most":

Just when I need Him, Jesus is Near,
Just when I falter, just when I fear;
Ready to help me, ready to cheer,
Just when I need Him most.

God walks with us from the beginning of the journey to the gates of eternity. When we are ready to acknowledge His presence and live according to His wishes, we begin to live triumphantly. David, in the Twenty-third Psalm, wrote, "The Lord is my shepherd; I shall not want" (v. 1). What did David mean? He meant that as long as we follow the Good Shepherd, we shall never lack the refreshing water of divine love. God shall lead us in green pastures where we shall find the spiritual strength to meet every situation with faith and courage. When the soul needs to be restored, God shall forgive us. When we face the dark valleys of life, we need not be afraid because God's hand shall steady us. When our hearts are broken and the lights of joy have been all but extinguished by the rains of sorrow, God shall stand by us to comfort and strengthen us. David was saying, "The only way you can reach your destiny is to walk with God." The journey through life may not be all you want it to be, but that does not mean that God has forsaken you. Write these three things upon your heart: (1) God walks with us; (2) God loves us; (3) with God, we can be triumphant.

(2) When you compare your disappointments and trials to those our Lord knew, you must conclude that yours are rather insignificant. Jesus was a perfect Man. By that, I mean that Jesus never disobeyed His Father. He loved God with all His heart, soul, mind, and strength. He was constantly praying that God would guide Him safely through temptations. More than anything else, Jesus wanted to be sure He marched by

divine music rather than the music of the world. There were many voices, but the voice He wanted most to hear was the voice of God.

In spite of His goodness, Jesus was troubled. What do you suppose He thought when He saw the shadow of the cross in His path? Do you suppose He said to Himself, "This isn't fair. I do not deserve this terrible experience. Why must I suffer so much when I have tried to live according to My Father's will?" One thing for sure, Jesus never accused God of being unfair. He never indicated that He would abandon His faith in God because of the suffering He had to endure on the cross. He was troubled, but never defeated. He suffered, but that drew Him closer to God. Jesus said, "Now is my soul troubled; and what shall I say? Father, save me from this hour: but for this cause came I unto this hour" (JOHN 12:27). He did not wish to turn back. When suffering is ours, let us march on, like Jesus, in faith, believing that somehow God will see us through. One thing I have observed, and that is that no person has ever been defeated who has kept his faith in God.

(3) Remember that you and I are not pioneers in facing the trials of life. The path over which we travel is stained from a host of bleeding feet that have passed the same way. The centuries of yesterday shout words of cheer and hope to those of us who march under the load of heavy burdens: "Don't give up! It isn't far to the top. Stop and rest awhile if you like, but never conclude that life is hopeless."

Norman Vincent Peale relates a story that took place during World War II. He was waiting in a railroad station, and when the train came in, the huge gateman let the soldiers pass through ahead of the civilians. A mother torn with grief hung onto her young soldier son who was about to leave. The boy, gently but firmly trying to free himself from his mother's grip, was obvious to all. He planted a kiss on his mother's cheek and hurried through the gate. As he passed out of sight, his mother leaned against an iron rail and sobbed bitterly.

The gateman, watching the woman closely, left his post and went over and spoke to her. Immediately a change came over her and she controlled her sobs, and the gateman helped her to a seat where she sat, calm and relaxed. As he walked away, the gateman said, "Now remember what I told you."

Dr. Peale was anxious to know what the gateman had said to the woman, so he engaged the man in conversation and asked what he had said. A little embarrassed, the gateman replied, "Well, it's this way. I saw that she had lost her grip, so I just went over and said to her, 'Lister, Mother, I know exactly how you feel. I have been through it myself. Lots of people have, but you have just got to forget these things. I don't mean that you are going to forget the boy, but you are going to forget your fears.' Then, I just added, 'Put your faith in God, and He will see both you and the boy through.'"

When the future is blurred, when the load is heavy and you seem to be alone, be quiet and let Christ speak to you. If you are sensitive to His voice, I am sure you will hear Him say, "Forget your fears. You are not alone in this. Put your faith in God, and He'll carry you through."

Robert Louis Stevenson wrote to a friend: "For fourteen years I have not had one day of real health. I have wakened sick and gone to bed weary, and yet I have done my work unflinchingly." Stevenson was saying, "Don't give up just because you don't get everything your way in life. In spite of your circumstances, you can achieve the goals God has set for your life."

Paul prayed that God would free him from the thorn in his flesh. That was a burden Paul did not wish to carry for the rest of his life. No doubt he felt that it would surely send him down to defeat. God did not remove the thorn in the flesh. He said to Paul, "My grace is sufficient for thee . . ." (II CORINTHIANS 12:9). You may be sure that God's grace is adequate for your every need.

(4) Whether you become a bitter person or a better person depends upon you. The way you react to life will send you

either to the pits of despair or to the mountain tops of victory.

A letter came from a young woman who had lost her twenty-three-year-old husband after only a year of marriage. "We loved each other so deeply and my husband had so much to offer, I find it impossible to understand why he should die." Then she wrote, "But I believe that God does all things well, and to become bitter against God would only multiply my problems. I keep going in the faith that God loves me, and if I am faithful to Him, He will sustain me." What a grand attitude in the face of such a tragedy! I have never seen a person gain inner peace or spiritual strength from becoming bitter toward God. On the other hand, I have seen many people stagger up the hill of hard circumstances with a light of faith in their hands and a divine hand upon them to guide them through the tragedies they could not answer.

J. Wallace Hamilton tells a story about an old hermit who once lived in the mountains of Virginia. He was a wise man, gifted with a rare insight some are able to acquire "through close contact with nature and the God of the Garden." Some of the young boys of the village laughed at the old patriarch. "I know how we can fool him," one suggested. "I'll take a live bird," he continued, "and hold it in my hand and ask him what it is. When he answers, I'll ask, 'Is it dead or alive?' If he says it is dead, I'll let it fly away; if he says it is alive, I'll crush it." They went and found the old man standing in the door of his little hut. "Old man," said one of the boys, "I have a question for you. What do I have in my hand?" After carefully observing the boy's hand, the hermit replied, "Well, my son, it looks like a bird." "That's right," the boy replied, "but tell me, is it dead or alive?" The hermit looked for a moment and then answered, "It is as you will, my son."

It is as you will. You determine what you will do with your life. You and I may not choose the colors, but certainly we choose the pattern. No matter how many sorrows you know or how many disappointments you experience, how you face them is up to you. If you face them alone, you will fail; but if you face them with God, you will be triumphant.

4

Somebody Loves You

There is a grim scene in Maria Cummins' book *The Lamp-lighter*. Little Gerty, who is only eight years old, lives with Nan Grant. Gerty's mother had died in Nan Grant's house five years before, and little Gerty had been tolerated but never loved. Her daily diet, since her mother died, consisted of abuse and vulgar language. She was beaten, called an ugly, wicked child, told that no one loved her, and that she belonged to nobody.

Gerty loved to watch an old man light the street lamp in front of her house. To see the torch flicker in the wind, and to watch the old man hurry up the ladder and light the lamp, was a ray of joy in a desolate heart to which gladness was a stranger. The one bright spot in her long day was the moment when Trueman Flint, the lamplighter, came down the street, leaving in the shadows of night a flickering light on every lamp post.

One night, as darkness fell, Nan Grant sent Gerty down the alley for milk. She returned just in time to see Trueman Flint climbing the ladder. At the foot of the ladder she stood gazing intently, and as Trueman came down he bumped into Gerty, knocking her down and causing her to spill the milk. He turned quickly and picked her up. "What will your mammy say?" he asked. Then, looking into her sad face, he continued, "She won't be hard on such a mite as you are, will she? Cheer up, . . . I'll bring you something tomorrow that you'll like. . . ." Gerty brushed her ragged clothes, and said, "I was seeing you light the lamp and I ain't hurt a bit; but I wish I hadn't spilt the milk."

Just then Nan Grant came to the door and, seeing what had happened, pulled Gerty into the house amidst blows and profane, brutal language. The lamplighter tried to appease her, but she slammed the door in his face.

The next night Gerty was waiting and the lamplighter was late, but quickly and carefully he pulled a tiny kitten out of his big coat pocket and gave it to Gerty. She showered the kitten with love and shared her meager food with it. For a month, she kept it hidden, but one cold night the kitten slipped into the house.

"Whose kitten is this?" Nan asked. "It's mine," Gerty replied. A few moments later, Gerty turned in time to see Nan Grant snatch the kitten from the table and throw it across the room. It landed with a splash in a pot of boiling water, and a few minutes later died in torture. Gerty, in a fit of anger, picked up a stick of wood and flung it at Nan and struck her in the head. The blood gushed from the wound, but Nan hardly felt the blow. She caught Gerty by the shoulder and pushed her out of the house, saying, "You'll never come in this door again," leaving her alone in the cold night.

The lamplighter came by a few minutes later and, finding the child crying and shivering in the cold, asked her the trouble. She told him the story and finally said, "She won't let me in! And I wouldn't go if she would." "Who won't let you in?" inquired Trueman Flint; "Your Mother?" "No! Nan Grant." "Who's Nan Grant?" "She's the wicked woman who drowned my kitten in boiling water." "But where's your mother?" "I haven't got one." "Who do you belong to, you poor little thing?" Trueman Flint asked. "Nobody; and I've no business anywhere."

This is the depth of human despair. This is the darkest night of the human soul. It is a desert where parched tongues and cracked lips find no water. No one had taught little Gerty that she was a child of God. No one had told her that Christ died for her sins and that He could light up the darkness within.

Life isn't worth living until you feel that you belong to somebody. You can't linger near Calvary without believing that your life does count. God's love for you becomes indescribable and undeserved.

I once held in my hand a note written by one who later placed a revolver to her temple and pulled the trigger. "Life holds no meaning for me. I see no reason why I should hang onto broken dreams and hopes that will never come true. What's left?" she wrote, moments before she pulled the trigger.

The woman lived in a beautiful house. Her bank account was bulging with money. Her closets were filled with lovely clothes. A new automobile was parked in her garage. She had friends by the score. Her life had been filled with gay parties and social activities. A desert had gradually filled her soul, and darkness hid the decent lights that give meaning to life. "She must have been mentally sick," some said. I am sure they were correct. When you empty life of compassion for others and concern for a starving world, a part of your soul becomes numb. When our little concerns hide the hurts of others, we become lonely and empty, and self-pity becomes our daily diet.

"What's left?" she had asked. There were thousands of people living in her city who needed shoes for bare feet, clothes for skinny backs, and food for empty stomachs. There were hundreds of hospital rooms filled with sick people who needed someone to come by for a visit. There were many little girls who needed someone to teach them how to cope with the problems they faced. That's not all! "What's left?" There is God. There is always God. He may not be all you want, but He is all you need in order to find meaning in life and walk triumphantly through the inevitable experiences that come your way.

We all want to be important and achieve distinction. There is, in most of us, a burning desire to lead the parade. Alfred Adler, one of the fathers of modern psychiatry, points out that the dominant impulse in human nature is the desire to be somebody, the wish to be significant.

We are skilled in our ability to gain attention. We are clever when it comes to methods that usher us to the center of the stage. Some seek attention by sitting on flagpoles. Others cross the Atlantic in a small boat. Still others wear loud clothes, and some turn to gossip. A few become criminals, and others let their hair grow long like the Beatles.

Praise never makes us despondent. Compliments never make us sad, even when we know we do not deserve them. Jesus spent very little time talking about the faults of people. He did not dwell on their sins, but on God's forgiveness. He challenged humanity to stand tall, and pointed out what we could become with God's help.

Some months ago, I was asked to visit a patient in one of our hospitals. She was a very sick woman, but was able to carry on a conversation. She complimented me more than I deserved. She said, "I've been to your church, and you are the best preacher I have ever heard. I've read some of your books, and you are a great author. You are the sweetest, kindest person in the world. You are a very handsome man." About that time her special nurse came in. I offered a prayer and left the room. The nurse very kindly walked to the door with me. She gently closed the door, following me into the corridor, and said, "Dr. Ozment, I don't know what the patient might have told you, but she is gradually losing her mind, so don't believe anything she said." "She carried on a perfectly grand conversation," I replied, "and I believe every word she said."

The advertising world appeals to our desire to be important. Ads tell us we should drink a certain brand of liquor if we want distinction. They advise us to smoke a certain cigarette if we want to be popular. They remind us to wear a certain make of clothes if we want to achieve success. We must drive a certain car if we want others to be envious of us. Ads even tell us what kind of deodorant to use if we want to keep our friends; they warn us about being half-safe, whereas, if we use a certain brand, we are supposed to be safe for twenty-four hours. When I was a lad, we took a bath that would last a week. If you take a bath with a good strong soap, it will still last you a long time.

Ego that is untamed or undirected can be vicious. Carl Sandburg, in his biography *Abraham Lincoln,* had this to say about John Wilkes Booth, the man who shot Lincoln: "He did what he pleased and took what he wanted. . . . They saw vanity grown in him—vague, dark, personal motives . . . to be feared; projects and purposes vast with sick desire, dizzy with ego." Has history concluded that a giant tree was felled in the forest of civilization by the hand of one sick with ego?

There isn't anything wrong with our desire to be somebody. Evil enters when we push others down in order to push ourselves up. On the other hand, it is wrong to be content to be a nobody.

A bishop in the Methodist Church, examining a group of young candidates for the ministry, asked if they had any desire for preeminence in their work. All of them answered in great humility that they had none. "Well," the bishop said, "you are a sorry lot, all of you." The young men stood embarrassed, and the bishop continued by reminding them that no person ever fired the ambitions of men like the Master. It was Jesus, more than any other person, who made little people feel big and important.

If I owned a bank, I wouldn't hire a man who didn't want to be president of the bank. If I owned a department store, I wouldn't hire a person who didn't want to be manager. Reality never outruns our dreams. You may never attain all your dreams, but you will never go beyond them, either.

Remember that scene in the New Testament where James and John slipped around to ask Jesus for a special favor? "Give us the best places in the Kingdom," they requested. They wanted to lead the parade. There was no consideration given to Peter, Andrew, Thomas, and the rest. James and John wanted to sit one on the right and the other on the left side of the Master. Those were the places of honor in a monarch's court.

Did you ever stop to think about the response our Lord gave to that request? He did not rebuke His disciples, neither did He suggest that their ambition ought to be curbed. Jesus

45

suggested that they did not know the depths of their request. Then He asked them two questions: ". . . can ye drink of the cup that I drink of? and be baptized with the baptism that I am baptized with?" (MARK 10:38). Jesus went on to explain that a place of honor could not be given away: it had to be earned.

J. Wallace Hamilton, writing about the incident, said that Jesus might have spoken in this fashion: "You want to be important. You want to surpass others and be great among men. All right. You should! To be My disciples, you must! But be sure that it is real greatness you are after. Be sure it is a greatness worthy of God. If you would excel, excel in goodness. If you want to be first, be first in moral excellence."

Greatness is the fruit of Christian service. Jesus said, ". . . whosoever will be great among you, shall be your minister: And whosoever of you will be the chiefest, shall be servant of all" (MARK 10:43-44). He encouraged His disciples to be superior. ". . . what do ye more than others?" (MATTHEW 5: 47). ". . . your righteousness shall exceed the righteousness of the scribes and Pharisees . . ." (MATTHEW 5:20).

The man who works for himself is selfish, but the man who works for others is a servant. An eloquent parade of great souls have dedicated themselves to a cause that reaches beyond personal ambition. Greatness is not achieved under the glitter of bright lights, but in the dark jungles of human need; in little rooms of dedication; in the halls of discipline, and in dimly lighted laboratories. Louis Pasteur is a star in the constellation of greatness. He often said, "In what way can I be of service to humanity? My time and energy belong to mankind." Albert Schweitzer could have lived in luxury, but he felt compelled to give himself to a suffering humanity. Madame Curie and her husband Pierre refused to exploit the commercial aspect of their discoveries. Concerning their research with radium, Madame Curie said, "If our discovery has a commercial future, that is an accident by which we must not profit. And radium is going to be of use in treating disease. . . . It is impossible to take advantage of that."

David Livingstone dedicated himself to lighting some lamps in darkest Africa. His greatness was found in the depth of his willingness to serve. Once he said, "I will place no value on anything I have or may possess, except in its relation to the Kingdom of God. Anything I have will be given, or kept, according as giving or keeping it shall I most promote the Kingdom of my Saviour."

What would Jesus say if He were to speak to us this day concerning our desire to be somebody? He might say, "You are important. God made you to be great. Don't ever settle for less than true greatness."

When the people of France put Louis XVI and his queen to death, there was left a little boy, who, if the monarchy had stood, would have become Louis XVII. The boy was put into prison and surrounded with vicious and vulgar men. Their mission was to teach his mind to think vulgar thoughts and his lips to say evil and depraved things. When someone would suggest that he say a vulgar word, the boy would reply, "No, I will not say it. I was born to be a king."

You were born to be a king, and you can be. If you feel that your life does not count, read the words David wrote when he looked at God's great universe: "When I consider thy heavens, the work of thy fingers, the moon and the stars, which thou hast ordained; what is man, that thou art mindful of him? . . . For thou . . . hast crowned him with glory and honour" (PSALM 8:3-5). Read the words of Jesus: ". . . the very hairs of your head are all numbered" (MATTHEW 10:30).

Go back to Calvary and take another look. You'll come away with a new sense of appreciation of yourself. You are important. You can be somebody. Resolve to be great, but be sure your greatness is worthy of God.

5

Things We Do Not Deserve

When life knocks you down, you have three choices: (1) you can stay there; (2) you can turn to a bottle and try to forget your burdens and drown your sorrows; or (3) you can turn to God and ask Him to help you. When life falls apart, you decide whether you will stay in the valley, try to cover your hurts, or, with God's help, rise above them.

Let none of us march out into the world armed with the false notion that when a man is committed to God, he is placed under a protective shell that keeps him from the dark nights of life. Neither let us fortify ourselves with the idea that when life is dark, all we need to do is call upon God to remove the darkness. We cannot use God as men use radar to guide them around the storms of life; nor should we think of Him as a force that sends us, like spacecraft, above the frictions of earth. God is that power which makes life possible when it appears impossible. God doesn't lift us out of the bloody battles, but He keeps us steady during the struggle. God isn't a "problem solver," but He is that majestic force in life which enables us to live triumphantly in spite of the burdens we carry.

The question is not, How will I react if trials descend? The question is, How will I react *when* trials come? Hardships come with life, and we cannot live without suffering. Life has always been that way. Optimism, good fortune, and riches may make life easier when the hardships descend upon us, but they won't do away with the uninvited guests.

It was a dramatic moment when King Charles and Joan of Arc came face to face. The king questioned Joan about the voices she claimed to have heard. Irritated, the king suggested that the voices should have come to him, not to a mere subject. "I am king, not you," he proclaimed. With gentleness that reflected compassion, and with fortitude that expressed an undaunted faith, Joan replied, "They do come to you; but you do not hear them. If you prayed from your heart and listened, you would hear the voices as well as I do."

That's our problem! We are so busy nursing our hurts and bathing in our self-pity that we do not pray with our hearts and listen for God to speak to us. Often we denounce Him and display our lack of faith by asking, "Where is God?" But we neither offer our hand to God nor listen for His voice. Little wonder that we see only despair when life falls apart.

When a man faces God, he always leaves with a word of hope. God lights a candle of hope in every person who comes seeking help, no matter what the circumstances of that person's life. Jeremiah made excuses because he could not speak for the Lord when God called him. Then God said, "Be not afraid . . . for I am with thee . . ." (JEREMIAH 1:8). When God called Joshua to lead the Hebrews into the Promised Land, the task seemed beyond Joshua's strength. But Joshua went about his task with these wonderful promises ringing in his ears: ". . . I will not fail thee, nor forsake thee. Be strong and of a good courage . . ." (JOSHUA 1:5-6).

Remember that thrilling incident in the Old Testament when David went to the front lines to visit his brothers while Saul and his men were facing the Philistines? When the giant Goliath challenged anyone from the armies of Israel and defied the armies of God, something stirred within David. He offered to fight the giant. His brothers, as well as other soldiers, thought he was foolish. Even Saul tried to persuade young David that he didn't have a chance against the giant.

49

David convinced Saul that the Lord was with him and Saul gave his consent for him to fight Goliath. With a simple sling and some carefully chosen stones, David conquered the giant. Previous to that simple act of courage and trust in God, the armies of Israel had trembled with fear each time the giant appeared. It's amazing what one can achieve when he anchors his faith in the goodness of God and walks with Him. It is also amazing to see how little are the things that make us stumble when we do not walk with God.

Frances Shumate does not like to think of herself as being handicapped, but the scars of cerebral palsy are evident. It has left its mark on her speech and her ability to get around, but her spirit has upon it the touch of the Master's hand. In her book *From My Window*, she writes about the tragedy of a hunchback:

> One day he felt his hump dissolve until his spine stood
>   straight.
> Still he saw nothing but the patch of ground beneath his
>   feet;
> His only pleasure was retelling his catalogue of hate;
> He'd let affliction twist his soul out of shape.

We can let bitterness twist our souls out of shape, seeing only the tears of today and never picturing in the mind the dawn of tomorrow. That is one way to face life when dreams are shattered and eager hopes are dashed to bits.

Frances Shumate refused to share the despair of the hunchback. Like all mortals, she felt the pain of disappointment when her dreams were crushed. In these words, she opened for a moment the door of her soul:

> I know there is grief deeper than mine.
> But, my grief is mine. It is my heart
> Which feels the teeth of despair
> Feeding bit by bit, tearing apart

The pattern I had dreamed.
May I be given the gift of grace
To welcome His choice for me,
To accept the pattern chosen to replace
The design of my desire.

When we learn to pray from a genuine heart for the grace of God which will enable us to accept that which cannot be changed, God will grant that strength and we will be well on our way to victory.

Life falls apart for many under the stress and strain of sickness. The achievements of the past are not sufficient to support us during a long period of sickness. When we are alone, we see wasted opportunities, selfish moves, and ugly deeds. It's easy to become a battered victim of despair.

A few months ago, I visited a man in a hospital who had been critically ill. For some days, he lay near the brink of death. During the long weeks of convalescence, he told me about his fears and hopes. He had spent most of one night considering this one question: "What if I don't make it?" He couldn't think of any achievements of which he was proud. Yet he thought of many deeds that brought shame to his heart.

"I have learned one thing from this sickness," he said. "I can tell you that the really important things are the things I have so often taken for granted. I didn't know before that I had been such a selfish man," he continued. He had been so busy making a living that he hardly knew his own children and they didn't really know him. He promised to be a better husband and father. He assured me that he wanted a place to serve in the church and something to do that would be an expression of his gratitude for the privilege of life.

In the New Testament we find a tender scene between Jesus and a woman who had been sick for twelve long years. She probably suffered from a chronic hemorrhage, which was not only embarrassing, but impoverishing and discouraging. She wanted so much to be well and had spent all her savings go-

51

ing from one physician to another. The primitive methods of the medical profession had failed to help her. Little was known about disease and few remedies ever brought relief in those days.

The woman had done all she knew how to do. Little hope was left. Now she must accept her poor health and learn to live with it. Then she heard about Jesus; His fame had spread quickly. He had healed others, and perhaps He could do something for her.

The news spread through Capernaum that Jesus had arrived. A crowd quickly gathered around Him. In that crowd many people held on to their fragile hopes. Among them was Jairus a leader of the synagogue; his little girl was dying and he begged Jesus to heal her. As the woman marched with the others through the dusty streets, hope leaped in her heart. How could she approach Jesus? He was in the company of important people; she was unclean. Blotches of blood could be seen on her clothing. "If I could only get close enough to Him," she thought to herself, "to touch the hem of His garment, I would be healed." Shyly, but with great determination, she stumbled through the crowd and gently touched His robe. "Only the Master can put my life together again," she thought. Jesus turned around and looked into her face and said, ". . . thy faith hath made thee whole . . ." (LUKE 8:48).

Life also falls apart when we lose our faith. The very first step on the ladder that leads to success is faith. Next are discipline, effort, patience, fortitude, and enthusiasm. You see, you can never conquer a problem until you believe it can be mastered. You can never achieve a goal until you are convinced that you can do it.

The disciples must have related to many who were filled with fear the incident that took place on the Sea of Galilee. The night was dark and the Master was asleep, when suddenly the placid little sea became a mountain of swirling and churning waves. Water splashed over the bow and it appeared that the boat would sink.

52

"Do you remember," Peter must have said to James, "we were tugging with all our might to keep the boat headed into the waves, and Jesus was sleeping peacefully?" "Yes," James probably replied, "and someone shouted, 'Master, don't You care if we perish?'" "Then," said Peter, "Jesus rebuked us for our fear and lack of faith. What a Man!" Peter mused, "He is the Son of God. There are no storms that He cannot calm. There are no lives that He cannot redeem. There are no problems that He cannot solve."

One theologian, writing about the question, "Master, don't you care if we perish?" remarked: "Stupid question." It is not stupid at all. When men are filled with fear, they lose their faith, and many a person has let that question fall from his lips. When the waters of earth threaten our happiness, or the happiness of those we love, it is not difficult to ask that same question.

I know a family who recently walked through one of life's darkest valleys. They hold today the broken pieces of what was a joyous dream. Slowly and painfully they are, under the guidance and help of God, putting life together again. The scars of sorrow will never be removed, but because of their faith in God they will find not only the strength to endure, but the joy of new adventure and the satisfaction of seeing new dreams fulfilled.

Faith overcomes other handicaps. Louis Pasteur was stricken with a paralytic stroke at forty-six. Some might have placed their tools on the shelf, but Pasteur worked on with an undaunted faith and unwavering courage. Helen Keller was both blind and deaf, and fear might have kept her locked in a tiny room until death. Instead she chose faith to produce the music by which she marched. Paul was the victim of a "thorn in the flesh," for which he prayed more than once that God would give him relief. His relief came in the form of God's strength to march on in spite of the "thorn in the flesh." Fear tells us that we do not count, that God does not need us. Faith proclaims, "You are important, and God can use

53

you." When we follow faith, even a life that has been dashed to pieces can be put back together.

When we lose one who is close to us, life can fall apart. Sometimes the tears of Calvary hide from our minds the truth of Easter. As long as we focus our attention on the hurts of Calvary, we cannot hear the bells of Easter.

Three crosses silhouetted against a blue Syrian sky, with three men slowly but surely dying, made a grim scene. After almost six agonizing hours of suffering, the soldiers examined the three men. One soldier pierced Jesus' side with a spear. Before they marched back to their barracks, they were satisfied that Jesus was dead. His death was also reflected on the faces of the disciples. As the shadows lengthened, the disciples gazed at each other with puzzled looks of grief. "He's dead," said Simon Peter. Not only were the Roman authorities satisfied that Jesus was gone forever, but even the enemies of Jesus were happy to know that He would never get in their way again.

To take every possible precaution, the enemies of the Master asked Pilate to set a watch of soldiers at the tomb for at least three days. The haunting words of Jesus would not let them rest. "He said He would rise again after three days," they kept reminding one another. Pilate granted their request, saying: "Ye have a watch: go your way, make it as sure as ye can" (MATTHEW 27:65). The soldiers sealed the grave and left a detail to watch.

Then came the first day of the week. The Good News was announced. The truth of Easter was not accepted without evidence. The disciples at first refused to believe. Then Jesus appeared unto them and fresh hope filled their lives. Despair was changed to unwavering conviction. Fear was transformed, and humble disciples were filled with enthusiasm. Dr. George A. Buttrick said, "Why did these men suddenly rise from their bemoanings and, with light on their faces, fairly spring on the world with the message of a living Saviour for Whom they were willing to suffer any persecution?" The answer could be found only in the unequivocal knowledge that Christ was alive.

Do you believe the story of the resurrection? If you believe it and trust in God, the shattered pieces of a life broken by sorrow can be put together again. To believe this story will cause little flames of hope to leap from the cold gray ashes of sorrow.

If we do not believe it, then we must conclude that it is a shameful lie. God has deceived us and life is a big joke. If this story is not true, the Gentle Galilean was a filthy liar who painted pictures of hope on fragile parchments that disintegrate when the winds of reality blow. But the story is true, and death is merely the door that leads to the living room of God.

Finally, sin results in life falling apart. Evil separates us from God. It does not separate us from God's love any more than a wayward son could be separated from the love of a devoted mother. God has chosen to love us regardless of the thoughts of our minds, the deeds of our hands, and the attitudes of our hearts.

When life is torn apart by our ugly deeds, the only source of help is found in God. We cannot cover the stains of sin with good deeds. We cannot erase the sins of yesterday by making noble resolutions today. Our sins can be absolved only as we bring them to God in a spirit of penitence.

A few days after His triumphant march into Jerusalem, Jesus was with His disciples in the upper room. When the Master revealed the shocking news that one would betray Him, the disciples asked, with puzzled looks, "Lord, is it I?" (MATTHEW 26:22).

Before the last rays of a crimson horizon gave way to the darkness of night, Jesus said, "All ye shall be offended because of me this night . . ." (v. 31). There must have been a look of dismay on the faces of the disciples, and after a moment of silence Peter spoke: "Though all men shall be offended because of thee, yet will I never be offended" (v. 33). Jesus, in

His gentle way, replied to Peter, ". . . before the cock crow, thou shalt deny me thrice" (v. 34). Peter fortified his first statement by saying, "Though I should die with thee, yet will I not deny thee" (v. 35).

From the upper room, Jesus and His disciples made their way through the shadows to the Garden. There He was arrested, and Peter was ready for the conflict. It was evident that Jesus was in danger of losing His life, and the hostility was greater than Peter had imagined. Before the morning sun chased the shadows away, Peter denied Jesus three times. Then, in the distance, Peter heard the cock crow. He had forgotten. The cock crowed again. He remembered! He slipped away and buried his face in his hands and wept.

"Look what an awful mess I've made!" Peter cried. "Will He forgive me? Can I ever look Him in the face? What can I do to make this up to Jesus?" Peter discovered that the past cannot be changed, but he soon learned that yesterday's deeds could be forgiven.

On the slopes of Galilee, Jesus came to His disciples, and when Peter recognized Him, he made a dash for Jesus. Peter had loved Him, had denied Him, and he still loved the Master. There in the freshness of a new day, Peter responded to the forgiveness of Jesus and went about feeding the sheep.

Have you ever loved Jesus? Have you ever denied Him? Do you still love Him? Will you come back, like Simon Peter, and let Christ cleanse and redeem you? The deeds of yesterday may be ugly and they may cause you to weep, but Christ can change all that. He will, if you give Him your permission.

6

Patch Up the Past

"What do you consider to be the main business of the Christian church?" someone asked me recently. Without hesitation, I replied: "The church exists for only one purpose, and that is to present the God we see so unmistakably in Jesus Christ to a staggering, weary, and undeserving humanity."

Our major business is not to promote little programs, nor to spend our time presenting lectures on current events sprinkled with irresistible charm. The church should not be a place where we come to be entertained, or to make friends. It must be a place where those who walk in the darkest night of life can see a star of hope and find spiritual strength. The church must keep the lights of hope lit. It is our task to bring people face to face with God, and thereby keep the torch of courage and faith burning bright. Let us proclaim the faith we see in the early Christians. They approached their task armed with the belief that nothing was impossible when God and man worked together.

When a man comes to church holding his shattered hopes and broken dreams, we can say, "Don't give up. All is not lost!" When a woman comes with her soul covered with the stains of many sins, we can shout, "God loves you and will forgive you! No person is beyond His redemption." When a young person brings a heart full of jagged disappointments, we can tell him about a God who knows the secrets of the heart, and whose grace is adequate for every situation.

I agree with James S. Stewart, the eminent Scottish preacher, who said, "Christianity, therefore, is right, absolutely right, when it refuses, in spite of a barrage of criticism, to be deflected from the one object for which it exists, which is to hold up Jesus." When we fail to lift up Jesus Christ, Christianity loses its power and is robbed of its vitality.

There are times when the sermon may pour out healing oil on wounded souls. At other times, the sermon may be compared to a painful operation without the comfort of a numbing anesthesia. Not only must we see our ugly deeds and filthy sins, but we need to experience the Christ who can cleanse us from our transgressions and transform us into new creatures.

No one would deny the fact that all of us need to see our faults; but I am convinced that a lot of preaching falls short. That is to say, it merely points out the evils of our society and fails to proclaim the message of redemption. Some preaching could be compared to a doctor's examination which clearly defines the disease but refuses to prescribe a cure.

It is not enough to be against hate; we must be for love. It is insufficient to make a stand against deceit; we must wave the flags of honesty. We fall short when we merely disdain a falsehood; we must crusade for truth. We cannot measure up to the standards of Christ by simply opposing infidelity; we must march in that army whose motto is "fidelity."

Some months ago, I received a letter from a woman in the Midwest. She thanked me for one of my books which she had just finished reading. Near the end of her letter was a sentence that stood out like a towering redwood in a pine thicket. It has caused me to consider very carefully the content of my own preaching. Here is the sentence: "Our preacher doesn't seem to be against anything and, furthermore, he isn't for very much." What a pity! The church cannot afford to drift with the crowd. It must be the compelling force which pulls man toward his destiny and the lighthouse by which men are guided safely through the storms.

After preparing each sermon, I ask myself some questions. Is there anything in here that would help guide a person who has lost the purpose of life back to God? Is there any grass in these words that will feed the hungry sheep? Is there a word of hope for the hopeless? Is there a bit of comfort for those who bear the burden of sorrow? Is there some courage for those who have lost their grip on life? Is there anything here that will offer a little light of faith to those who walk through the valley of uncertainty? Will this sermon bring people into the presence of God? I have come to believe that if a sermon does not bring worshipers face to face with God, the preacher's efforts are in vain and the congregation's time might well have been wasted.

Our preaching must not reside in the chasms of condemnation; it must climb the steep slopes of Calvary where the battle of good and evil was fought and won. Let us bring the weary to Christ, where they can find strength. Let us bring those who struggle under the weight of sin to Christ, where they can find release.

Jesus did not spend much of His time condemning the things that were wrong in His day. He talked about the God who could redeem and forgive. He was never without a word of hope and courage. Walk with Him over the dusty streets of Jericho and Capernaum. Travel with Him by the shores of Galilee. Ride with Him in the little boat across the sea. Listen to Him talk!

When Jesus heard the cry of blind Bartimaeus, He did not remind him of his sightless eyes and his bleak world of darkness. Jesus asked, "What do you want me to do for you?" Bartimaeus replied, "'Oh, master, let me see again!' 'Go on your way then,' returned Jesus, 'your faith has healed you'" (MARK 10:51-52, PHILLIPS).

One day as Jesus taught, a crowd gathered at the Mount of Olives. Very soon a poor woman was brought to Him and her sin was exposed to all who were near. She had been taken in adultery. Jesus did not condemn her. Why? Because her evil deed had condemned her already. He did not need to magnify the ugliness of it. She needed to be redeemed. Therefore,

59

Jesus said unto her, ". . . go, and sin no more" (JOHN 8:11).
Our churches are filled with spiritually sick people who are
desperately searching for a prescription that will make them
well again. The church has such a prescription.

I talk with a lot of people who are in trouble. No matter
how dark and stormy the night, with God's help I can find a
star of hope. In most counseling sessions I do little talking.
Counseling is mostly listening. All the advice I ever offer is
based on one principle: I believe in the sovereignty of God;
God is behind life; He is the Ruler of the universe. You and
I were created by Him and we never get—even for one moment—out of His sight. The gospel tells us many things, but
one truth that rings loud and clear is this: Your life can be
changed, or you can be transformed in your present situation.

I know a man who was indifferent to God and the church.
As a matter of fact, he was bordering on cynicism and bitterness toward God. One day the storms of sickness descended
upon him. He was rushed to a hospital. I went to see him
and we had prayer together. He was sick for several months.
We both prayed that God would spare him and make him
well. Of course, we prayed, "Thy will be done. . . ." During
the dragging days and long nights, he was forgiven of his sins
and accepted Jesus as his Saviour. His whole attitude
changed.

One day, when I entered his room, he talked very freely
about his own situation. Among other things, he said, "This
sickness has brought me to God. I only regret that I did not
know Him before, so I could have lived for Him. I was afraid
to die until I met God. The doctors have told me that I probably won't get well, but I am no longer afraid." God did not
change the circumstances that surrounded that man's life, but
He transformed the man in spite of his circumstances. If the
wise God does not lift the load we bear, He will provide the
inner strength we need to keep walking without ever falling.

Have you ever heard of Death Valley, California? It borders
on the State of Nevada, and is the lowest, hottest, and driest

land in the United States. Normally, there are only a few inches of rainfall in this valley each year, not enough for the plants to grow. While the land is not entirely lifeless, it is ordinarily a desolate valley of sand dunes. Ironically, only eighty miles away stands the awe-inspiring Mount Whitney, which is the highest point in the United States.

During the month of May, 1930, rain fell in Death Valley for nineteen consecutive days. During those days, seeds that must have been dormant for years sprang to life, and parts of the valley became a carpet of beautiful wild flowers. Buttercups, Indian paintbrush, poppies, larkspur, and other flowers transformed the ugly, dry desert into a gorgeous flower garden. It was reported that a hundred varieties of flowers were found within a half hour in one small area.

Many of us live in a desert without faith or hope. When we put our faith in God and let Him occupy the center of our lives, the dull sand dunes of the soul are transformed into a garden of beauty. The flowers of hope and courage bloom everywhere, and suddenly the gray yesterdays are changes into bright tomorrows.

H. G. Wells, in his book *God the Invisible King*, wrote, "Religion is the first thing and the last thing, and until a man has found God, he begins at no beginning; he works to no end." It is quite evident that a host of people do not believe the truth of that profound statement. The man who tries to manage his life without the help of God is like a captain trying to bring his ship to harbor without either an engine or a rudder.

We live in a world where our sense of values has become confused. Many of us have grown to be selfish and cruel. Money has become more important than morality. Position, for some, has become more desirable than integrity. Others would rather achieve power than moral stature.

Our society reminds me of the story about several boys who broke into a department store and for several hours changed the price tags on the merchandise. They put three-dollar price tags on five-thousand-dollar mink coats, and five-thousand-dollar tags on three-dollar handbags. The clerks discovered one-dollar price tags on two-hundred-dollar suits, and two-hundred-dollar tags on one-dollar ties.

I once noticed a woman who attended church every Sunday and sat in the same seat. She was not a member of the church and never participated in other activities of the church, but she was always in her place when the worship service began. One day I had an opportunity to visit with her, and I asked her why she felt it necessary to attend church every Sunday. I told her that she came more faithfully than some of those who belonged to the church. She was a very humble woman and one who loved God. She said, "I carry many burdens which most people do not know about. I work hard all week and the nature of my work often causes me to become depressed. I come to church each week in order to give God a chance to speak to me. I get my empty buckets of hope and faith filled in church each Sunday, and God sends me back to my work with all the strength I need to carry my burdens.

Dr. Pierce Harris was for twenty-five years pastor of Atlanta's First Methodist Church. One day a member said to him, "I first came to this church because I liked you. Then I came for a while because I enjoyed the church and the people who come here. Now I come to church because I love God." To fill empty hearts, and to teach people to love God and follow His teachings ought to be the goals of every church.

The Christian church must become like a lighted torch in a weary world of doubt and frustration. I remember a young minister who called and wanted to see me. He was disturbed about his Christian faith. "I'm afraid I will be a failure as a minister," he confided. "If you believe in a God who is big enough to solve the problems of humanity and provide the strength to be triumphant, you preach it and leave the rest up to God. If you have that kind of faith, God will see to it that you don't fail. If you don't have that kind of faith, you might as well get started in another profession." He confessed to me that he had some serious doubts. "Well," I told him, "I don't know many people who have not entertained some doubts at one time or another in life. You preach your faith and pray about your doubts, and God will see you through." It is our business to proclaim the faith, not talk about our doubts. Bishop Arthur J. Moore wrote: "We sing a song at midnight, not because of the darkness, but because we are sure the morning will appear."

I have discovered, in the course of counseling, that we must constantly remind ourselves of four major truths concerning the Christian faith. They are truths that Jesus taught, and by which He lived His own life. They are like lanterns guiding us safely through the dark nights of life:

(1) Reconciliation between God and man is possible. Two churchmen were discussing the unsearchable riches of Christ, and one said to the other, "Tell me, what is the best news you know about God?" His companion replied, "He forgives my sins."

I'll have to confess that I do not fully understand how God can forgive us our ugly sins. However, I am fully convinced that everywhere in the life, death, and the resurrection of our Lord we see evidence of God's unfathomable love, which is behind His forgiveness. The sins of our lives repudiate this divine love. In spite of this fact, God continues to love us and is willing to forgive us.

Suppose Jesus had said to the woman at the well, when she freely admitted that He knew even the secrets of her heart, "You are just a poor, sinful woman whose deeds are so evil and whose soul is so stained that you are beyond redemption." He didn't say that. Instead, He told her of the water that would last her an eternity. When Jesus revealed Himself unto her, she hurried back to the city, leaving her water jug, to tell others that she had seen the Christ. Her life must have been transformed, because many of the Samaritans believed because of her testimony. Others believed because they, too, heard Jesus speak.

63

Suppose Jesus had said to Peter, when he denied Him, "You have had your chance. I cannot forgive you." Jesus did not say that. Instead, He recommissioned Simon Peter to do His work. Jesus said to Peter, "Feed my lambs. . . . Feed my sheep" (JOHN 21:15-16).

When Jesus heard the sincere cry of the thief who was dying beside Him on another cross, He did not say, "You must pay for your crimes." The thief admitted his ugly sins; he said, ". . . we receive the due reward of our deeds . . ." (LUKE 23:41). When he said to Jesus, "Lord, remember me when thou comest into thy kingdom," Jesus replied, ". . . Today shalt thou be with me in paradise" (LUKE 23:42-43).

You see, God forgives us even when we do not deserve it. I suppose, if the truth were fully known, we never deserve His forgiveness. Dr. E. Stanley Jones once told of a government official in India whose job took him away from home weeks at a time. He was greatly tempted and soon fell into the ways of shame and dishonesty. His wife was a devoted Christian, and the man's sins continued to haunt him, so one day he decided to tell his wife the whole wretched truth. He called his wife into his room and told her the sordid story. It came as such a shock that she fell against the wall and stood there with tears streaming down her face. She looked as though she had been struck with a whip, and her face turned pale as death as the meaning of his words began to dawn on her. Later he said, "In that moment, I saw the meaning of the cross. I saw love crucified by sin." When it was all over, she told him that she still loved him and would not leave him, but would help him back to God and a new life. That is what God has been saying across the centuries. God says, "I won't leave you; I'll help you back to life if you'll just give Me your hand."

I like to read the want ads. Recently, I saw a little two-line ad that really intrigued me. It read: "Dear Carolyn: Come back home. We can patch things up. I love you. Chuck." I wonder why Carolyn left home! Perhaps it was because of

Chuck. But then, it could have been because of her own wrongs. Actually, it doesn't matter why she went away. The only thing that matters now is that Chuck loves her and things can be patched up. God has been telling us that for centuries. It does not matter what sins cause us to be away. God keeps saying, "Come on home. Things can be patched up. I love you. God."

(2) Don't be afraid of life. Fear paralyzes us. It robs us of our effectiveness. Faith and confidence give us strength. All through the Bible, we are told to trust God. He keeps us from being afraid. After the death of Moses, Joshua was chosen by the Lord to lead Israel. Of course, the task was too big for mere human strength. God frequently gives us opportunities that we could never achieve alone; we must have His strength. Listen to the word of the Lord, speaking to Joshua: "Be strong and of a good courage; be not afraid, neither be thou dismayed: for the Lord thy God is with thee whithersoever thou goest" (JOSHUA 1:9).

The Lord was saying some very significant things to Joshua: (1) He was urging him to remember his own abilities and strength; (2) He was stressing the importance of faith—"Keep your courage high"; (3) He was reminding Joshua to guard against fear and dismay, telling him never to look at a task and say, "I will fail," even before he began; (4) the Lord was assuring Joshua that He would go with him every step of the journey. Victory is assured, when we know God is with us. What more do we need than to hear God say, "I will be with thee: I will not fail thee, nor forsake thee" (JOSHUA 1:5)?

Remember that thrilling story about a very important man who ran to find Jesus? His name was Jairus. His little daughter was critically ill and he was making a desperate attempt to save the one who was close to him. When he told Jesus about his problem, Jesus knew how much the little girl meant to her father, and He agreed to go and help. While they were on the way to the home of Jairus, a servant came and said to Jairus, "Thy daughter is dead: why troublest thou the Master any further?" Jesus heard the report and turned to Jairus and said, "Be not afraid, only believe" (Mark 5:35-36). As long as we live in the presence of God, we need not be afraid.

While preaching in another state, I was asked to visit a saintly lady who was critically ill. I didn't look forward to the visit, but after it was all over, I was mighty glad I saw her. It was not difficult to see that her life was ebbing away. Yet on her face was a radiance that expressed her faith in God. I am sure she was an inspiration to all who knew her. She was not afraid to talk about death. For her, it was merely changing her place of residence. Like Paul, she believed that ". . . the sufferings of this present time are not worthy to be compared with the glory which shall be revealed in us" (ROMANS 8:18). She said "I have spent the past fifty years walking with God and I am not afraid of tomorrow." When we walk with God as that woman walked with Him, we shall find the inner strength to face each tomorrow without fear.

God does not send us into unknown lands; rather, He invites us to follow Him. You may be certain that no matter how steep and rugged the hill, or how deep and black the chasm, or how big and heavy the burden, if you are sensitive to God you can see His footprints and feel the touch of His hand. When you walk through some dark valley, remember Gethsemane; and when the weight of the world is upon you, remember Calvary.

(3) God never fails us. In one of the great affirmations of faith, we read that God's Will "is ever directed to His children's good." We also believe that in God we can find an adequate supply of "strength and help in time of need." That is to say, God's grace is adequate for man's every need. Not only is it adequate, but it is also available to the last and the least.

I often say to people, "You may not get what you want out of life, but if you will accept it, God will give you what you need." The one thing we ought always to remember is that we may not always get our way, but we always have God.

I think of St. Paul as a spiritual giant. Yet he knew the hard realities of life. He was shipwrecked, beaten, ridiculed, and cast into prison for his faith. He also suffered from a physical handicap. He referred to it as a "thorn in the flesh."

In spite of the persecutions Paul endured, he was able to say, "I can do all things through Christ which strengtheneth me" (PHILIPPIANS 4:13). Paul did not get the exact answer he wanted from God when he prayed for the "thorn" to be removed. Nevertheless, he had God, and he discovered that no matter what a person must bear, if God is with him he can be triumphant.

We do not always know what God said to Jesus in answer to His many prayers. We have every reason to believe that when Jesus prayed, He always left the place of prayer, knowing that God was with Him. Once Jesus prayed, ". . . My God, my God, why hast thou forsaken me?" (MARK 15:34). Had that been the last word Jesus uttered on the cross, I would be greatly disturbed. Yet He continued to speak, which was evidence that He felt God's presence. His final word from the cross was one of perfect trust and confidence: "Father, into thy hands I commend my spirit . . ." (LUKE 23: 46).

God never promised to make life easy for us. He never promised to keep us free from disappointments and hardship. He did not say, "Don't worry, you won't ever be hurt." The promises are: "My grace is sufficient . . . ," "I will be with thee . . . ," "I will not fail thee."

(4) God created us for eternity. This is God's gift to man. None of us would claim that he has done anything that makes him worthy of an endless life, but this is our claim because it is God's promise.

Many people look with great dread upon death. For the Christian it is merely a second phase of life. The Christian passes through the valley of death with great expectations and holy aspirations. I am convinced that he will not be disappointed.

At our house we have two small boys who are learning the Twenty-third Psalm. I often need to prompt them when they forget the next line. After the phrase, "Yea, though I walk through the valley of the shadow of death, I will fear no evil . . . ," I often have to help them. I simply say, "Why won't you be afraid?" That is all I need to say. They continue, ". . . for thou art with me; thy rod and thy staff they comfort me" (v. 4).

J. Wallace Hamilton reminded us of the famous king who appointed a man to say to him each day, "Philip, remember thou art mortal," lest he forget his kinship with God and eternity.

I have always been fascinated by the story of the prodigal son. I have often wondered about the feelings and thoughts of the father. I have an idea he was very restless every moment his son was away. He must have thought, "I could not keep him from going away because he is a grown man and can choose to live as he pleases."

How did the father know that his son was coming up the path? Do you suppose the father sat by the window, looking down the path? Did he take a chair and sit on the front porch and wait? The Scripture reads, "But when he was yet a great way off, his father saw him, and had compassion, and ran, and fell on his neck, and kissed him" (LUKE 15:20).

How long the young son had been away, we cannot tell. I do not believe the father just sat down and waited. That was not in keeping with the character of God as revealed in Jesus Christ. Maybe the father had said to a servant, "I can't stand it any longer. I am going to look for my son." With that, he walked down the path at the very moment his son approached. Before he traveled very far, he saw his son coming up the path and ran to meet him.

No matter for what reason we approach God, we will always find Him coming down the road to meet us. Perhaps we come to Him in search of forgiveness. If so, He will be looking for us, and will even meet us along the road. When we pass from the lights of the earth through the valley of death, we will not be alone. God will be waiting for us with His lantern of love in the darkest valley of all. Let us try to be worthy of such a God.

7

But What Can I Do About My Problems?

A defeated man walked to the center of the Brooklyn Bridge. An eye-witness reported, "He climbed up a part of the superstructure. He paused! Then he jumped!" A few days later the body was found, identified, and buried. In a dingy apartment, a note was found among the man's personal effects: "Life is hell and I have come to the end of the way. I find no purpose in my existence. There is no alternative."

The man did not need money; he had a small fortune in the bank. He could have worn expensive clothes and lived in an exclusive apartment. He chose to live alone—so much alone that he excluded God from his life. When a man commits his life to God, there is never "an end of the way." We come to the end of the way only when we search in our little bags of intellectual achievement and human frailties for the wisdom and strength to face life.

There is always an alternative. There is my way, and there is God's Way; I must make the choice. My way leads to defeat and frustration. God's Way may bring me through a dark Gethsemane, up the slopes of Calvary, or through a lonely valley, but it never comes to a dead end. His Way will eventually bring me to victory. When I enter tunnels of trouble, I can have the comfort of God's presence. When I bear my burdens, I can have divine strength. When the way is blurred, He offers His hand to guide me.

Two things keep sending me back to the workbench: namely, God has a purpose for every life, and He has the answer to every problem. It is not always easy to find His purpose; nevertheless, He has a purpose for each of us. Like our Lord, we struggle through Gethsemanes in search of answers to our problems. We may not always find the answers we want, but God has an answer for every problem we face.

Recently I was visiting a lovely lady in a hospital, and she told me about a conversation she had had with her doctor. It went something like this: The doctor placed his hand on hers, looked straight into her eyes, and asked, "How much do you want to live?" "I want to live more than anything in the world," she replied. "I love life," she continued. "Well, you must stop smoking immediately," the doctor replied.

Now, I want to ask you a question: How much do you want to live? If your answer is the same as the answer of the woman, then I would reply, "You must stop trying to live alone, and let God have first place in your life."

One of my favorite stories in the New Testament is the one about the healing of the nobleman's son. In this simple little story, we discover some simple steps that will bring us from hopelessness to hope, and from defeat to victory.

A few days before the incident, Jesus had been in Jerusalem. There, many people heard Him speak and some were healed of their diseases. Then, in Samaria, many believed. Christ's fame was spreading, but the people of Galilee seemed to be indifferent to Him. But when He reached Cana of Galilee, the people received Him gladly. Many of them had been in Jerusalem during the feast and had heard Him speak, and they were impressed with the sensation He caused.

People flocked around Him, hoping He would perform some exciting miracle. Strange rumors about the power of Christ had spread throughout Galilee. They reached a nobleman in Capernaum who walked the floor with a sick son. At such a time, when we have done all we know how to do, and still failure seems evident, we all scan the horizon to see if we can find a glimmer of hope. Suddenly the nobleman thought of Christ. "Someone told me Christ was in Galilee. Yes," he said to himself, "Christ is in Cana. That is not more than twenty-five miles away. I will go to Cana and see if Christ can help me." So he took the first step: (1) let's call it resolution; he made up his mind.

To paraphrase Shakespeare, "Experience teaches us that resolution is the only help in time of need." Resolution may not be all the help available, but we must admit that it is the first step. Resolution is a dream that has not yet come true.

Do you have a problem that needs to be solved? You can be a better husband, wife, son, or daughter. You can be a better neighbor, employee, or employer. You can be a better student. But first you must resolve to be *better*. Some people are just about trapped by evil habits. They can be mastered. There are the evil habits of drinking, cursing, gambling; the sins of gossip and promiscuous sexual activity. They can be conquered. The first step is resolution.

You will notice that the man whose son was at the point of death did more than make a resolution: (2) he followed through. He was a busy man, but he let other things wait. He could have made his resolution and left it there. He could have said to himself, "I will just wait, and perhaps Jesus will come to Capernaum." No. First on his agenda was to find Christ.

All of us face the danger of making noble resolutions and then failing to follow through. A young couple decides, before marriage, that they will attend church together. Then there is the temptation to sleep late on Sunday morning, and soon other activities begin to fill the Lord's day. They made a good resolution, but they failed to follow through. A student may decide, at the beginning of the quarter, to study diligently and to improve his academic record. Suddenly, he finds himself facing final examinations without having followed through on his resolution.

I remember visiting a family almost ten years ago and talking about the church. This family never attended church. The father said, "We know we should be attending church, and we will get started as soon as summer is over and school starts." School began, fall came, and winter's snow glistened on the trees, and still the family had not been to church. Another call brought a similar confession: "We know we should be in church, and we have all agreed to come. We will begin after Christmas." Christmas came, and the flowers of spring waved gently in the breeze, and the family did not come near the church.

The years slipped by, and one day a tearful mother came to the office. "I don't know whether you remember me or not, but you came to see us and invited us to your church. We never came, and perhaps it's too late now. My husband is home drunk and my young son is in the juvenile jail. Will you go visit him?"

I went to see the boy, and when his case came to court the judge asked the young man, "Do you attend church?" The boy stammered and then gave that embarrassing reply, "No, sir, your honor." "Do your parents go to church?" was the next question. A big lump came into the boy's throat, and he dropped his head, "No, sir!" Then the judge looked at the boy's parents and said, "This does not excuse the boy of the crime he has committed, but I don't see how you can expect much more from your son unless you try to teach him and set a good example before him."

George Eliot wrote, "The only failure a man ought to fear is failure in cleaving to the purpose he sees to be best." Just one question: Do you follow through in the purposes you believe to be best in life?

Notice the next step the nobleman took: (3) he asked for help. "Sir, come down ere my child die" (JOHN 4:49). Jesus said, "Go . . . ; thy son liveth" (v. 50). Many people lose their faith if prayer does not always bring the results they want. There are some sweeping promises in the New Testament concerning prayer. They are frequently misunderstood. Jesus said to His disciples, "If ye shall ask anything in my name, I

73

will do it" (JOHN 14:14). This means that you must ask in the Spirit of Christ. It means praying the prayer you believe Christ would pray, if He were in your place.

I received a letter from a woman who had read one of my books: "I prayed, as you suggested, but my prayer was never answered." Then she wrote about losing her husband and how hard the past year had been. This was my answer: "God does not always take our advice when we ask Him to remove some burden or lead us around some storm, but He will give us the strength to bear the load and lead us safely through the storm, if we will ask for His help." This I believe.

The nobleman believed: (4) he was willing to trust Christ. He did not hurry home. He knew within his heart that his little boy would get well. The next day his servants met him and told him his son had had a change for the better. The news came as no surprise, because the man had believed the words of Jesus.

So many of us are afraid to trust God. I remember the story about the woman who boarded the streetcar, carrying a heavy bag in one hand. She paid her fare and held onto her luggage. The conductor said, "You can put your baggage down, lady; the streetcar will carry it for you." That is a parable of life. We have a lot of baggage that ought to be committed to God through prayer. Let us not carry these cares, worries, and fears around with us. Let us give them to God and He will carry them for us.

We are actors in the drama of life. The Author chooses the parts we should play. The Greek philosopher Epictetus reminded us: "If it be His pleasure that you should act a poor man, see that you act it well; or a cripple, or a ruler, or a private citizen. For this is your business: to act well the given part; but, to choose it belongs to Another."

Dr. Samuel Shoemaker told the delightful story of an elderly woman who was knocked down by a tire that flew off a passing truck. The accident left her with a broken hip and confined her to a small room for the rest of her days. There is

74

always the chance that one will grow bitter, or at least become impatient with such circumstances. Not that lovely lady! When Dr. Shoemaker stood by her in the hospital, she looked up from her bed of intense pain and, with a wonderful smile, said, "Well, I wonder what God has for me to do here." Is our faith in God that strong? Do we believe that, regardless of the circumstances that surround us, God has something for us to do? Such a wholesome attitude toward life will keep us from growing sour or denouncing the wisdom of God and doubting His love.

The belief that God will keep His promises to us will relieve us of loads of anxiety. To believe otherwise buries us under a mountain of futility and hopelessness.

"But what can I do?" you ask. You can resolve to be better. You can follow through on your resolutions. You can ask God to help you. You can, by the grace of God, trust Him.

8

Five Steps to a Better Life

There is a gripping scene in Harry Wilson's book *The Seeker*, where young Bernal comes to his grandfather to inform him that he has decided not to enter the ministry, and cannot accept the traditional views of God that his grandfather preaches. After a lengthy discussion, the old man looks into the face of his grandson and says, "I have no claim upon you; and I shall be glad to provide for you—to educate you further for any profession—away from here—from this house."

They were stinging words. Bernal did not expect them from his granddad. "Thank you, sir," he replies. "I could hardly take anything further. But I will go . . . I will take a small sum to go with—enough to get me away. . . ." Slowly, the boy turns and walks away. The old man falls on his knees and prays for Bernal. His sobs choke and shake his body.

At early twilight, Bernal comes to say good-bye to his grandfather. He makes his way to the study door for a final word: "I believe there is no One above Whose forgiveness I need, sir—but I shall always be grieved if I can't have yours. I do need that." The old man stands by the open door. "You have it," he says. "I forgive you any hurt you have done me. . . . For that Other forgiveness, which you will one day know is more than mine—I—I shall always pray for that."

As Bernal walks slowly out the door and across the lawn, Nancy calls to him. They talk for a while, and finally Nancy

76

asks a burning question: "What are you, Bernal?" "Nothing, Nance—that's the trouble," he replies. "But, where are you going, and what for?" she continues. "I don't know either answer . . . ," he retorts.

It is not enough to know many fascinating theories about God. One may know the doctrines of the church and the latest twist in theological thinking, but unless he comes face to face with God, and commits his soul to the keeping of the Great Shepherd of the sheep, he will feel the emptiness of soul that Bernal's answer reflected when Nancy asked, "What are you?"

We know God did not make us to be a "nothing." He made us to be noble and to live on life's highest plateaus, where the breeze can be heard through the tall pines like the song of a mockingbird. Little wonder that Bernal didn't know where he was going and for what. The purpose of life is always blurred when one is not committed to a purpose beyond his own selfish desires.

If we are to find the purpose of life, we must look beyond selfish ambitions, which, after our goals have been attained, bring only pleasure to ourselves. Material things have a way of blurring our vision and blinding us to the sunlit peaks of spiritual achievement. A man must look at the stars and listen for the whispers of God before he discovers that his life counts; before he sees, on the distant horizon, an eternal purpose for his existence.

A man called and wanted to know if I would see his son. "If your son wants to see me, I'll be glad to talk with him," I replied. "He'll see you," the father responded. The appointment was made and the young man came. I believe in direct counseling, so I began by saying, "Your dad tells me that you are a little confused about the purpose of life!" "That's right, sir," he said, "but I believe my dad is a little mixed up, too." "Tell me," I asked, "what do you want out of life?" "What I want out of life," he answered, "could be summed up in one word —money."

The young man is not unlike a lot of other people I know.

I haven't met a man in my life who wouldn't like to make a million dollars, and I know some people who have already reached the million mark and they want to make more.

"Son, I pity you. Even if you make ten million dollars, you will be, of all creatures, most miserable. Money can buy luxurious mansions, flashy sports cars, fine clothes, and adventure, but these will never satisfy the deepest longings of the soul. You know the things that money can buy, but let me tell you some of the things money cannot buy. The richest man in the world cannot buy health, love, and happiness. I don't care how much money you have, you cannot buy courage, forgiveness, and the inner peace that comes when one is sure that all is well with his soul. These are the things that make this journey through life worthwhile."

There was a long pause and I could tell, by the look on his face, that the young man was giving some consideration to what I was saying. "I'd never thought of it that way," he answered. "Maybe I have been wrong," he continued; "I'll think about what you've said."

"There isn't anything evil about money," I told him. "The evil slips in at three points: how you make it; why you make it; and how you spend it. Lift your sights until you see something greater than just making money, and move in that direction." He thanked me and left.

How can we make life better? Did you ever give any serious thought to that question? If General Motors didn't give some serious thought to the question of how to make better automobiles, it wouldn't be long before they could hang a sign on their factories which read, GONE OUT OF BUSINESS.

I want to suggest five steps that you and I can take in making life better, not only for ourselves, but for those around us:

(1) Be cheerful. Jesus said, ". . . be of good cheer . . ." (JOHN 16:33). It isn't easy to be cheerful all the time, but most of us could be cheerful more often than we are if we worked at it a little harder. No one likes to be around a gloomy person. An old grouch who sees the world through

78

glasses of pessimism won't be bothered with friends dropping by to see him all through the day.

While visiting a lady who had been on a sickbed for more than fifteen years, I was amazed at her cheerful spirit. She had no hope of ever taking a walk among the flowers and trees she loved so much. Poor health sentenced her to that bed until death released her. Yet there was a cheerful smile on her face as I entered the room. She talked about the beautiful flowers in a vase on the little table by the bed. She expressed her gratitude for the green leaves that waved in the breeze outside her window. She spoke freely about her many friends and the goodness of God. When I complimented her on her cheerfulness, she replied, "I decided two things a long time ago. First, complaining will neither help me nor those who pass this way. Then, since this is the workbench where life has placed me, I want to show those who come this way that God provides the power to walk triumphantly through the dark valleys of life."

Jesus, more than anyone else, knew the hard realities of life. He felt the sting of disappointment in those in whom He had placed His trust. He knew what it was like to be hurt by those closest to Him, and He experienced the pain of the leather whip on His back, the bits of jagged metal tearing His flesh. Yet our Lord said, ". . . be of good cheer . . ." (JOHN 16: 33).

A governor of one of our states tells the story of a patrolman who had a grand sense of humor. The governor was always glad to see the patrolman coming because he knew he would have a funny story to relate. After dealing with the perplexing and pressing problems of the state, the governor was able to relax in the presence of a cheerful person. To be able to see the cheerful side of life, and to pass it on, is a ministry that will help lighten burdens and release the pressures of our tense world.

(2) Encourage the people you meet on the path of life. History is filled with thrilling stories of those who were ready

to give up on some problem, only to be encouraged by a friend and then moved on to victory.

Thomas Edison invented the phonograph, but the first phonograph didn't sound like stereo. Its high tones were harsh and its low tones were muffled. Edison employed a man to correct the situation. The man worked diligently for two years on that one problem and, after so many fruitless experiments, he became discouraged. One day he approached the great inventor and said, "Mr. Edison, I have spent thousands of your dollars and two years of my life, and have accomplished nothing. Surely, if there were a solution to this problem, I would have found it by now. I wish to resign." Edison paused for a few minutes, looked the man straight in the eye, and said, "George, I believe that for every problem God has given us, He has a solution. We may not find it, but someday someone will. Go back and try a little while longer."

It's easy to become discouraged when you meet failure at almost every bend of the road. No man ever climbs to the peak of success who gives up in despair. Edison was a man of tremendous patience, perseverance, and faith. It is difficult to defeat such a combination. When you are about ready to give up on some problem, remember "that for every problem God has given us, He has a solution. . . . Go back and try a little while longer."

When Daniel Webster was a lad of only fourteen, he was enrolled in the Academy at Exeter, New Hampshire. He did well in all his work except declamation. Each student was required to speak twice each month, and young Daniel was timid. He was horrified at the very thought of standing before his fellow students to speak. He studied his speech and committed it to memory, but when he mounted the platform his mind went blank and he could not recall a word of it. It was a moment of great embarrassment as he stood speechless on the stage. He made a second attempt and failed. Suppose no one had offered a word of encouragement to Webster. He would have finished his studies and probably would have gone back to New Hampshire to work on his father's farm. But his principal encouraged and helped Webster over his speaking difficulty. Because someone encouraged him, Webster went on to serve his country admirably and was acclaimed one of the greatest orators of his day.

Jesus was forever encouraging and challenging people to a better life. You, too, can offer a word of encouragement to those who walk beside you down the road of life. You'll be better for it, and the world will be better too.

(3) Remember that a little word of kindness can change a life. Phillips Brooks said, "If there is any good that I can do, or any kindness that I can show, let me do it quickly, for I shall not pass this way again." Today is the time to be kind to those around us; tomorrow may be too late. A little more kindness in some instances could change a cold business office, with its constant clink of machines, into a warm and friendly place to work. Kindness can transform a tense home into a beautiful place where laughter is heard and love lives. Kindness has a way of bringing the best out in us.

Once a little boy who had caused his mother great pain and disappointment because of his naughtiness was changed almost overnight. All of a sudden he was thoughtful and kind. He didn't talk back to his mother anymore, and when she asked him to do something, he did it with a smile. Instead of a source of trouble, he became a source of joy. The lad's mother asked, "What has happened to you, John? You have changed so completely!" "Well," John answered, "the other Sunday, as I left church, the preacher put his hand on my head, and said, 'You are a fine lad.' I knew he would be greatly disappointed if he found out that I wasn't a fine boy, so I decided to be as good as possible."

Kindness is a mighty important stone in the foundation of marriage. I was talking to a friend who told me about an incident in his own life. He was a successful businessman, and most of the time he was absorbed in his work. His wife, in addition to the responsibilities of the house, had offered some

81

of her time to worthwhile civic projects. "Suddenly we found ourselves growing apart," he said. "She had her interests and I had mine, and they were taking us in different directions. I was giving too much time to my work and not enough of myself to the family. I got up early and came home late. Then, one day, while sitting at my desk, I began to take inventory of the things that were really important to me. I wrote the names of my children and wife at the head of the list. I realized that they had been pushed out of first place by my work and other things, so I left the office early that day and went by the florist and bought the loveliest bouquet of roses you have ever seen and took them home. You know what my wife said?" he continued. "She said, 'I didn't know you cared any more.' Ever since that day, I've tried to remember that the most important thing in my life is my family, and I can tell you that we've been happy ever since." Kindness is the one ingredient that stirs within each of us the desire to become the best possible person.

Paul wrote, ". . . be ye kind one to another . . ." (EPHESIANS 4:32). Kindness doesn't cost anything, and all of us have the capacity to be kind. There is an old proverb which reminds us that "One can pay back the loan of gold, but one dies forever in debt to those who are kind."

(4) If you want to make life better for yourself and those around you, live your faith. Faith is the basic stone in the foundation upon which progress is achieved. You see, men never accomplish that which they believe is beyond their reach. Columbus discovered the New World because of his faith. Cyrus Field labored thirteen years in preparation to bring the Old World alongside the New. He believed a cable could be placed on the floor of the ocean and speed communications between Europe and America. Two failures were enough to cause every member of the syndicate, except one, to advise Mr. Field to abandon the project. His faith and perseverance were rewarded; the cable was triumphantly laid and communications were established between the two continents.

Faith climbs mountains that doubt can never ascend. Faith will bridge chasms that doubt could never cross. Christian faith keeps us going, no matter how dark the night or how heavy the burden. Do you remember those thrilling words of Tennyson:

> . . . cling to faith. . . .
> She sees the best that glimmers thro' the worst
> She feels the sun is hid but for a night,
> She spies the summer thro' the winter bud,
> She tastes the fruit before the blossom falls,
> She hears the lark within the songless egg,
> She finds the fountain where they wail'd "Mirage!"

> "Faith"

A young college student, whose cynicism seemed to be his most distinguishing characteristic, almost lost his grip on life. Like a flash in the night, he thought of his old professor of religion, in whose class he had sat for a quarter. The professor had lost a son during World War II. Later he watched his wife suffer for months with an incurable disease. Then he suffered a heart attack, and for four weeks lay flat on his back. Yet, through all of it, he had an unwavering faith in God.

The student, in his desperation, turned to the professor. "I guess I haven't found the meaning and purpose of life," he confessed. "Do you know God?" the professor asked. "I have never believed in a personal God," the student replied, "but I'll believe in God because you believe in Him." I dare say the professor had never received such a glorious compliment in all his life! All of us know that it is not sufficient to believe in God because someone else believes in Him, but it is a good place to start. We must believe in God because of what He does for us. The question I want to ask is this: Would anybody believe in God because of your faith?

Jesus didn't shrink from the cross. He prayed that God would provide some other way, but He also prayed, ". . . thy will be done" (MATTHEW 26:42). That is the presence of faith. Jesus was saying, "Father, I'll trust You. If I am placed upon a cross, I know the cross is Your will and is best for humanity." That is the kind of faith that always triumphs.

(5) Finally, life is better when we forgive those who hurt us and find God's forgiveness for our own sins. Forgiveness is a divine quality that heals our broken relationships. It makes us feel clean on the inside.

Jesus didn't come to coddle the rich, pamper the intellectual, or humor the upper crust of society. He made His mission unmistakably clear: He came to seek and to save the lost, and to redeem humanity.

Take a look at that enthralling scene recorded in Luke. The disciples had been fishing for a long time without success. Jesus asked Peter to launch out into the deep and let down the nets. Peter responded only because it was a request from the Master. He didn't expect to catch any fish, and when the nets were lowered, they caught so many fish that help was summoned to bring them to shore. Then Peter fell down before Jesus, and said, "Depart from me; for I am a sinful man, O Lord" (LUKE 5:8).

Two things were evident to Peter. He discovered, in that moment, the unsearchable riches of Christ and the spiritual poverty of his own soul. He knew that he was dependent upon the mercy of God and needed forgiveness.

Simon Peter was not always Saint Peter. The writer of the Gospel did not try to conceal his stumbling footsteps. He was impatient, crude, and often egotistical. He made many blunders, but we find it easy to forgive Peter because of his unwavering faithfulness and perseverance. His life didn't end with a blunder. When Peter came to the end of his earthly journey, flags of victory were flying and bugles of triumph were blowing.

After the crucifixion, the mourning women came to the tomb early in the morning on the first day of the week. Do you remember the message our Lord left with the one standing guard? ". . . go and tell his disciples, and Peter, that he will be in Galilee. . . . You will see him there . . ." (MARK 16:7, PHILLIPS).

Simon Peter must have been brooding. He had failed his Master; he had denied Him at a crucial point. Could he ever feel clean again? Even if the Master were alive, could Peter ever look Him in the face? Perhaps he thought of the words of Jesus: "No man, having put his hand to the plow, and looking back, is fit for the kingdom of God" (LUKE 9:62). That message, ". . . tell his disciples, and Peter . . . ," must have been like a drink of fresh water to a man whose throat was parched and whose lips were cracked. Peter hung onto every word that fell from the lips of the messenger. "Did He really call my name?" Peter listened again as the messenger repeated those words. Peter must have said to himself, "He still wants me! Even after what I did the night of the trial and the day of the crucifixion? That means He still believes in me, and I'll have a place to work for Him."

Can't you just see Peter on that dusty trail as the disciples tramped toward the Sea of Galilee? He walks ahead of the group, his heart beating with an exultant joy. Now there is hope in his heart where there was once failure and shame. The past is stained with ugly deeds, but the future is full of hope! Peter is on his way to see Jesus, and that makes the difference.

Now, when we come face to face with ourselves, and see the ugly deeds of our lives, and feel the hopelessness that Peter felt, let us listen for that message that comes from the Master. He will meet us and forgive us and put the stars back in our lives. The Master gave Peter another chance. He gave the adulterous woman another chance. He'll give us another chance if we will come to Him. He will not turn us away.

Not only do we need God's forgiveness, but we need to forgive each other. There is a thrilling story in Ian Maclaren's book *Beside the Bonnie Brier Bush* which illustrates this fact. The young minister John Carmichael and Lachlan Campbell, one of the leading members of John's church, had engaged in some unpleasant words over some of the things that had been said from the pulpit. After prayer and some discussion about the problem with a saintly member of his congregation, the young minister decided to visit Lachlan.

As the young minister approached, Lachlan was busy binding up the wound of a lamb that had lost its way and hurt itself. When the wound was thoroughly cleaned and bound up, Lachlan stood and looked into Carmichael's face and held out both his hands to greet him.

The young minister spoke first. "You and I, Lachlan, have not seen eye to eye about some things, lately, and I am not here to argue which is nearer the truth. . . . But once I spoke rudely to you, and often I have spoken unwisely in my sermons. You are an old man and I am a young man, and I ask you to forgive me and to pray that both of us may be kept near the heart of our Lord, Whom we love and Who loves us."

Campbell replied, "You have done a beautiful deed this day, Mister Carmichael; and the Grace of God must have been exceeding abundant in your heart. It is this man that asks your forgiveness, for I was full of pride, and did not speak to you as an old man should; but God is my Witness that I would have plucked out my right eye for your sake." They knelt down together and prayed.

No matter what our station in life is, we need God's forgiveness and we need to forgive one another. This is not an easy step to take, but it'll make our lives, as well as those around us, better.

9

How to Get Rid of Self-Pity

The world is full of sick people. The No. 1 disease in this country is one I choose to call selfishness. It is easy to become intrigued with the self. Those who have will admit that it is a one-way street.

The symptoms of selfishness are discontentment and unhappiness. Our world becomes so little that God's purpose cannot be seen. We lose sight of the horizons that challenge us. The call of adventure slowly fades into the distant hills. The horizons that challenge are still there, and the echo of adventure still calls, but we can neither see nor hear. We have become infected with ourselves.

The most miserable people in the world are those who feel only their hurts, and remember only their disappointments, and are interested only in their own victories. I didn't always agree with Bertrand Russell, but he spoke to this point with an amazing insight into human nature. "Nothing is so dull," he wrote, "as to be encased in self, nothing so exhilarating as to have attention and energy directed outward."

The most difficult mountain to climb is the mountain of selfishness. The person who conquers himself stands ready to serve a needy world. Louisa May Alcott wrote a little verse called "My Kingdom":

I do not ask for any crown
    But that which all may win;
Nor try to conquer any world
    Except the one within.
Be thou my guide until I find,
    Led by a tender hand,
The happy kingdom in myself
    And dare to take command.

The road to selfishness will eventually bring us to the house of self-pity. Here we lament the misery in our hearts. In such a condition we often get the feeling that no one really cares about us and the world has been unfair to us. We pull the shades, close the doors, turn out the lights, and curse the darkness. One would think that here was a place from which there was no return.

I keep saying to people who bear heavy burdens, experience deep sorrow, and face anxiety that no situation is ever hopeless. God will never give us a task that is impossible to achieve if we are faithful to Him. Jesus said, ". . . for with God all things are possible" (MARK 10:27).

Let me make some practical suggestions that will help us to move out of the house of self-pity and away from the road of selfishness toward a life of happiness and service:

(1) Take a look around. If you feel that all the trouble of the world has settled in your backyard, it won't take you long to see the folly of such a belief. Even the casual observer will be able to see the bleeding sores of a staggering humanity. Jesus warned, "In the world ye shall have tribulation . . ." (JOHN 16:33). He never suggested that there was even the slightest possibility that you could pass this way without ever feeling the sting of disappointment or the sharp pain of grief. This is a part of the price you must pay for the mountains of joy you know as you pass through life.

If you ever get the idea that God has singled you out and placed the heaviest cross upon you, come by my office and let me share with you some of the morning mail. Linger for a while and listen to the people who come in search of a light of hope. Go with me to the hospitals and visit the rooms in which you can almost hear the flutter of an angel wing.

Any self-pity that you may have will be easily transformed into compassion when you see the troubles others bear. I wish you could have been with me recently when I walked into Room 2219 in Egleston Hospital. In that room was a mother, a father, a grandfather, and a sick little boy. The little patient was not yet six years old. I helped the little fellow put a toy together. He won't get to play with it very much. Before long, he'll be playing around God's great throne.

I wish you could have heard that mother say, "This thing is hard to accept, but with God's help we will accept it. We are mighty thankful that thus far our boy has been able to be up and to play a little each day. This is not what we want, but we know God will give us the strength we need to face it." You couldn't stay there very long before a big lump crawled into your throat. When you left, you wouldn't be thinking of a single problem that was yours. Rather, you would go away saying a prayer for that little boy and his mother, father, and grandfather. You would likely ask God to give them strength, and before you said "Amen," you would probably thank God for some of your own blessings.

If you take the time to look around you, you will also discover that others have been triumphant in spite of their troubles and sorrows. The trials and tribulations of life need not defeat us. When Beethoven lost his hearing, he did not place the tools of life upon the shelf and quit. He went on to write his greatest music, and it will inspire and thrill the souls of men as long as good music is played. Milton was completely blind at the age of forty-five. Yet he continued to write, feeling that blindness was no excuse to hide the talent God had given to him. Pasteur suffered a paralytic stroke at forty-six and was handicapped for the rest of his life. Yet he continued to give himself to his work, and all of us would agree that much of modern medicine rests upon his labors.

Take a look around you at the troubles and handicaps others know and remember that many have been triumphant. With God's help, you can be victorious.

(2) Ask God to help you become the person you were made to be. God did not make any of us to be self-centered and miserable. I am convinced that He wants each one of us to be happy.

My mother and father had five children. They taught us to love and respect one another. They took us to church and prayed with us. More than anything else, they wanted us to be Christian. They believe, and I have a feeling that they are absolutely right, that you cannot be genuinely happy unless you are at peace with God.

I once talked to a couple who were having a hard time on the sea of matrimony. The young woman was a patient and devoted wife. She loved her husband and wanted to save their marriage. "I don't believe that divorce is right," she said, "and I'm willing to do anything to make my marriage succeed." I learned that she had gone the second mile and had often turned the other cheek. The husband was a very selfish person who believed that God made him to occupy a throne and, at the same time, live as he pleased. He was stubborn and full of pride. I don't know whether my counsel helped them or not, because I never heard from them again. I had the feeling that the young wife was doing her best, but the husband didn't seem to think he owed anything to the marriage. The truth is, you can't make much of a marriage unless both are willing to try.

The husband expected his wife to have the meals on time and keep the house in perfect order. I told him he had a double standard: one standard by which he wanted to live, and another by which he expected his wife to live. That is true in many marriages. One good rule to remember is this: Make every effort to become the same kind of a person you expect the one you love to be. That is to say, don't make any

90

demands on others that you are unwilling to make on yourself.

We do not achieve happiness by being served, but by serving. For example, there is a lot more happiness in giving a bouquet of roses than in receiving one. Happiness is like a boomerang; it always grows when we make others happy.

When the cultured, rich man came to Jesus, he asked, "Good Master, what shall I do that I may inherit eternal life?" It was evident that he was a student of the Scripture and a good, moral individual. He didn't commit adultery; he did not steal; he had never committed murder, and had always honored his father and mother. In spite of that, the man was not sure of his salvation and knew that he was not completely happy. He was selfish and greedy. Jesus said, ". . . sell whatsoever thou hast, and give to the poor, and thou shalt have treasure in heaven: and come, take up the cross, and follow me" (MARK 10:17, 21). Would it be a bad interpretation to indicate that Jesus was saying, "If you want eternal salvation and genuine happiness, do something for someone else, and in so doing, you will become the person God expects you to become"?

(3) Let God use you. It may be that God will not always permit us to work where we want to serve, but He has work to be done wherever we find ourselves. You see, we often forget that the stars must have a supporting cast, or else there can be no play.

Several months ago, while speaking in another church, I noticed a woman who was facing the sunset of life. After the sermon, I saw her move slowly toward the pulpit; to walk was a real effort. She gently squeezed my hand and told me how much the sermon had meant to her. Then she said, "I retired a few years ago, and there were so many things I wanted to do in the church. I had dreamed of giving all my time to God and His church. Shortly after my retirement, I was stricken with arthritis. I can't do the things I dreamed about, and there are times I can't even attend." With tears falling from her cheeks, she said, "But I can do something: I can pray." We are never useless tools if we place ourselves at God's disposal.

A preacher once quoted a saintly old woman as saying, "God takes a hand whenever He can find it. Sometimes, He takes a bishop's hand and lays it on a child's head in benediction; then He takes the hands of a doctor to relieve pain; the hand of a mother to guide her child; and, sometimes, He takes the hand of an old woman like me to comfort a neighbor." No matter where we are, if we will hold up our hands God can use them.

There are times when we get in God's way. Instead of being stepping stones, we are stumbling blocks. We influence others by the way we live.

Once, when a leading businessman was approached by a minister about becoming a member of the church, the businessman said, "It might surprise you, preacher, but three of your leading members have blocked the door for me. You know them at church," he continued, "but I know them in the business world." That was a flimsy excuse, we would all agree. God doesn't measure His expectation of me by what others do. Yet, we must remember that, in some measure, we are responsible for our influence. Paul wrote, "It is good neither to eat flesh, nor to drink wine, nor any thing whereby thy brother stumbleth, or is offended, or is made weak" (ROMANS 14:21).

Let us live in such a way that our lives will be a light for those who walk in the darkness, and strength for those who bear heavy loads, and courage for those who are afraid. A blind Englishman was noted for a lantern he always carried. People often asked, "What use is the lantern to you, since you are blind?" The wise old man replied, "I do not carry it to prevent my stumbling over others, but to keep them from stumbling over me." Herein lies the challenge of the Christian faith we profess. Let us make certain that no one stumbles because the faith we profess and the faith we practice are so different.

(4) Be willing to start. Many of us are like the old man who prayed, "Lord, use me in an advisory capacity." I know a lot of people who would be proud to be generals in the Lord's army, but God needs a host of privates.

A man said to me recently, "I volunteered to do the dirty jobs in the church, and I didn't realize there were so many dirty jobs that folks don't like to do." The Lord needs some privates who are willing to say, "Send me down to the front lines where the bloody battles are fought."

This word *readiness* is exceedingly important, and our psychologists have recognized its significance. A child does not talk until he is ready. He doesn't walk until he is ready. You and I must be ready to venture for God before He sends us on a divine mission.

God had a hard time persuading Moses to lead the Hebrews out of Egypt. Before Moses began his difficult mission, he said, "Let me go . . ." (EXODUS 4:18). God calls constantly, but we must respond.

Isaiah had a glorious vision in the temple. God needed a messenger to speak to His people, and suddenly it occurred to Isaiah that he could be that messenger. He responded by saying, "Here am I; send me" (ISAIAH 6:8).

Procrastination is one of Satan's most powerful weapons. If he can persuade one to defer making a decision, he is satisfied. A young couple may be convinced that they should become active in a church. Evil agrees, but it whispers, "Wait until next week." A man convinces himself that his drinking is a problem. It is a problem at work and at home. He tells himself that he ought to quit. Again evil agrees, but it whispers, "Sure, you ought to quit, but wait until next month." A person becomes unfaithful to a marriage vow and is aware of the evil involved. It isn't difficult to convince one that such is wrong. Still evil agrees, but it whispers, "Sure it's wrong, but don't decide today; wait until tomorrow."

You and I do not become spiritual giants overnight. But everyone knows that if we are ever to become the persons God expects us to become, we must take the first step.

An outstanding man, one to whom I have already referred, came to Jesus in quest of the good life. No one had to convince him that to be like Christ was the ideal way to live. He wanted the inner peace that comes to the person who follows Christ, but he was unwilling to make a decision for Christ. Decide, this very moment, that you will make every effort to be the person God created you to be. Keep in mind that you cannot be that person unless you say "Yes" to the claims He has on your life.

I say to a lot of people, "Don't be sorry for yourself; wake up and live." Life may not be all you want it to be, but we can wave the flags of victory if we say "Yes" to God. The circumstances that surround life may not be very pleasant, but the power that can be ours through God is totally adequate.

10

Things I Know About God

The other day a little boy died in a hospital. For several weeks he had suffered from a tumor of the brain. He had the best medical care. In spite of it, he died. Someone asked, "How do you explain something like that?" My reply was, "You don't explain it, but you have to accept it."

Actually, we could make some feeble attempts to offer an explanation. One might say, "It's God's will." I would answer, "Oh, no! I do not believe that!" I cannot reconcile such a death with the Christ who walked the dusty streets of Jericho and the shores of Galilee. I am fully convinced that God wants us to find the answer to such conditions.

Another may say, "This is one of the risks we must assume." All of us know that the privilege of life does not carry with it an immunity from sickness, sorrow, and tragedy. Even this explanation is completely inadequate to assuage our grief and answer the restless questions of the heart.

What are we to do when we fail to find answers to many baffling questions that grow out of our experiences along the road of life? Shall we turn away from God and utterly desert Him because we do not understand all of life? Shall we deny the knowledge of God we do have because we cannot know all about Him? Shall we abandon the faith we have because we do not have all faith?

When reason fails us and logic evades us, we need our faith more than ever. If we trust in God regardless of the circumstances that surround us, He will neither fail nor forsake us. Have you ever thought about the magnanimous faith of Job? How could Job ever have found his way through the tragic events of his life by means of reason and logic? He finally concluded that no human answer to the problems that plagued him would satisfy. Therefore he said, "Though he slay me, yet will I trust in him . . ." (JOB 13:15). He affirmed his faith in God's goodness, and was determined to hold onto it, because faith in God was his only hope.

A friend of mine owns a small plane. When the clouds are low and the fog is thick, he never flies. When the weather is bad, he is quick to tell you there are two good reasons why he wants both feet on the ground: he does not like to take unnecessary chances, and he does not have the instruments to fly in bad weather.

Some months ago, I was flying to New York. The captain spoke to us through the intercom system: "We regret that this part of the trip may be a little unpleasant due to inclement weather. We will be flying through some clouds and may experience a little bumpy flying." Then, with complete confidence, he concluded by saying, "Don't worry, our instruments are working fine and everything is under control."

The big planes continue to fly through the clouds because they have instruments to guide them when the pilots are unable to see where they are going. That is the difference between the man who has a genuine faith in God and the fellow who doesn't. When the storms of life descend upon the person who has no faith, the pressure makes him fall. On the other hand, when trouble comes to the person who really believes in God, he keeps going. His faith keeps him steady.

When Jesus faced Calvary, He couldn't find a logical explanation for the brutal cross. Even though He did not understand the full meaning of it, He knew it must be, and His faith in a God who was both good and wise kept Him from falling. Faith is that quality of a man's soul that compels him to believe and trust God when all the lights of reason have been extinguished.

I know a man who doesn't have a college degree, has never even registered at one of our great universities. If you measure wealth by stocks, bonds, money, and real estate, then he would be listed among the poor. I do not mean that he is poverty-stricken. He owns his own home, has a good job, and drives a nice automobile. If, on the other hand, you measure wealth by character, gentleness, concern for one's fellow man, and love, then this man is one of the richest I know. I could find an army of people who would tell you that his life has greatly influenced theirs. They could list many good deeds that he has done for them and others. I am certain that he has never read a book on theology. He probably wouldn't know who Barth, Tillich, Bultmann, and Kierkegaard are. He couldn't tell you what Brunner thinks about God, but he knows what Jesus thought about God. He could also tell you a great deal about Moses, Joshua, and Jeremiah. He could talk for a long time about Paul, Andrew, and Peter.

There are many things that this man cannot tell you about God, but what he knows about God is worth remembering. The things he cannot explain about God don't cause him to abandon his faith. One might say that he doesn't know much theology, but he knows God. The reason I know so much about this man is that he is my father.

In spite of the fact that a part of God's nature remains concealed, there are some things we know about Him beyond any doubt. Let me suggest some of them:

(1) God comforts us when the walls of sorrow surround us. I often tell people that in all my searching, and in the searching of men of other centuries, no one has found a way around sorrow, but many have found a way through. The psalmist was not exempted from sorrow, but he was fortified with a faith that kept him steady during the trials of life. He said, "Cast thy burden upon the Lord, and he shall sustain

thee: he shall never suffer the righteous to be moved" (PSALM 55:22). He spoke like a man who knew what he was talking about.

Henry Wadsworth Longfellow expressed a keen insight into life when he wrote:

> Be still, sad heart! and cease repining;
> Behind the clouds, the sun's still shining;
> Thy fate is the common fate of all,
> Into each life some rain must fall,
> Some days must be dark and dreary.

> "The Rainy Day"

I am not sure that some days *must be* dark and dreary, but I am certain that some *are*.

When sorrow comes, you can find genuine comfort only in God. Sir Harry Lauder, the great Scottish comedian, upon receiving the news that his son had been killed during World War I, remarked: "In a time like this there are three courses open to a man. He may give up in despair, sour upon the world and become a grouch. He may endeavor to drown his sorrow in drink or by a life of waywardness and wickedness. Or, he may turn to God."

The best-known psalm in the Bible is the Twenty-third. Unnumbered millions have committed it to memory. The psalmist admits that he does not know of a detour around sorrow, but he expresses his faith in God's goodness: "Yea, though I walk through the valley of the shadow of death, I will fear no evil: for thou art with me: thy rod and thy staff they comfort me" (v. 4).

I know a man who watched his wife slowly die. He was very much afraid that he could not endure the grief that would come when she died. I tried to assure him that God would not ask him to bear a burden that he was incapable of bearing. After his wife died, the man said, "I realize that before her death I did not have the strength to bear such a

98

heavy cross, but God gave me the strength I needed." The psalmist said, "I laid me down and slept; I awaked; for the Lord sustained me" (PSALM 3:5). We have the assurance that, in all of life, God will supply the comfort we need to meet the sorrows of life. That should not surprise us. Jesus said, "Blessed are they that mourn: for they shall be comforted" (MATTHEW 5:4).

As a minister, I have been privileged to walk with many people through some mighty dark valleys. Most of them have walked triumphantly. A few of them have been defeated by a heavy blow of grief. Those who walked triumphantly accepted divine help and held on to the hand of God. Those who were defeated chose to walk alone and refused to accept God's hand. Jesus said, "I will not leave you comfortless: I will come to you" (JOHN 14:18). He is near when our hearts are broken. His comfort is available, but we must accept it.

(2) God sustains us when our strength fails. Most of us do not travel far down the path of life before we discover that human strength is not enough to cope with our gigantic problems. There may be times in life when we feel that faith in God is not an essential ingredient to successful living. Then there are days when we know that faith in God is imperative. There comes a time when divine strength is the difference between faith and fear, victory and failure.

I remember reading about a young man whose boat capsized about three miles from shore. He began the long swim toward the beach with fear in his heart. While still several hundred feet from shore, he became exhausted. "I prayed," he said. "I don't think I have ever prayed so hard. I told God that either He must take over or I was going under. God took over and I made it to the beach." There are times in every life when either God must take over or a man will go under.

I wonder if Jesus ever prayed for additional strength. Do you suppose He prayed only for insight? He felt the need of constant communion with God as He faced the major decisions of His life.

Go back for a moment and stand in the shadows of Gethsemane and listen to the words of the Master. Who can understand the agony of His heart? "Father, if thou be willing, remove this cup from me . . ." (LUKE 22:42). What a terrible hour to be deserted by His closest friends! They could have supported Him by remaining with Him. Instead, they all went to sleep. Jesus was well fortified after His experience of prayer. Anyone could look in His eyes and see that He was ready.

After Jesus prayed, the Bible tells us, ". . . there appeared an angel unto him from heaven, strengthening him" (LUKE 22:43). In every trial and during each storm, we can, through sincere prayer, find divine strength.

There is a quotation in which an old Rabbi asks, "What is the worst thing the evil urge can achieve?" and he answers, "To make man forget that he is the son of a King." When your strength fails and human resources fade, don't forget that you are the child of a King, and His riches and resources can be yours.

(3) God loves us with a love that is unfathomable. There may be many unrevealed characteristics about God's nature, but surely humanity cannot misinterpret the many expressions that reflect His love. How else can we explain the incarnation, except to say that it was a message of love wrapped up in the person of Jesus Christ? "We do not deserve such love," you say. You are quite right. Divine love can never be merited; it is always a gift from God.

I once asked our two small sons to tell me why they loved me. Immediately, they began to list the many things that normal parents provide for their children. "You buy our food, clothes, and almost anything we want," they replied. "You buy us candy and toys," they continued. Then I asked them another question: "Did you ever stop to think why I love you so much?" For a moment they were silent. "I'll tell you why I love you so much," I responded. "I love you because you are my sons. I love you because I cannot help it."

Perhaps we have some good reasons why we love God. His gifts are more than we deserve. Did you ever stop to wonder why God loves us? He loves us because we are His sons and daughters. He loves us because it is His nature to love us. Charles H. Gabriel, the writer of the great hymn "My Saviour's Love," wrote about the wonderful and marvelous love of God:

> I stand amazed in the presence
> Of Jesus the Nazarene,
> And wonder how He could love me,
> A sinner, condemned, unclean.

We may never know how God is able to love us, but we know that He does.

God's love is indestructible. Robert Southey wrote,

> Love is indestructible,
> Its holy flame forever burneth;
> From heaven it came,
> To heaven returneth.

"The Curse of Kehama"

It is hard to conceive that God's love is greater than the love we have for our children. Yet that is certainly true.

My two sons could do many things that would hurt me deeply and disappoint me beyond description. They could possibly make me ashamed of them; but I am certain that they could never make me stop loving them. God's love is very much like that. You and I do things that hurt and disappoint God. He is not very proud of many of the thoughts we think or the deeds we do, yet we can always be assured of God's love. The man who lives in the gutter and breaks every moral law can still stand up and say, "God loves me." He would be absolutely right.

I'm glad we celebrate Easter each year. While lingering at the cross, we catch a new glimpse of the endurance of divine love. The cross stands as a challenge to each of us. It compels us to give ourselves unreservedly to God. It would be impossible for an observing student of history, or one who is sensitive to the blessings of life, to deny the fact that God loves us. I like J. B. Phillips' translation of the last lines in that great thirteenth chapter of Paul's First Letter to the Corinthians. It reads, "Love knows no limit to its endurance, no end to its trust, no fading of its hope; it can outlast anything. It is, in fact, the one thing that still stands when all else has fallen" (I CORINTHIANS 13:8).

(4) God forgives us when we do not deserve it. Forgiveness is not a beggar's refuge; rather it is the fruit of divine love. Someone has said that the degree to which we are willing to forgive others corresponds to the amount of Christian love in our hearts. When God forgives our sins, He looks beyond all that is ugly and evil about us and claims us as His own.

God has that amazing power to forgive our sins and forget them. The psalmist wrote, "As far as the east is from the west, so far hath he removed our transgressions from us" (PSALM 103:12). God is gracious to forget. "I, even I, am he that blotteth out thy transgressions for mine own sake, and will not remember thy sins" (ISAIAH 43:25).

Once a cleaning woman said to Charles Spurgeon, "I doubt that God will ever forgive my sins. But I tell you, if He ever does forgive me, He will never hear the last of it!" There is a joy that defies description when one has accepted divine forgiveness.

The Good News that God would have us remember is that our sins can be forgiven. Everybody ought to be reminded of this fact each day. No matter how blighted our past may have been, our future can be bright because God stands ready to forgive all our sins. A host of His disobedient children pass by God's throne of mercy each day, and find forgiveness. If our hearts cry out for pardon, we will hear the Master say those thrilling words that He spoke to the woman almost two thousand years ago: "Neither do I condemn thee: go, and sin no more" (JOHN 8:11).

I don't know all I want to know about God, but what I do know is sufficient for this life. What I know about Him, compels me to trust Him to do what is best when the storms of life descend upon me.

11

You Can Be Forgiven

"Can my life be changed?" people frequently ask me. Many people feel the utter despair that covered the soul of the young woman who wrote, "When I look at my past, I am deeply ashamed, and when I get up each morning to face a new day, I tremble with fear." Then she asked the question that a host of people ask at one time or another in life: "Is there any hope?"

God has been lighting candles of hope through centuries of darkness. Micah proclaims, "... he will have compassion upon us; he will subdue our iniquities; and thou wilt cast all their sins into the depths of the sea" (MICAH 7:19). Moses said to Israel, "The eternal God is thy refuge, and underneath are the everlasting arms . . ." (DEUTERONOMY 33:27). God is our refuge from the storms of life. He is our refuge when temptations constantly threaten us. He is our redeeming refuge from the sins of life.

God never spoke more clearly concerning our salvation than when the cross was planted on Calvary's hill. The cross is an expression of God's unfathomable love, but equally significant is its magnanimous message of redemption. Here God is revealing to a hostile world that did not understand Christ, and to an undeserving humanity, His plan for divine pardon. There were other ways in which God could have expressed His love for us, but the cross was the only plan He designed to redeem us.

When I write about the need for forgiveness, I know it applies to everyone who reads. Who among us would dare claim that he has lived a perfect life? Our deeds and thoughts would speak out against us. "All we like sheep have gone astray; we have turned every one to his own way . . ." (ISAIAH 53:6). Then, when I write about the possibility of forgiveness, it strikes a responsive chord upon the keyboard of each heart. Paul wrote, "For whosoever shall call upon the name of the Lord shall be saved" (ROMANS 10:13). When I read, "all . . . have gone astray," I am sure it includes me. When I read, ". . . whosoever shall call upon the name of the Lord shall be saved," I am fully convinced that I am also included. You see, no one is ever excluded from God's measureless mercy and complete forgiveness.

Yes, life can be changed. I know a man who at one time was a slave to liquor. It ruined his life, robbed him of his job, and more than once caused him to spend some time in jail. His language was profane and his deeds brought disgrace to himself as well as shame to those who loved him. Then he met the Master, and like Saul who persecuted the Christ, he was changed and became Paul the gallant soldier proclaiming the good he had once despised. Today he lives not merely a respectable life, but a life of honor. His language is no longer vulgar and his deeds bring neither dishonor to himself nor shame to those who love him. When Christ came into his life, he became a new creature. The pages of history are filled with records of those who were locked in dungeons of self-defeat and have emerged triumphantly.

The one hope that remains for humanity is found in God's forgiveness. This is our only means of escaping the consequences of our sins. Bishop Everett W. Palmer, in his book *You Can Have a New Life!* wrote, "Where we need changing, there can be change. A bitter spirit can become sweet with forgiveness and kindness. A sharp tongue can become gentle with love and forbearance. A fear-ridden mind can find the clarity and serenity of faith. A degrading habit can be replaced by noble thought and action. Cowardice can be exchanged for courage; weakness for strength." A miracle can take place in our lives, and our thoughts and actions can be brought into harmony with God's will.

I am one of those who believe that God's forgiveness is of such a magnitude that finite minds will never fully understand it. Perhaps it is just a fact of God's gracious character that we must accept without really knowing how it takes place. We are like the lady who commented, when the mechanic came to repair her automobile, "I just drive the thing; I do not understand how it runs." There are, however, some things that we know about forgiveness:

(1) Forgiveness is largely a divine act. It is the supreme way in which God expresses His love for us. Once, while teaching a membership class of young people, this question was asked of me: "Exactly what takes place during forgiveness?" I tried to explain it. "Forgiveness," I told them, "is a divine act. It is like taking a trip on an airplane. You may pack your bag, make your reservations, purchase your ticket, and even board the plane. You might fasten your seat belt and relax for the trip. That is all you can do. The next move belongs to someone else. The pilot must start the engines and release the brakes before the big plane leaves the ground. Forgiveness is like that. We acknowledge our wrongs and repent of our sins. We come, asking God to forgive. That is all we can do. The next move belongs to God. He never disappoints us. He covers our ugly sins with His divine love. That is forgiveness."

(2) Forgiveness is something we neither earn nor deserve. What could we possibly do that would suggest that we merited forgiveness? We will always be in debt to God because His divine mercy has been extended to our hearts. But we are also indebted to a host of people who lived before us. We are indebted to Isaac Newton, Johann Kepler, and Marie Curie. We are indebted to Beethoven, Benjamin Franklin, and a host of others.

Not too long ago, I found myself sitting at a head table with several people who were being honored. I have never felt more out of place than I did during that event. I can't speak for the dog world, but I felt the way I think a hound dog would feel at a poodle convention. There were several distinguished people; among them my good friend Dr. William R. Cannon, whose outstanding achievements towered above anything I have ever done. When it was my time to speak, I simply said, "I deserve this honor least of any who sit here, but I dare say that no person appreciates it more than I." That is precisely the way I feel when I think of God's forgiveness. I deserve it least, but I am profoundly thankful that He forgives me.

I have more friends than I have earned. I've got friends from Maine to Florida, and from California to Georgia who are better to me than I deserve. A letter came from Florida, from a man who owns a motel. He wrote, "Come and stay as long as you like. It won't cost you a cent." From all over America, I get mail from people who tell me they are remembering me in their prayers. I have said, over and over again, to so many, "I do not deserve your friendship, but I am grateful for it." I feel the same toward God's forgiveness.

(3) Forgiveness is an outright gift from God. I do not agree with George Bernard Shaw that "Forgiveness is a beggar's refuge; we must pay our debts." I just thank God that Shaw was not right.

While walking down the street with me recently, a friend asked me how much I paid for the coat I was wearing. I replied, "It didn't cost me a penny." "Do you mean they are giving them away?" he responded. "The man who brought me this one was giving them away," I answered. You may be certain of one thing: when you see a man whose sins have been forgiven, the clean coat he is wearing is a gift from God. Forgiveness didn't cost him a thing. Actually, it is sin that has the big price tag hanging on it. Sin will cost you inner peace and will separate you from God. It will eventually cost you your soul, unless you repent and accept God's forgiveness.

(4) James S. Stewart wrote: "Forgiveness is not the remission of a penalty; it is the restoration of a relationship." Forgiveness is not so much getting out of paying the price of our sins as it is coming into a right relationship with God.

Perhaps I ought to illustrate the difference between spiritual and physical consequences of our sins. Once God forgives us our sins, we are no longer separated from Him. We can say, with Johann Bengel, "O God, there is nothing between us." There is no longer the burden of guilt or the feeling of estrangement. We are overwhelmed with the feeling that we are at one with God.

On the other hand, one must frequently pay the physical and, sometimes, mental consequences of his sins after he has been forgiven. Take the man who falls into ways of evil living. One day he becomes engaged in a drunken brawl and loses the sight of one eye. While in the hospital, in a critical condition, he realizes the folly of his ways. During the long days of convalescence he spends a lot of time in serious thought, and gives his heart to God. From that time on, he remains faithful to God. In spite of the fact that he has been forgiven his sins, he must pay the physical penalty of his wayward years. Nothing will ever restore the loss of his eye.

The prodigal son was forgiven his sins, and I am certain that his father never mentioned his being away from home. That does not mean that his brother did not remind him of his evil ways. No doubt, the prodigal thought of the days when he was cold and hungry. He must have recounted the days of loneliness and despair. It was not easy for him to readjust to things at home. There is some great consolation in having a right relationship with God, regardless of the consequences we suffer. That was very true with the prodigal. Better to face the consequences of his sins at home where he knew he had the love and understanding of his father. Dr. James S. Stewart, considering this point, wrote, "There might be bitter things to be endured, but what really mattered was that the broken relationship had been restored." Of course,

108

he was thinking about the relationship being restored between the son and father.

I spend a lot of my time offering a word of hope and courage to those who feel that life is no longer worth the struggle. I tell them God can change them. It is sometimes very difficult to scrape away from the flickering lamps of faith the corrosion that is caused by skepticism. Only the power of God can clean those fading lamps again. I am never more keenly aware of the presence of God than when broken relationships are being restored. It is there, more than any place else, that we are dependent upon God.

God's first business is restoring broken relationships. He is trying to make obedient children out of a hostile world. He stands at the door of our hearts, waiting patiently for us to invite Him into our lives. Bishop Arthur J. Moore tells of a lecturer who showed colored slides on religious subjects before the days of motion pictures. One night, the lecturer was in Manchester, England, showing his slides to a great hall crowded with miners and their families. As he flashed Holman Hunt's famous picture "The Light of the World" upon the screen, he stood quietly, because the picture carries its own message. In it, the masterful artist has portrayed the door of the human heart, barred with rusty hinges and nails. Wild grass and brambles cover the threshold. Jesus stands with a lantern in His hand, which represents the light of conscience, and the light on His face glows with assurance and symbolizes the hope of our salvation. He waits patiently because the latch is on the inside of the door.

Suddenly a little girl's voice broke the silence of the hall. "Daddy," she asked, "why don't they let Him in?" "I don't know," her father whispered softly; "you must be quiet." She was silent for a few moments and then, overcome with anxiety, she asked again, "Daddy, why don't they let Him in?" Rather impatiently, the father answered, "Hush! I don't know." Then, as the audience studied the picture, the little girl shouted and all could hear, "Daddy, I know why they don't let Him in. I know why. They must live in the back of the house."

Do you live in the back of the house? If you are lost, you may be certain that it is not God's fault. Calvary is more than you could ask or expect, even from a God whose mercy is everlasting and whose love cannot be measured. Christ stands at the door. He knocks, and waits patiently. Do you hear Him?

Do you have some relationships that need restoration? Some may be filled with resentments and unwarranted prejudice. Others may have a deep sorrow that needs divine healing. Still others may be caught in the grip of some evil habit. Some have the burden of guilt because sins need to be pardoned. Then there are others who need more spiritual strength and fortitude to face the irritating problems of daily living. Whatever your spiritual needs are, they can be met in Jesus Christ. I do not know what your spiritual needs are, but I do know a God who can supply your every need, and who can give you the grace to walk triumphantly through all of life. No life is beyond His help. Jesus said, ". . . for with God all things are possible" (MARK 10:27).

12

When the Lamps of Faith Flicker

A young college student, questioning the Christian faith he had learned as a lad, began to take off what he considered to be the old-fashioned garments of faith and hope. His parents had taught him that God made this marvelous universe, and that apart from God life has no genuine purpose. At the end of the young man's first year in college, he came home to visit his humble parents; he was wearing the garments of skepticism and doubt. He questioned the existence of God.

One day the lad sat with his father under a big oak tree near the woodpile. The old man picked up a piece of soft pine and began whittling. They sat in silence for a while, and finally the boy asked this penetrating question: "Dad, how can we know that God made this universe?" The old man paused for a few minutes and then slowly closed his pocket knife and placed it carefully on the log, along with the piece of wood he had been whittling. Without saying a word, he took his pocket watch out of his pocket and removed the back so the boy could see the many moving parts.

"Son," he began, "look at that watch. There must be more than a hundred little wheels, springs, and gears in that watch. We could carefully take every tiny part out of the case and throw them on the ground, and no matter how many times you repeat that act, those little delicate parts would never accidentally fall into their proper place. Only a master watchmaker could have made that watch in the first place, and only a good watchmaker could make it run again if it stops. Son, all around me I see the footprints of God, and no one could ever convince me that this world just happened. I do not understand all the mysteries of life, but as long as I can see the footprints of God, I know all is well." The saintly old man's faith could see beyond the young man's logic and reason.

Few men stand so far removed from God as to argue with you concerning the existence of some intelligent mind behind this amazing universe. It is rare to find one who will seriously defend the position of an atheist. The evidence in favor of God is so overwhelming that those who are inclined to doubt His existence find little ground to stand upon in the world of reason and intelligence. With one great chorus, and in almost perfect cadence, humanity stands to proclaim our unwavering belief that God is behind the universe. There is too much intelligence and precision in our world for us to be so naïve as to assume that the author of it is mere chance.

Great and humble minds of every century have reverently tipped their hats to a God they did not fully understand, and very often to a God to whom they did not give themselves, but to a God they knew exists. None of the intellectual giants of history have ever claimed to understand God, but most of them have acknowledged His presence and felt His power.

Most of us have little difficulty in believing that God exists and is the Author of the universe. Like men of the past, we acknowledge the footprints of God. Many people with whom I talk are having trouble finding God in the everyday experiences of life. It is not enough to see God's footprints—we must hear His voice and feel the touch of His hand upon us.

We are convinced that God created this universe, but the deep question that cries for an answer in every man's heart is this: "Is God still interested in His creation?" Christianity must be more than a creed. It must reach beyond a set of beliefs that we so glibly say in unison each Sunday.

I talk to people almost every week who find little comfort in knowing that God is behind this creation. If I were to try to comfort some by whispering, "Did you know that God is the Creator of all we see about us?" they might feel like saying, "So what!" People want to know if God is still a part of His creation, or if, perhaps, He has stepped aside to see the show. Does God make up the audience, or is He on the stage of life, prompting those of us who forget our lines and make a miserable mess of the play? Can God be found as we walk across the parched desert, with sand burning our bleeding feet, while lifting the heavy burdens of disappointment and loneliness? Is He near when the human heart is crushed with unexpected sorrow? Is God close by when we sit quietly with our fears and hold in our hands the shattered pieces of what yesterday were noble dreams? Are the words of hope and courage we hear from the pulpit only empty echoes of what the preacher wants to be true? Did Jesus deceive His disciples when He challenged them to stand as true soldiers and promised to be with them in all their struggles? If we can trust the integrity of those giants who have moved across the pages of history, we can conclude that God is inexorably mixed up in the affairs of man. He is near to sustain us when human strength fails, and to guide us when human wisdom deceives us.

Harry Emerson Fosdick wrote, "God outside us is an hypothesis; God inside us is an experience." It is not enough to know about God; we must talk to Him each day and walk through the paths of life with Him if we would be victorious.

Soon after the new clergyman moved into the parish in which Thomas Carlyle lived, he called upon that very wise man. While discussing the needs of the parish, Carlyle said, "What this parish needs, before everything else, is a preacher who knows God other than by hearsay." Well, that is what every church needs, and that is the need of every individual. When a troubled world like ours hears and obeys the voice of

God, we will experience much peace, and love will be the motivating force behind our thoughts and deeds.

Men lose their fear when they feel the touch of God's hand upon them. Humanity refuses to give up as long as it feels the power of His presence.

Robert Louis Stevenson felt the touch of God's hand during his long days of illness. During a decisive period in his life, when the light of the future seemed to fade, Stevenson found his way by responding to the gentle touch of God's hand upon him. "I came about like a well-handled ship," he wrote. "There stood, at the wheel, that unknown Steersman Whom we call God."

The one thing that sends me back to the workbench is not the victories I have known, but the undying belief that God is in life; that if we are sensitive to Him, we will find the grace that forgives our sins, the strength to lift our burdens; that we will feel the touch of the divine hand that will keep us steady during the temptations of life.

I wonder if Breton's beautiful picture "The Song of the Lark" thrills you as it does me. Did you ever notice that there is no lark in the picture? The artist captured the thrill on the face of the peasant girl as she walked toward the field of labor at daybreak. She hears the divine symphonies in the song of a lark amid the common tasks of earth. Flash that picture across the screen of your imagination. Look at the girl. She is on her way to hours of weary labor. Instead of concentrating on the tasks that await her, she hears the song of the lark as it soars through the trackless sky. The melody she hears in this moment will sing in her soul and bless every hour of her toil. You cannot see the lark in this lovely picture, but no one would ever doubt the fact that the peasant girl with the majestic look on her face has heard its thrilling song.

Not too long ago I spent some time with my good friend Henry L. Willet, who is one of America's foremost stained-glass-window artists. As we were driving from my office to his hotel, Henry told me about Bill, who was the vice president of his company. Only a few weeks before, Bill had died suddenly while out of the country on company business. "It fell my duty," Henry Willet said, "to break the sad news to his wife and young son. The day Bill was due back home, we received news of his death." Henry went to Bill's home, and in response to the doorbell Bill's lovely wife came to the door, expecting to find her husband. "Oh, it's you, Mr. Willet," she said, with an obvious look of disappointment on her face. "Yes, it's me," he replied, "and I've got terrible news for you." She interrupted, "It's Bill, isn't it?" "Yes, it is," Mr. Willet responded. "He's dead!" she said, knowing it must be true but waiting for him to confirm it. "I just shook my head, and she knew," Henry told me.

After the terrible shock of that dreadful moment was over, Bill's wife prayed: "O God, thank You for the gracious things You have done to make our life together so wonderful. Give me strength to face these days and to carry on as Bill would want me to if he were here. . . ." She knew God was near and she knew how to find Him. There have been many lonely days and weary nights when all the stars seem to fade from sight, but that young widow has marched with an unfaltering step. "Tell me," I asked, as we rode along the expressway, "what was her secret?" I knew the answer, but I wanted to hear what my friend would say. "Her faith in God was her secret," he replied. "You know," he continued, "as long as a man hangs on to his faith in God, he can face anything life brings him."

After Henry Willet walked away, and on my way back to the office, I got to thinking about what he said: "As long as a man hangs on to his faith in God, he can face anything life brings him." "That's what Jesus was saying to the disciples when they faced an almost impossible situation," I said to myself. Jesus reminded them that "with God all things are possible" (MARK 10:27). That is also the answer Paul received when he prayed for the thorn in the flesh to be removed, "My grace is sufficient for thee . . ." (II CORINTHIANS 12:9). When

115

you and I come face to face with what appears to be the end of the road, let us never forget that "with God all things are possible."

I've lived long enough to know that man must respond to the voice of God if this journey through life is to be meaningful. There are times in almost every life when a man feels that he can get along without God. He plays in gardens of beauty and runs across plains of joy without giving a serious thought to his need of God. In these circumstances, God seems more like a luxury than a necessity. Such moments are exceedingly short in most lives. At other times, God is never considered a luxury but a necessity. When a man climbs over the jagged rocks of temptation and struggles up the steep paths of disappointment, he needs God. When he walks through the deep valleys of sorrow where the lamps of faith flicker, he needs God. When human strength would camp in valleys of defeat and despair, a man must have that divine strength that keeps him marching toward the morning.

Zechariah spoke to a disheartened people. The exiles had returned to a land of ruin, and Zechariah warned them that there was no hope without God. He urged the people to turn back to God, and in Him they would find their true purpose. Zechariah told the people that God had spoken to their fathers, but they would not listen. Now he warned them to listen to God's voice and obey it. "Be ye not as your fathers, unto whom the former prophets have cried, saying, . . . Turn ye now from your evil ways, and from your evil doings: but they did not hear, nor hearken unto me . . ." (ZECHARIAH 1:4).

The exiles wanted to live as they pleased, yet they wanted the peace that comes from knowing God. They were eager to achieve the goal without paying the price. Such thinking prevails today among many of us. Many of us know how we could improve our marriage relationship. Some of our daily acts do not conform to God's will. Some of our young people know how to make their homes happier places to live in, but they aren't willing to do their part. All of us are caught in the grip of some habits that we know we ought to commit to God, and by doing so we would become better husbands, or wives, or sons, or daughters. Yes, God still speaks, but many of us fail to hear Him.

I like what George MacDonald, the Scottish poet and novelist, said more than half a century ago: "You are like little children sitting on the curbstone hunting in the gutter for things. Behind you is a King's palace, finer than Buckingham. In it your Father sits. But you won't listen. You won't even turn around to look. You just keep on hunting in the gutter for things, and it doesn't matter whether it's rotten vegetables, or pennies, or shillings, you find there. They can't make you happy without your Father." God still speaks, but we don't have to listen.

God is still saying what He said to the psalmist: "Be still, and know that I am God . . ." (PSALM 46:10). Waiting very often challenges the very best that is within us. All of us are filled with goals to achieve and destinations to reach. We get irritated when we are hindered by detours or delayed by circumstances. We must be busy meeting appointments and fulfilling the very often ridiculous demands we have made upon ourselves. Most of us have reserved little or no time for waiting.

There are times in life when we are forced to wait. One would find it difficult to imagine the difference we would see in our lives if, at the beginning of each new day, we sat quietly and centered our attention upon God. Our sense of values would change. The tasks to which we give ourselves might be altered. Our working day might be a little shorter. We would be able to face the events of the day with greater confidence and poise.

Sometimes the only thing we can do is wait. If waiting is all we can do, we can be sure that waiting is best. I once read a story about a young lad who had only recently been employed in a coal mine. Soon after entering the dark tunnel, his lamp went out. Fear filled his heart and he hardly knew what to do;

the mine was dark, and to move around might bring sudden death. He decided to sit down and wait. Waiting was hard, but it seemed the best thing to do. In the utter dark, every little noise seemed like the thunder of doom. Looking down that dark tunnel, he saw the faint glow of a lamp in the distance and heard a friendly voice say, "Don't be afraid. I've come to get you."

When troubles descend, and you feel there is nothing but darkness around, "Be still," and listen for the voice of God. You can hear Him say, "Don't be afraid. I have come to get you." God waits in the shadows to lead us safely through the dark places when our little lamps go out.

13

Life Is a Million Little Things

Happiness is not an impossible achievement. If you really want to be happy, you can.

A wise man once suggested nine requisites for the person who finds contentment in life: he must have enough health to make work a pleasure; enough money to support his needs; enough strength to battle with the difficulties of life and overcome them; enough grace to confess his sins and forsake them; enough patience to work until some good is achieved; enough charity to help him see some good in his neighbor; enough compassion to move him to help others; enough faith to make real the things of God; enough hope to live above anxious fears concerning the future.

It is impossible to find purpose and meaning in human existence until we relate ourselves to God. It is like trying to tell time by a clock without hands. The prodigal son tried to live without his father; he found only poverty, hunger, and disappointment. I can imagine the prodigal son giving advice to others who were looking for adventure in the far country. "Don't go," he would tell them; "the lights of excitement soon fade, and the fires of adventure turn to cold, gray, and disappointing ashes."

Evil always deceives us. It never satisfies the deep longings of the soul. It may appease us for the moment, but it will never give us the inner peace we need. Evil that brings contentment is like something bought on the installment plan: someday the account must be settled; the consequences of an evil life must be faced. The Bible makes it very clear that our sins will be exposed if they are not forgiven. Life offers every man a choice. He can take what he likes, but he must pay the price.

A man called me one day and asked if I would see him. He insisted that I visit him in his home. I drove out to his house and we sat down in a sparsely furnished room that was in bad need of some major repairs.

"Preacher," he began, "you may not believe my story, but I want to tell you, anyway. I have ruined my life, lost my family, and must face the rest of my days alone. Ten years ago I was making thirty thousand dollars a year. There was laughter in this house, and the furnishings were as fine as money could buy. I sold the furniture and bought whiskey. I beat my wife, and said ugly things to those I love. You are looking at a man who has been defeated by liquor. I am paying for the sins of yesterday." That man could have said, with John Donne, "I count all that part of my life lost which I spent not in communion with God, or in doing good."

I often talk with young couples who are disappointed in marriage. If they begin such a noble adventure with the feeling that it's going to be one long honeymoon, they will become discouraged. There are no moonbeams in a dishpan full of dirty dishes, and there is no stardust on an ironing board loaded with wrinkled clothes. Actually, marriage is composed of a series of little things.

A well-adjusted person is one who is able to cope with the irritating problems of everyday living. Life itself is not one big deed; it is a million little things. It's watching a bird build a nest. It's taking time to pat a little boy on the head. It's looking into the eyes of a pretty little girl. It's walking through the woods on a summer day. It's admiring the lovely clouds as they float overhead. It's going to church. It's discovering the beauty of a sunset. It's finding satisfaction in doing a simple deed for a friend.

You would be unwise to defer this business of living. You may never paint a picture or write a book that will be recorded in history. You may never build a statue or perform some outstanding deed that will assure you of a place in history. But you can leave your mark in a simple and unselfish deed.

History has a way of remembering, with love, those who have lifted the burdens of humanity, brought joy to others, dispersed the clouds of ignorance and superstition, and permitted the light of truth to shine upon man's way. You will never find the names of all the great men and women in our history books. Many great people walk an obscure path.

Greatness is not measured by fame. Elizabeth Taylor is famous, but I dare say she would make no claim to greatness. Cassius Clay is a name known throughout the sports world, and in spite of the fact that he claims greatness for himself, I venture to suggest that he does not measure up.

Greatness is not measured by one's wealth. You may have the ability and opportunity to make money, but along with money comes a responsibility to use it wisely. You do not measure greatness by the size of a bank account.

Greatness is measured by how closely our lives resemble the life of the gentle Galilean. You may be rich or poor, educated or ignorant; you may live in the bright lights of fame or in the shadows of obscurity; but you can never achieve greatness until your thoughts and deeds resemble the thoughts and deeds of Jesus Christ.

There are two primary ways to measure a man. You can measure him on the outside and get his physical dimensions. Then, if you want to determine his spiritual dimensions, you must measure him on the inside. I know a man who isn't over five feet ten inches tall, and he weighs less than 150 pounds. His outside dimensions are average, but on the inside he is well on his way to becoming a spiritual giant.

You are never made great by what you have. Greatness is the result of what you are. What you are is expressed in what you do. Many of us say we believe in God each Sunday. Do we? Do we believe in Him enough to give generously to His work? Do we believe enough to give Him first place in our lives? Is our belief strong enough to stir within us genuine compassion for those who suffer because of poverty, ignorance, and disease?

Recently there was a discussion on television about Dr. Albert Schweitzer and his work in Africa. One man claimed that Schweitzer was an egotist, that he did what he did for himself, and that all his service and sacrifice was an attempt to satisfy his own oversized ego. The other speaker claimed that Dr. Schweitzer's compassion was his motive in giving himself to the dying black men of the jungle. It's strange how we judge the motives of others. If a man keeps everything for himself, we are quick to say that he is selfish. If he denies himself for others, we accuse him of having an oversized ego.

I do not know how God will judge Dr. Schweitzer's work, but I suspect his chances of hearing that "well done, thou good and faithful servant," will be better than that of his critics. He left the comforts of home and moved to the jungles of ignorance, disease, poverty, and suffering where he built fires of healing and lit candles of truth. Did he not go to the "least of these My brethren," to express, not only with the words of his lips but with the deeds of his hands, the Spirit and teachings of Christ? I don't know of another man in this century who has relieved more suffering and lighted more candles of hope in a dark world.

Jesus talked about the importance of simple deeds that grow out of love and concern. He talked about giving a cool drink to the thirsty, sheltering the stranger, feeding the hungry, visiting the sick, and clothing the naked. Whenever we meet a human need with love, we are doing the work of God.

Two men, James and John, with their families, lived as neighbors for many years. They were neighbors in the true sense of the word. One day John's wife became critically sick, and before the crimson colors of the setting sun turned to black shadows, she died. Jim came over to John's house. He didn't have much to say. He didn't know what to say. He put his arm around John's shoulder. They stood for a moment in silence. Jim stayed all night with John. He chopped the wood, kept the water bucket full, and tended the fire. Weeks later, the two men were talking about that long night. "I felt as if I was in the way," Jim said. "You gave me strength," replied John; "I don't think I could have lived through the night, if you had not been there." It was a simple deed, but it was worth doing.

We cannot be Christian in theory only. Christianity cannot be tied up in a neat little bundle of philosophical or theological discussion, no matter how exhilarating it may be. Christianity cannot be confined to the four walls of a lovely sanctuary, or limited to a well-equipped educational building. We cannot restrict Christ to our place of prayer. He must be exemplified by our deeds as well as expressed by our lips.

Roy Angell tells us about an experience that came out of his seminary days. Just before dark, one bitter cold evening, he answered a knock at the small house in which he lived. He found the pastor of a nearby church standing at the door, with flakes of snow covering his coat. Angell invited him in and asked, "What are you doing out in this cold weather?"

There was a glow on the pastor's face as he answered: "I have just seen something that I want to share with somebody. Just outside of town, at the foot of the hill, there lives a little elderly widow. Our church takes care of her. I went to see if she needed anything during this bitter cold weather. As I entered her living room, I saw a little mischief in her eyes as she took me to the kitchen and pointed to a basket of groceries, and a man's coat was draped across the chair. 'You have a man hiding here! Where is he, Auntie? Trot him out.'

With a smile on her face, she said, 'You'd be surprised—no, you wouldn't, because you know him. Come to the kitchen window.'"

Near the kitchen window the preacher heard the ring of an ax. After scratching the frost off the window, he saw the president of the seminary chopping wood under the wood-shed. Writing later about this incident, Dr. Angell said, "Here was a man with an assignment, a God-given assignment, who had turned aside from his teaching to release some of the Spirit of Christ that so filled his life." The Christ we teach in the classroom and preach in the pulpit must be lived in the street, and in the office, and in the home.

Most of us may never have a chance to do just one big thing in life, but all of us have the opportunity to do a million little things for the King. If we are faithful to the opportunities of each day, we can look back over life when it is over and feel that the journey was worthwhile.

14

All Things Are
Possible With God

Frederick Atkins wrote a book entitled *Standing Up to Life,* and the title suggests two things: one can stand up to life, and one can be triumphant. All of us need a faith that sustains. God did not give us the strength to face life alone, but He did make it possible for us to find in Him the strength we need.

When I was a lad, we lived about two hundred yards from a small country store. Frequently, in the evening, my father would ask me to go to the store for fruit, candy, or something he wanted. I was afraid of the dark and never looked forward to the trip. While it was only a short distance, that did not calm my fears. My father knew I was afraid, and he would always turn the front light on and frequently walk down to the mailbox and wait for me. I could look back and realize that I was never out of my father's sight. I could always hear his voice and see the light shining on the front of the house.

Life is like that. You and I are never out of sight of the God who created us. Neither are we out of sight of the lights of the Father's house, nor the sound of His voice.

The Hebrew poet walked out under the Syrian sky and looked at the stars and moon, and was overcome with a sense of God's greatness: "O Lord our Lord, how excellent is thy name in all the earth! . . . When I consider thy heavens, the work of thy fingers, the moon and the stars, which thou hast ordained; What is man, that thou art mindful of him?" (PSALM 8:1, 3, 4). That's a good question—What is man? It is a question all of us ought to consider.

Back in 1926 a chemist decided he would analyze the human body in order to discover its commercial value. He discovered that if you weigh 160 pounds, and are five feet ten inches tall, your body contains enough iron to make one nail; enough phosphorus to make 2,200 match heads; enough fat to make seven bars of soap; enough sugar to fill a small dish; enough lime to whitewash a chicken coop; and a little magnesium, potassium, and sulphur left over. The commercial value of all this was 98 cents back in 1926. Due to inflation, and on today's market, you would be worth about two dollars.

Is that all there is to man? No person in his right mind would put himself up for sale at such a price. You are made in the image of God, and you can be filled with the Spirit of God, and you are here to do God's will. To believe this about man makes a big difference.

What a man believes about himself will determine how he lives. If you are dust, and only dust, why not have your fling and satisfy the desires of the flesh? If you are only dust, go ahead—eat, drink, and be merry. Live the way you want to. But give everybody else the same privilege you take for yourself.

Man is more than flesh, blood, and bone. There is something deep within the soul of man that calls to us. It calls us to stand tall, walk straight, and live unselfishly. Until we respond to that call, we can never be happy. Unless we live by some sort of moral compass, we will soon be lost in a world of hopelessness.

A young man was brought before a judge to be sentenced for a crime for which he had been convicted. The judge saw some good qualities in the boy and talked to him in his private chamber. "Tell me, son, why did you do it?" The boy replied, "I guess I just lived up to what people expected me to do." Our children sometimes do the things they think we expect them to do. Well, God expects us to attain a spiritual level of living that most of us have not yet attained.

A few days ago I ran out of gas. Fortunately I was in front of a service station. It doesn't take much city driving before your tank is empty. You may have the finest car money can buy, but unless you keep gasoline in the tank, you don't have transportation. Today's automobiles will not run on kerosene or diesel fuel; they are made for gasoline.

You may fill your days with fun and frolic, but your soul remains empty until you open your heart to God. The circumstances around your life may be exactly what you want, but the soul remains dull and lifeless until you accept God as your partner.

Dr. Ellis Fuller once preached a sermon on the far country. One normally thinks of the far country as a desolate place where the scum of society have settled. It's easy to think of the far country in the words of Kipling: "Where the trails run out and stop." Dr. Fuller said the far country is "Anywhere . . . a man tries to live without God." That's a good definition. The far country could be the house in which I live, or the one next door. It could be on the loveliest street in the city where the lawns are trimmed and the houses are decorated with sparkling chandeliers. When a man fails to follow the footsteps of God, he is already in the far country. He doesn't have to wait until his bank account is exhausted and there are patches on his pants and holes in his shoes.

When life appears meaningless, remember your heritage. It is a marvelous thought to know that you were made in the image of God. You may feel defeated, but you have tremendous possibilities. Don't let life defeat you. Remember, you are a child of the King. If you believe that, then act as if you do.

There always seems to be a breakdown of morals during the crisis of war. On hearing of the immorality between American soldiers and German girls, a father was concerned about his son, who was stationed in Germany. When the boy came home, the father said, "Son, I've got to know. Did you follow the crowd?" The young man looked his dad in the face, and replied, "Dad, don't you know that there are some things men with our name can be trusted not to do?" That was all the answer the father needed.

There are some things that you can trust people not to do if they bear the name of Christ. They will not cheat. They will not lie. They will not take unfair advantage of another.

Remember Susan Warner's book *The End of a Coil,* in which Rupert and Dolly visited the ruins of Rome? Dolly reminded Rupert that most of the emperors of Rome died a violent death. They were murdered or committed suicide. "Some were really great men, weren't they?" asked Rupert. "Here is Trajan," said Dolly. "He was a philosopher and a distinguished man in the arts of war and peace. Yet, he ordered any who professed Christianity to be put to death. Do you think he was great in the sight of God? Here is Marcus Aurelius. He was what the world calls a very great man. He was wise, strong and cultivated. He sought out Christians, east and west, and had them tortured and killed. What do you think the Lord thinks of such greatness?"

"Well," asked Rupert, "what is greatness? What is worth trying to achieve?" "Only that which will last," answered Dolly. "What will last?" asked Rupert. "Only the work you do for God." "But what about all the other work we do?" questioned Rupert. "All our work should be done for God," Dolly replied. "The merchant ought to make money for His service. The lawyer ought to bring justice to all; break every yoke; let the oppressed go free. Soldiers ought to fight to protect the weak people from violence and wrong."

"Why should a man try to improve himself?" asked Rupert. "So he can serve God better," Dolly answered. "If you are right," Rupert said, "then the rest of the world is wrong." "Yes," Dolly replied, "the Bible says: 'The wrong way is the broad way where most of the people go.'"

When life seems hopeless, remember that God is not only

your Creator, but that He is with you. Jesus said, ". . . with God all things are possible" (MATTHEW 19:26). This is a daring faith. What did Jesus mean? Surely He meant that no situation is hopeless. Certainly He meant that no matter what the circumstances of life are, we can be victorious. Above all, He meant that human personality does not travel a dead-end road. It runs through deep waters and up steep mountains, but at the end of the journey there is light and peace for those who have been faithful to God.

The psalmist learned the truth of this point a long time ago. It is reflected in his wise words: "Yea, though I walk through the valley of the shadow of death, I will fear no evil: for thou art with me . . ." (PSALM 23:4). There is no way around that valley, but His is a hand that will keep us steady as we make the journey.

There is a story about Billy Hicks, a petty officer in the British Navy. He was finally promoted to the captain of the foretop. He knew it was a dangerous post and that two men who had held the post had fallen to their death. Billy was afraid.

A few nights before he was to assume his new post, Billy was seen working with the signal apparatus as if he were sending an urgent message. When he was to make his first climb, he went aloft like a seasoned sailor and came down safely. He was a changed man, but no one knew why.

The secret of his transformation was not discovered until an officer of another vessel was a guest on board. The guest asked the captain if had a man on board by the name of Billy Hicks. When the captain told him he did, the visitor said he had noticed a signal coming from the ship and had asked his signal officer to take down the message. This was the message:

"God, this is Billy Hicks speaking. I'm not afraid of no living man. . . . I'm not asking for special favors except one. . . . When I climb the foretop tomorrow, let it be with the courage of a man who is clean. And, O God, if it's just the same with You, from this day on, give me the feeling I used to have long ago when I knelt at my mother's knee and said, 'Our Father. . . .' Good night, God."

Life is hopeless without God. With God, the burdens of life can be endured, and you and I can be triumphant.

On my way to the church one day, I heard a new song; or at least it was the first time I had heard it. It was entitled "Life Is Empty Without You." The writer was not thinking of theology when he penned those lines, but if you think of human life in relation to God, there is some mighty good theology in those words. Life never loses its meaning if you feel the touch of God's hand, and if you believe that He is the creator and the Goal of life.

15

Take a Look at Yourself

"What do you like most about your work?" a friend asked. "I love to preach most," was my reply.

Week after week and year after year, the minister stands behind the pulpit to speak to his people. He has a marvelous opportunity as well as a tremendous responsibility. There is always the temptation to echo the mind of the congregation. One is likely to get the feeling that some people are interested in hearing about the sins of other generations, but have no interest in exposing the sins of our society. The minister who is true to his calling must get his message from God and speak clearly and profoundly to those who sit in the pews each Sunday. If his message comes from God, he will hit his target Sunday after Sunday. God does not require us to be successful, but He does demand that we be faithful.

There was a preacher who went to serve a new congregation, and he called a meeting of his officials soon after arriving. The officials seemed eager to assist the preacher by suggesting certain subjects that should not be expounded in his new parish. "Don't say anything about liquor," one suggested, "because one of our largest contributors owns the biggest still in these parts. Don't talk about gambling, because some of your prominent members have a little poker game each week." "I would advise," said another, "that you go easy on the subject of gossip, because this is a prevailing pastime in this town." The startled preacher asked, "What on earth can I preach?" "I know," exclaimed one member; "Talk about the Jews. There isn't one in a hundred miles of this place."

Jesus was a successful preacher because He spoke to the needs of people in a language they could understand. You cannot separate the teachings of Jesus from life.

Every sermon ought to do at least two things: it must magnify man's weakness, and remind him of his need for redemption; then it must bring man to the place where he can see the greatness of God and His eagerness to help. As a minister, I feel compelled to remind people that a new birth is necessary if we are to reach the destiny for which God created us. The minister will denounce some things, but he must be careful not to remain too long in valleys of denunciation. He must warn us of impending dangers and decry the evil that parades in garments of respectability and social charm. He must not only talk of the dark and evil night through which we pass, but he must tell of a morning that is possible.

The minister is charged with the awesome responsibility to proclaim the Good News. Now comes the big question: What is the Good News? The most thrilling news I know is that Christ died for our sins. Jesus gave us a grand picture of God's character, and everywhere in His teachings we see evidence of a good God who stands ready to forgive us. The life and death of Jesus also express the fact that you and I, through daily communion with God, can overcome all the evil that plagues us.

Another great challenge in preaching is to keep people growing in the Christian faith. You may be able to read music, but that will never assure you of being an accomplished musician unless you pay the price of long hours of practice. You may plant the finest rose bushes available, but you cannot expect to enjoy a beautiful rose garden without keeping the weeds pulled up. You may go to the altar and respond to the marriage vows with a heart full of dreams, but your noble hopes will turn to gray ashes unless you keep the fires of love burning and work to fulfill your dreams. You can walk around in the woods with a perfectly good compass in your pocket and remain lost unless you have learned to use it. You and I must sit at the feet of the Master and learn the lessons of life that will enable us to be victorious in facing the little irritating cares, as well as the great tragedies, that lie in the future.

A good deal of preaching must be directed to those who have set sail on the sea of Christian living, but who still need words of courage to keep moving. Suppose you were to go to see your physician while in great pain. You might even feel that death might be near. Your physician examines you and then says very gently, "You are a mighty sick man." You wait for a word of hope and, after a long silence the doctor repeats his first statement: "You are a mighty sick man." You might respond by saying, "Yes, doctor, I know that, but is there anything you can do to help me?" You would not be interested in hearing how sick you were; you would be eager to know if there was a prescription that would make you well again.

Jesus never left anyone without a word of hope. Even the rich young man who came to inquire about eternal life was assured of an open door through which he could walk. The young man had permitted wealth to build a wall between God and himself. No matter what difficult problem we are facing, there is always hope, because with God all things are possible. Preaching must wave a flag of hope before a weary humanity.

While walking through a crowded department store, I noticed a little boy crying. I walked over and stooped down before him and asked him to tell me why he was crying. "I can't find my father," he said. "Don't you cry," I said to him, "and I'll help you find your father." That brought him courage and he dried his tears as we headed toward the Lost and Found Department. Little help I would have been had I said to him, "Son, you are lost, and that's too bad. Maybe you will never find your father." When we reached the Lost and Found Department, there was his father. The man gathered his little boy in his arms and said, "I'm sorry you got lost. I have been looking everywhere for you. From now on, you must let me hold your hand."

We often get lost, and perhaps it's because we do not want the Father to hold us by the hand. We want to walk alone and do as we please. Like the little boy, if we let God hold us by the hand, we will never get lost. Jesus is constantly saying to us, "Come with Me, and I'll show you the Father."

God doesn't take our human freedom away once we are saved. We are not mere puppets on a string, in spite of the fact that we have surrendered our wills to Him. We can still deny God and refuse to do His will. We can, by sheer selfishness, push Him from the throne of our lives and give Mr. Ego control again.

Let me suggest three simple steps that will lead you to a new life:

(1) Don't be afraid to admit that you have been wrong. Once a man called me and asked if I would talk to his son. "Tell me," I asked, "what seems to be the trouble?" "He thinks he knows everything, and that he is never wrong. Just tell him that everybody is wrong sometimes." There is no help for the person who refuses to admit he is wrong. You can't help such a person because he doesn't even recognize the problem, let alone feel the need for help.

In counseling with couples who are drifting on the sea of domestic storms, I know my job is a difficult one, if not impossible, when two people come in and tell me that the trouble does not lie with either of them. When a woman tells me all the fault is with her husband, and when her husband tells me it is all his wife's fault, I know there isn't much help I can offer until they are able to see their own mistakes. Admitting your faults is the first step in becoming the person you can become.

(2) Ask God to forgive you. There is no record of anyone being turned away who has come to God forsaking his sins and seeking forgiveness. Dr. James McConnell of Oklahoma City told a story many years ago about a day when he was fishing on the Missouri River. Dr. McConnell looked up and

134

saw a small boy frantically waving a red flag from a home-made dock jutting out into the river. He also saw a large Missouri River steamboat coming down the river. It looked as if the boy might be trying to stop that boat, so Dr. McConnell moved down to where the boy stood and asked, "You don't mean to tell me that you are fool enough to think that great riverboat will respond to your signal and try to stop at this little dock on the bend of the river?" "Sure I do, mister," the boy replied confidently, "it'll stop, all right. It'll stop." "That boat couldn't possibly stop in this swift water, even if the Captain wanted to stop," Dr. McConnell answered. "They'll stop, all right, mister, they'll stop. I ain't afraid they won't stop!" Just then, Dr. McConnell saw the great boat make a sudden swerve and heard the whistle blow twice in recognition of the boy's signal. The steamboat slowly made its way over to the boy's homemade dock and the gangplank was run out and the boy stepped on board. He looked back over his shoulder at the stranger and said, "I ain't no fool, mister. My father's captain of this boat!" Need any more be said? You wave your little flag and ask God to forgive you, and He will. I have never been more sure of anything in my life.

(3) You must believe on the Lord Jesus Christ. Remember the story of Paul and Silas having been cast into prison because they were accused of disturbing the peace and teaching customs that were unlawful for the Romans to follow. After they were publicly beaten, they were thrown in what would be called a "maximum security" prison, and the jailer was sternly charged to see that they did not escape. At midnight, while the prisoners were praying and singing, an earthquake shattered the prison doors and every prisoner could have walked to freedom. The Philippian jailer awakened and drew his sword to kill himself, supposing the prisoners had escaped. Paul urged him to keep calm and assured him that all prisoners were present and accounted for. The jailer was afraid that he would be put to death if the prisoners escaped. He came trembling to Paul and Silas and fell on his knees and

asked, "Sirs, what must I do to be saved?" They replied, "Believe on the Lord Jesus Christ, and thou shalt be saved . . ." (ACTS 16:30-31).

Now just what does that mean? Does it mean that we are to give intellectual assent to Jesus? Many people believe that Jesus lived, but mere belief has made little or no difference in their lives. Look up the word *believe*. It means to "accept," to "have faith in," and to "trust." To believe on the Lord Jesus Christ is a transforming experience. It means living by His teachings and following in His footsteps. Polycarp, a first-century Christian, expressed this belief when men were being fed to the lions and burned at the stake for their faith. He was arrested and asked to denounce Christ. The Roman officer who arrested Polycarp tried to persuade him to say, "Lord Caesar." Polycarp said, "I am a Christian." "Just pay your respect to Caesar and save your life," the proconsul urged; "Reproach Christ and you will be free." Polycarp said, "Eighty and six years have I served Him and He never did me an injury; how, then, can I blaspheme my King and my Saviour?" He was led to the stake and burned alive. Never once did he flinch from the pain. That is what Paul meant by believing. We must trust and follow.

To believe on Jesus is more than a mere tip of the hat on Sunday; it is taking hold of His hand and walking confidently through life with Him. To believe on Jesus is to trust Him when the shadows fall around us; it is to believe that He is a true revelation of God's character, and that His life expresses God's care and concern for us. It is to believe that through Him we can be redeemed, and by His example we can meet all the problems of life successfully. To believe on Jesus is to follow Him through the dark tunnels of suffering and through the deep valleys of sorrow and disappointment, knowing that on some tomorrow He will bring us to the sunlit hills of that land where sorrows are not known, suffering is only a faint memory, and disappointments are forgotten.

Let God's love flow through your life. God's love is deep and

136

unfathomable. Human love is often shallow and superficial. Divine love moves in three directions: from God to man; from man to God; from man to man. Every man's life is either a channel for God's love or a stuffy storage bin for his own selfish desires. When we commit ourselves to God, life becomes a rippling stream as His love flows through our thoughts, deeds, and attitudes. If we fail to commit ourselves to Him, life becomes a pond stagnant with the stench of egotism, covered with the slime of selfishness.

It is thrilling to know that God can live within us. Paul expressed this when He exclaimed, "I am crucified with Christ: nevertheless I live; yet not I, but Christ liveth in me . . ." (GALATIANS 2:20). Jesus talked about this idea when He said, "As the Father hath loved me, so have I loved you: continue ye in my love" (JOHN 15:9).

Jesus knew that it was man's nature to love himself. Therefore, He never commanded us to love ourselves; but He did say, "Thou shalt love thy neighbour as thyself" (MATTHEW 22:39). He did not condemn man's love for himself. To care for ourselves is not necessarily evil, but to exclude others from the same concern and love we express for ourselves is wrong. Our greatest problem is not the task of loving ourselves. Our great challenge lies in loving ourselves in the right way, and loving others in the light of the teachings of our Lord.

A woman writes, "How can we know that God's love is within us?" There is only one answer to that question. Jesus gave us the answer on two different occasions. Once He said, "By this shall all men know that ye are my disciples, if ye have love one to another" (JOHN 13:35). A man can shout all day that he loves God with all his heart, but unless that love moves in the direction of his fellow man, you can be sure that God's love fails to flow through his life. Jesus also said, ". . . the tree is known by his fruit" (MATTHEW 12:33). A good tree will bring forth good fruit, and man will reap what he sows. That is God's law in nature as well as in the spirit.

When we relate ourselves properly to God, all our human

137

relationships will be Christian. The kind of love we express for one another depends upon the degree to which we love God. It follows that the evidence of our love for God will be expressed in the way we treat our fellow man.

Once a young man in a Midwestern city decided to leave home. He announced his intentions to his father and advised him that he would be leaving the next morning. "I have decided to leave," he said; "I am tired of your restraints and mother's piety." The night was long and restless for that father and mother. They loved their son and were afraid of what might happen to him in a large city without their Christian counsel. All night they turned restlessly and the stains of many tears were on the pillows.

The next morning they heard their son tiptoeing down the stairs an hour before he usually arose. The father jumped out of bed and went to the head of the stairs and called out to the boy who had already reached the front door. "Son, come in here for a moment!" The boy turned back and walked slowly to his parents' room. His father put his arm gently but firmly around the boy's shoulder and said, "Son, your mother and I have not slept all night. We are sure that there must be something wrong in our lives, and before you go we want to ask you to forgive us." The boy looked into the weather-beaten face of his father and saw the tears of love on his cheeks. "Father," the boy said, "the trouble is not with you and mother; the trouble is with me." Together they knelt by the bed and prayed. The boy got up with God's love flowing in his life. After that, home was the happiest place in the world for him.

16

Life Can Be Better

Some people are asking profound and significant questions: Where is God? How can I relate my life to Him? Can I be triumphant? Does my life have an eternal purpose?

I received an astounding letter recently from an academic dean in one of our great universities. He had read something I had written which was obviously basic in Christian tradition, and he wrote: "I'm glad to know that somebody still believes in the fundamental teachings of Jesus. I have just returned from a worship service in which I heard an eloquent preacher deliver a sermon, with proficient dullness, on psychological vibrations."

That phrase "proficient dullness" caught my eye. It reminded me of a story I heard some years ago. A pastoral relations committee asked for a new preacher on the grounds that the one they had was supernaturally dull. The bishop wanted to know what they meant by the term "supernaturally dull." "Well," said the spokesman for the committee, "no man could be as dull as our preacher without divine aid."

Man estranged from God is like a mighty ship without a captain. The potentialities are gigantic, but the ship sails to no harbor, delivers no cargo, carries no passengers, and reaches no destination without a captain. Without God, man drifts in a sea of frustration and uncertainty with his cargo of selfishness. The challenge of preaching has never been greater, and the harvest to garner has never been larger than it is in our generation.

Dorothy Sayers released a stinging indictment against those of us who stand in the pulpits of the nation when she wrote, "You have the greatest good news on earth—the incarnation of God in human life—and you treat it as an insignificant news item, fit for page fourteen in the chronicle of daily events." That is a scathing remark, but the tragedy lies in the fact that there is more truth in it than we ministers wish to admit. We must be alive to the needs of our people and also aware of the power of God to meet those needs.

Ministers must do more than proclaim the news events of the week or denounce the evil that surrounds us. We need to lift up Christ, who is the only Light that flickers in our dark world. We can get the news on TV, but it doesn't motivate us to make better news tomorrow. We can read fresh reports of what is happening in our world in the daily paper, but it is never redemptive. Preaching ought to be like a candle burning in a dark night, or like a drink of fresh water found in the midst of a parched desert.

Remember the words of the psalmist, as translated by Moffatt, "When I was hemmed in, Thou hast freed me often" (PSALM 4:1). Well, a lot of people are hemmed in today. They are hemmed in by their sins. They are hemmed in by their selfishness and disappointment. They are hemmed in by their fears and sorrows. The Good News we have to proclaim is that God can free them.

Catherine Marshall talked about that feeling of being hemmed in when her husband died. God can take the worst situation and make something good out of it. Calvary and the ugly deeds performed there were transformed into a place where all men can find the forgiveness they do not deserve. When Peter Marshall died, a prophetic voice was silenced at the age of forty-six. Catherine Marshall wrote: "On that chilly January morning in 1949—as I looked at my husband's face for the last time, then turned to leave the bare little hospital room—it seemed like whistling in the dark, to believe that God could bring good out of such tragic loss." She found release from that feeling, and through her writings has been able to minister to the needs of others.

Joseph R. Sizoo, in his book *Still We Can Hope*, tells us about the professor who was a brilliant Greek scholar and a wonderful interpreter of the New Testament. Once he taught a course on the Book of Romans. When he came to the eighth chapter of Romans, the grand old professor read that strange verse, "All things work together for good to them that love God." One of the students lifted his hand, and when the professor recognized him, he inquired, "Professor, you do not mean to tell us that a man with your intellect believes that?" "Yes," the professor replied, "I believe it with all my heart." Later in the afternoon, the professor and his wife went for a ride in their automobile. There was a terrible crash that left the professor unconscious and his wife dead. When the old scholar became conscious, he was in a hospital. A nurse stood nearby, and the professor asked her if she would telephone and ask the president of the institution in which he taught to come to see him. When the president entered the room, the professor said, "Tell my class what I said this morning about ROMANS 8:28 still holds good." Then he died.

Remember the agonizing prayer our Lord prayed under the shadow of the olive trees in the Garden of Gethsemane: ". . . nevertheless not my will, but thine, be done" (LUKE 22:42). Follow Him for a few minutes to the praetorium. Hear again the false accusations brought against Him. Watch Him stagger under the weight of the cross. Listen to Him pray. ". . . My God, my God, why hast thou forsaken me?" (MARK 15:34). Ask yourself the question: "Does His prayer in the Garden still hold good?" Sensitive hearts can hear Him whisper above the noise of gambling soldiers, "Father, what I said in the Garden of Gethsemane still holds good." All of us get hemmed in now and then, but we can be set free by the grace and power of God. That's Good News!

E. Stanley Jones once told a story about a Danish wood-carver who picked up a piece of driftwood along the shore in

Hawaii and, seeing its possibilities, carved a beautiful head of Christ. Without God, we are little more than driftwood on the restless shores of eternity, but God sees within each one of us a faithful disciple.

In the powerful little parable of the lost sheep, Jesus gives us a word picture of the pursuing love of God. He comes to us; He dogs our steps until we invite Him to live within. When we clog our souls with cheap deeds and waste our efforts in selfish pursuits, He knows that we could yet become obedient sons of God.

The major thrust of this parable is twofold: (1) God's ceaseless love for an undeserving humanity, and (2) man's need for redemption. Not only do we see the wonder of God's love, but the hopelessness of man ever finding his way back to the fold by himself.

A hundred sheep would have been a large flock in Palestine during the time in which Jesus lived. Yet the loss of even one animal would have sent a good shepherd into the wilderness to search for it. A shepherd with less concern might have been pleased to keep ninety-nine percent of his sheep. He might even have rejoiced in the fact that only one was missing.

In America, the average congregation has about twenty-five percent of the members present on a given Sunday. That leaves seventy-five percent of the flock unaccounted for. What is our attitude? How do we react? Do we say to ourselves, "Let them find their way back," or "They should know better than to stay away"? Or do we just forget them and, after a reasonable length of time, mark them off the records or place them on the inactive role?

Once a mother who had a rather large number of children was being interviewed by a newspaper reporter. He asked, "Which one do you love the most?" She was a wise woman and her reply indicated not only her wisdom, but a good mother's spirit. "I love the one most who is away from home until he returns; and the one who is sick until he is well; and the one who is hurt until the hurt disappears; and the one who is lost until he is found." Some scholars tell us that the sheepfold in which the shepherds herded the sheep at night was shaped like the capital letter "C"; and the shepherd wrapped himself in his garments when the shadows fell, and slept across the opening so that any animal that tried to ravage the flock first had to encounter the shepherd. What a grand picture of the shepherd! It reminds me of the words, "I am the good shepherd, . . . I lay down my life for the sheep" (JOHN 10:14-15).

There is a dramatic scene in Ian Maclaren's book *Beside the Bonnie Brier Bush* which relates the story of Flora Campbell running away from home. Flora's father, Lachlan, was deeply hurt and he struck her name from the family Bible. When Marget Howe came to talk to Lachlan, she found him hard, cold, and stubborn. "She is not anything to me," said Lachlan, ". . . she has been a black shame to her name . . . would to God that she was lying in the graveyard."

Marget Howe spoke softly, but firmly, "Just twenty years ago this spring her mother died. Not a woman to watch over her and she wandered from the fold, and all you can do is to take her out of your Bible. Woe is me if our Father had blotted out our names from the Book of Life when we left His house. But He sent His Son to seek us, an' a weary road He came. I tell you, a man wouldn't leave a sheep to perish as you have cast your child away."

Before many minutes had passed, Lachlan was on his knees, praying, "God be merciful to me a sinner." After addressing a letter Marget had written, begging Flora to return home, Lachlan cleaned the lamp that had been kept for show and had never been used, and he placed it in the window each evening. Every night its light shown down the steep path to Flora's home like the divine love from the open door of our Father's house.

Here is a question we should consider: How can we become more effective in our witness for Christ? We need to possess more fully three indelible qualities we see so clearly etched in the life of our Lord:

(1) Notice the unflinching allegiance Christ had for His

Father. Jesus had but one purpose: He wanted to please His Father and live God's will to perfection in His own life.

After a long, weary day, Jesus sat by Jacob's well and talked with a woman about living water, which she so desperately needed. The disciples had gone into the city to buy meat, and when they returned they begged Jesus to eat. He said, "My meat is to do the will of him that sent me, and to finish his work" (JOHN 4:34). Let us be careful that our purpose does not become cloudy with activities other than the Master's work.

Harold Bosley, in his book *The Mind of Christ*, opens his first chapter with a delightful little story that suggests the Christian strategy we need to follow. A missionary, who had just arrived at a new post in China, asked a little girl, who had been picked up as an orphan and cared for in the mission, whether or not she had heard the gospel. "No," she replied, "but I have seen it." Aye, that is far better than hearing the gospel. We ought to live such a life that others can see the gospel in us.

Jesus Christ was and is the gospel. Those who flocked around Him could see it at work in His attitudes as well as in His deeds of love. This day requires the church not only to proclaim the gospel, but to be the gospel.

(2) Notice the discipline Christ demanded of Himself. The work of His Father had priority in His life; it was always God first. Jesus studied the scripture and was often found at the place of prayer.

E. Stanley Jones tells the story of a monk coming to his abbot and saying, "I do not know what is wrong with me. I keep the rules, I fast at all appointed times. I pray according to the prescribed regulations for perfect monks. And yet, I am a complete failure. What is the matter with me?" The abbot lifted two fingers toward the sun until the monk noticed the light filtering through his fingers as red as blood itself. Then the abbot spoke: "You must become a flame of fire." That's the secret. Those of us who stand in the pulpits, and those who wave His banners and profess Him as Lord, must become flames of fire before our influence can be what it ought to be.

I am thrilled every time I read that story of the old slum woman who sat, Sunday after Sunday, in the congregation George Matheson once served. For a long time she had lived in a cellar. One day, to the astonishment of her neighbors, she moved from the dark, dingy cellar to a sunny garret. When her friends assailed her with questions, she answered, "You cannot hear George Matheson preach, and live in a cellar."

Every preacher who reads these lines could be a better preacher if he demanded more of himself. Everyday, when I look into the mirror to shave, I say to myself, "Bob Ozment, you could be a better preacher." To believe otherwise is to stop growing. Every layman whose eyes fall across these pages could have a greater influence for good on others if he demanded more of himself. The world is full of people who live in damp cellars. Your preaching and the way you live could cause them to change their residency.

(3) Notice the unfaltering compassion Jesus had for others. The Master loved people, not because of what they were, but because of what He knew they could become. It's easy to love nice people who do nice things for you. Such love is rooted in selfishness. God's love breaks through the bands of hostility and prejudice to love us for what we can become when we are fully consecrated to Him. I can think of a thousand reasons why I love my Saviour, but I cannot think of a single reason why He should love me.

When our Lord's fame spread throughout the land, He went from city to city and taught the multitudes and healed their diseases. He saw great numbers of people with so many burdens and hurts. Their lives had neither purpose nor direction. The writer of Matthew says, ". . . he was moved with compassion . . . because they . . . were scattered abroad, as sheep having no shepherd" (MATTHEW 9:36).

We can never earn His grace; neither can we deserve His forgiveness nor merit His love. Nevertheless they are ours. His grace is extended to our hearts, His love surrounds us; and when we turn from our sins, His forgiveness is ours.

Francis Bourdillon wrote:

> The mind has a thousand eyes,
> And the heart but one;
> Yet the light of a whole life dies,
> When love is done.

"Light"

There is a story about a Negro slave standing on the deck of a sinking ship with what looked like a heavy bundle in his arms. He was about to step aboard a lifeboat already over-crowded when a member of the crew shouted, "Come ahead, but leave the bundle behind. There is not enough room for both you and whatever you have in the bundle." The old Negro pressed the bundle to his bosom and opened its folds. There lay two small children who had been committed to his care. He kissed them and lowered them into the boat with this request: "Tell the master that I was faithful in fulfilling his charge." The boat pushed away and the dark man stood alone on the deck of the sinking ship. That's fidelity! That's discipline! That's love!

That is really a parable of Jesus staggering up the cruel slopes of Calvary. The cross was a heavy burden but Jesus was convinced that it was God's Way, and He was determined to be faithful. Listen to those agonizing words of victory as Jesus shouts, with the last ounce of energy, "It is finished" (JOHN 19:30). What did He mean? Did He mean only that a difficult ordeal had come to an end? Did He mean that the dying note of His earthly symphony was fading away? No! He meant that His work was finished, and that His life had been lived in perfect harmony with the will of God. Another translation

146

might read, "Father, I was faithful in fulfilling the charge committed to me."

Have we been faithful? Have we stood the test of living up to God's expectations of us?

17

Don't Be Afraid of Tomorrow

Bishop Arthur J. Moore, in his book *Fight On! Fear Not!*, reminds us of the divine power that can be ours during life's most difficult battles: "Christ does not take us out of the battle: He does something batter. He gives us trust and triumph in the battle and promises that, at the end of the struggle, a friendly hand will guide us into the presence of One Whose 'Well done, thou good and faithful servant,' will glorify the battle scars."

On his eighty-seventh birthday, Carl Sandburg said to a group of reporters, "Life is short. You'd better resolve that it is short." The swiftness of our earthly journey is frightening to some. I wish the poet had elaborated on his remark. He was reminding us to live each day fully, and to make every stroke on the canvas of life count. We have learned an important lesson when we discover that life is too short to be selfish, stubborn, and little. William Thackeray wrote, "Life is a mirror: if you frown at it, it frowns back: If you smile, it returns the greeting." That is not a new principle. Paul wrote in his letter to the Galatians: "Be not deceived; God is not mocked: for whatsoever a man soweth, that shall he also reap" (GALATIANS 6:7).

Mr. Sandburg could have said, "Life will bring sorrow, hurt, and disappointment. You'd better resolve that in your heart." I am sure of one thing: Man does not fail because life is hard; neither does man succeed because life is easy. The circum-

148

stances of life are beside the point. Man is driven to defeat and despair, or he climbs to the peaks of joy and triumph because of his attitude toward life and his faith in God.

God offers to every man the strength he must have in order to bear his load. The man who refuses that strength will be crushed, but the man who accepts it will be triumphant. Let me tell you about two men with whom I have been counseling in recent months. Both of them have been brought low by the problems they face. They are passing slowly and painfully through a dark valley. One man feels the hopelessness of utter despair; he believes that the only way out of his present misery is suicide. He is unwilling to face the consequences of his ugly sins. There can be no help for him until he commits himself to God. The other man has asked God for help, and while the night is still dark, he is marching toward the sunlit mountains of victory. Here are two men walking in the dark night of life. One man feels the heavy hammer of defeat, while the other holds tenaciously to the hand of God.

One of my ambitions has been to play the piano. I realize that I will never achieve that goal. To become an accomplished musician demands a lot of time, and I do not feel that I can afford the time it requires. It has been said that life is very much like a piano. One man sits at the keyboard and runs his fingers over the keys in a haphazard way. His efforts produce harsh music filled with discord that is unpleasant to the ear. Another man touches the keys with the hands of a master musician and sends out a succession of melodious sounds that are soothing to the ear. Both men use the same instrument, but one man produces discord while the other produces harmony. Of course, the difference is found in the fact that one man knows little about music, while the other has spent years learning to play the piano correctly. You see, it is what you bring to the keyboard of life that makes the difference.

Life is the same way. Live it according to the teachings of the Master, and it gives you harmony. Live it in the name of selfishness, and it produces discord. No intelligent person would say the piano is at fault when harsh notes are heard; and we cannot honestly say that life is at fault when the storms descend upon us.

Do you remember that thrilling story of the Israelites leaving Egypt under the leadership of Moses? What a magnificent sight it must have been to watch that nation leave a hand in which they had been enslaved, to march toward the Promised Land upon which the eyes of the Lord gazed constantly. The air must have been electrified with excitement as the people marched triumphantly out of slavery. It was not long, however, before the Israelites became discontented with their position. Whenever they confronted danger or suffered the hardships of life, they complained. Soon after they left Egypt and faced their first crisis, they murmured, "Let us alone, that we may serve the Egyptians . . . better for us to serve the Egyptians, than that we should die in the wilderness" (EXODUS 14:12).

Humanity tends to suffer from a chronic disease of complaining. Doubts concerning God's care and goodness arise, when life is hard and burdens are heavy. We often question the wisdom of God when the future is blurred and circumstances place upon us the crushing sorrows of life. When the Israelites complained, Moses, their stalwart leader, said, "Fear ye not, stand still, and see the salvation of the Lord . . ." (EXODUS 14:13).

Moses preached a mighty powerful sermon in that one statement: (1) He was saying, "Don't be afraid. Don't give up and turn back." (2) He was urging the people to stand still— "Get hold of yourself. Let's take a good look at the problem before we quit." (3) He was reminding the people to trust God.

When your troubles seem more than you can bear, remember the advice of Moses: master your fears, stand still, and look to God for the strength you need. For those who are faithful, God will provide the strength that is necessary to ring the bells of victory when they reach the end of their earthly journey.

The person who feels the gentle tug of God's hand will never be afraid on the road of life. Mrs. Carl Simon tells us a delightful story that illustrates this truth. When Mrs. Simon was a little girl, one thing to which she looked forward was a Sunday afternoon walk with the family. Often they would walk down along the railroad track into a lovely wooded area. There they would run and play, and in the spring they picked fragrant wildflowers. Like most journeys through life, there are always some unpleasant places through which we must pass. In order to get to the woods in which they played, it was necessary for the family to cross a high trestle that spanned a creek. The children would often run ahead of the parents, but Mrs. Simon said, "I always waited for my father a few feet this side of the trestle. I didn't dare cross it without him. Often my brothers would offer me their hand, but I did not want to walk with them. I wanted my father. With my hand in his, I stepped confidently across those ties with no sense of fear, knowing that he would guide me safely to the other side."

Before the children of Israel entered the Promised Land, Moses tried to impress upon them the importance of keeping the commandments. The theology one is likely to read in Moses' charge to obey the Lord might be expressed as follows: be good; keep God's commandments, and everything will be fine. Moses promised Israel that, as long as they loved and served God, the fields would yield a good harvest and grass would grow for the cattle. On the other hand, if they followed a false god, the rains would cease, the fields would not yield their harvest, and the grass would fail to grow. It does not take one long to conclude that the good are not always rich and the rich are not always good. God does not always reward righteousness with good health and material wealth. If He did, I know a lot of people who would be more regular in church attendance.

There is truth we can draw from this theological interpretation of Moses' words. We are all completely dependent upon the goodness and mercy of God, and to become aware of God's love and goodness will result in our keeping His commandments. To live otherwise spells spiritual disaster.

Jesus warned us not to be overly concerned about acquiring the material things of life. These are not really important when we see them in the light of eternal values. Do not worry about the clothes you wear or the food you need. God takes care of the lilies of the field and the birds of the air, and we can trust Him to take care of us. Jesus challenged us to "seek ye first the kingdom of God, and his righteousness; and all these things shall be added unto you" (MATTHEW 6:33).

Our Lord knew that we would be tempted to give priority to material things and neglect spiritual matters. All of us would agree that Jesus had a keen insight into human nature. I know people who are spending most of their time and energy with one goal in mind: the acquisition of things. They live in beautiful houses, buy exquisite foods, wrap themselves in the latest fashions while their souls starve for Christian nurture and shiver in the cold shacks of spiritual poverty. Whatever else the Master meant by "All these things shall be added unto you," He expressed His faith in the adequacy of God's power.

Jesus was suggesting that many of us live as if we were alone in the world without the sustaining presence of the God who loves us and who will take care of us. God provides, for those who love and serve Him, the necessary material out of which they can build victorious lives. Most of us are endowed with material blessings that we do not need, but few of us are overstocked with spiritual strength and fortitude.

There are three things Moses challenged the Israelites to do; they are also a challenge for us: (1) love the Lord; (2) walk in all His ways; (3) cleave unto Him.

I have never known a person who loved God, who walked in His holy ways, and who held to the hem of His garment, to be deserted by the Father and allowed to sink to the depths of despair. The psalmist expressed it this way: "I have been young, and now am old; yet have I not seen the righteous forsaken, nor his seed begging bread" (PSALM 37:25). God will never forsake us.

I talk with many people who are afraid of tomorrow. Fear of the future will paralyze us and keep us from present duties as well as rob us of the hopes that thrill the soul. The general rule usually follows that one who is afraid of tomorrow has failed to walk with God in the past and refused to give life his best; therefore, he cannot trust God for the future. To say it in a positive way, I have never known one to carry a big bag of fears in his heart if he has walked with God, given his best to the duties of today, and anchored his faith in God.

When Moses challenged the Israelites to walk without fear, he reminded them of God's goodness in the past. When fear fills our minds, let us remember the past. You may be worried, and perhaps you have good reason to worry, but I challenge you to sit down and write the things that worried you five years ago. I doubt that you will be able to think of many things to write down, but of the things you may be able to remember, I would suggest that most of them never happened.

Moses would not let the Israelites forget that God had provided for their every need. He protected them from their enemies. He provided both food and water in the wilderness. He guided them when the way was blurred. To remember the sheltering hand of God in the past is a source of strength for today and hope for tomorrow. The psalmist said, ". . . the Lord is the strength of my life; of whom shall I be afraid?" (PSALM 27:1).

Simon Peter was impetuous. He spoke and acted impulsively. He was always busy doing something, wise or foolish. His blunders, foolish words, and inconsistencies draw out our sympathy. There were times in Peter's life when he thought he knew more than the Master. In spite of his dedication to the Master, he made many mistakes. On the last night of our Lord's earthly life, Peter pledged his allegiance to Jesus. "Even if I must die with You," he declared, "I will not deny You." Fidelity could not be expressed more emphatically.

The faith Peter expressed so confidently in the upper room faded under the pressure of fear. He denied ever knowing Jesus. How could he ever forget such an ugly deed! Such a night, which was so indelibly etched in the heart of Peter, could not be forgotten.

More important, however, was the morning when Jesus ate breakfast with Peter and some of the other disciples in the Galilean hills. Peter would never forget that morning. That was the time Christ assured him that he had a place in the Kingdom. Then the Master sent him out to feed the sheep. A broken relationship had been restored; Peter had been forgiven.

Peter became a pillar in the early church. He preached in spite of the fact that his faith might have cost him his life. Many people were converted under his ministry, and legend reports that Peter suffered martyrdom in Rome at the time of the persecutions by Nero. Tradition tells us that, during the height of the persecutions, Peter's friends prevailed upon him to flee for his life. On the way out of the city, Peter saw a vision of his Master going toward Rome. He fell down before Jesus and asked, "Where are You going, Master?" Jesus replied, "To Rome, to be crucified anew." Peter turned back and walked to the city, where he was arrested and condemned to be crucified. He requested that he be crucified with his head down, because he did not feel worthy to be crucified as his Lord had been. He could not forget the past, and the presence of the Master kept him from being afraid.

If we want to face the future with confidence, we should take a quick look at the past. We have faced many disappointments and hardships. There have been sorrows through which most of us have passed. Days have been dreary and nights have been lonely. Most of us have come to the place where we wanted to give up and quit. All those experiences are in the past. We have managed, with God's help, to overcome them. We have shouldered loads we feared would crush us. We have mastered problems we thought would defeat us, and conquered mountains we did not believe we could climb. When we look at the past, we recognize that God has been with us, and the words of the psalmist take on fresh meaning: "Thou hast beset me behind and before, and laid thine hand upon me" (PSALM 139:5).

If we want to face tomorrow with confidence, we must do our best today. The man who refuses to give his best efforts to the tasks of today will not be prepared to meet the demands of tomorrow. When we do the tasks of each day well, we may be certain that tomorrow will not ask of us a task we are not prepared to perform.

That advice may be trite, but it is still true. No man can give his best to the duties at hand if he divides his attention between the problems of yesterday, the hopes of tomorrow, and the duties of today. I am saying what others have been saying for generations, and that is: live one day at a time.

Recently I was talking to a doctor in a hospital corridor outside a patient's room. He told me what he had prescribed for the patient. "It's an old drug," he remarked, "but it works, and that is all I am interested in right now." My advice may be an old prescription, but it works, and that's all I am interested in right now. I do know that unless we are faithful to the work of today, we will not be ready to face tomorrow. No student can understand the principles of calculus without first having some understanding of algebra and geometry. Unless we learn the lessons life teaches today, we cannot hope to face the future victoriously.

The campus of Northwestern University in Evanston, Illinois, is on the shore of Lake Michigan. There is a bronze plaque on that campus in honor of Edward W. Spencer. Over a hundred years ago there was a boat wreck on Lake Michigan, and Edward W. Spencer was on the scene. He heard the screams of frightened and dying men and women, and swam out into the swirling waters sixteen times and saved seventeen persons from death. Finally, he fell to the ground, exhausted. While gasping for breath, he was heard to say, "Did I do my best? Did I do my best?"

None of us would deny the fact that Edward W. Spencer did his best. What answer would we give to that same question when asked in relation to our lives? Have we done our best? Let us consider this question in the light of all our relationships with other people.

Finally, if we are able to face tomorrow without being afraid, we must learn to trust God. I was talking to a young man who has a brilliant mind and could make a marvelous contribution to society. "I can't believe in God," he said, "because I have never seen God." "Do you believe in love?" I asked him. "Yes," he replied. "Have you ever seen love?" I responded. "That's different," he continued, "Love is a relationship and a feeling that you have toward someone else." "Well," I said, "I believe in God because of my relationship to Him, not because I have seen Him."

I went on to tell the young man that each day I talk with God and I know He is real. "Suppose," I said to him, "that someone called you from New York and talked with you on the telephone. Just suppose that you did not know the person and had never seen him. When you finished with your conversation, you would believe that the person with whom you had been talking existed." "Of course I would," he replied. "You would have a hard time convincing the many people who talk with God each day that He does not exist. They believe in Him and trust Him, not because they have seen Him, but because of the relationship they have with Him."

Some find it rather easy to trust in God as long as they live in the sunshine and on the mountain peaks of victory. When the clouds descend, the winter wind blows, and they find themselves in the shadow of misfortune, they entertain some doubts concerning God's love and care, and even His very existence. Their faith in God hinges on the circumstances of life.

It is foolish to conclude that God's love and care are measured either by the victories we know or the defeats we suffer. We test our faith, not during the days of sunshine, but when the nights are darkest.

A mighty ship proves its worthiness, not in the calm waters of a harbor where it is sheltered from the rolling waves of the ocean, but in the midst of the gigantic waves that break over its bow. So it is with our Christian faith.

We do not commit ourselves to God only during days of good health and prosperity, but for all of life. The psalmist proclaimed his unswerving faith in the adequacy of God's grace: "Yea, though I walk through the valley of the shadow of death, I will fear no evil . . ." (PSALM 23:4). The psalmist had committed his life to God, not only for the days of victory, but for the moments when the shadows would surround him.

As a minister, I am frequently called upon to unite young couples in marriage. I like the phrase "till death us do part." It is a tragedy that so many take it so frivolously. Nevertheless they promise God and each other that they will live together, even though the future may bring sickness instead of health. They pledge their love, each to the other, whether they find a pot of shining gold or the hardships of poverty down life's winding road.

Our commitment to God must be equally complete. Our faith in His love and mercy is for all of life. This is difficult for some to achieve, but unless we can reach these heights in our trust, our faith is totally inadequate.

Ella Wheeler Wilcox wrote a verse that has come to be one of my favorites. It expresses undaunted faith in the face of defeat and disappointment:

157

I will not doubt, though all my ships at sea
    Come drifting home with broken masts and sails;
    I will believe the Hand which never fails,
    From seeming evil worketh good for me;
  And, though I weep because those sails are battered,
    Still will I cry, while my best hopes lie shattered,
    "I trust in Thee."

Whatever the future holds for us, we can be sure that God stands in each tomorrow, offering the hope we need to keep trying, giving the strength we need to bear our burdens, and supplying the faith we must have in order to see how to walk when the way is blurred.

You and I will never live on the spiritual heights for which God created us unless we walk with Him, give life our best, and trust Him. There just isn't any other road that leads to victory.

18

Discovering God's Will Through Prayer

"Everybody loves somebody sometime," is a line in a popular song. We love because it is necessary to fulfill our purpose. We love because we cannot help it. I want to change this line a little and use it in connection with prayer: "Everybody prays to something sometime."

Did you ever consider the question, Why do we pray? We pray because we cannot help it. We pray because it is evident to us that we cannot reach our destiny without the help of some power beyond ourselves. We pray because the path of life leads us through dark valleys and up hills that are too much for us.

Even people who do not profess a profound faith in God, pray. Hugh Walpole's Vanessa says to Benjie, in response to Benjie's question, "Why do you love me?" "I love you because you are all that I have in the world; because without you, I am always lonely; because I am not alive without you." Before that, Vanessa and Benjie had talked about God. Benjie did not believe in God, but Vanessa did. Then Benjie took Vanessa's hand and kissed it. "God helping me," he said, "you will not regret it. Although I don't believe in Him, I expect Him to help me, you see." The need for prayer is so great, and the urge is so strong, that you will find a prayer brewing in the hearts of people everywhere.

Some people think of God as a cold computer sending back His sometimes cruel and impersonal answers to requests.

Little wonder such people lose interest in prayer. We will never begin to understand prayer until we learn to think of God as a Father. In the true sense of the word, a father is one who loves his children and who has both an interest in, and a concern for, the welfare of his children.

To make certain we understand the full impact of God's love and interest in us, Jesus explained this "Father" characteristic of God and its relation to prayer: ". . . what man is there of you, whom if his son ask bread, will he give him a stone? Or if he ask a fish, will he give him a serpent? If ye then, being evil, know how to give good gifts unto your children, how much more shall your Father which is in heaven give good things to them that ask him?" (MATTHEW 7:9-11).

It may be hard for us to bring the deep hurts of the heart to some strange force in the universe which we do not understand, or to some power that is so great we cannot define it or even imagine it. Prayer is made easier when we come to believe that we are praying to a God who is like a perfect Father. When we see God as a perfect Father, we are never afraid to approach Him when the way is hard and sorrow fills our hearts.

Some people think it is futile to pray. We live in a world governed by law, they suggest. The movements of the earth and planets have been plotted for centuries yet unborn. We do not need God anymore, they reason. We just have to take life as it comes. To follow this philosophy to its logical conclusion, we need not pray for the sick, nor will it do any good to pray for strength. God placed the universe in motion, and it cannot be altered. Those who feel this way fail to see the truth behind and beyond the laws which they believe have imprisoned God.

It would be inconceivable to think of life without these laws. They are for our own good, and God expects us to cooperate with them. Bring upon the scene intelligence, and these laws can be used for our advantage.

There is a law that an object heavier than air cannot fly. Yet just the other day I boarded a giant airplane that weighed over a hundred tons and flew halfway across the nation within a few hours. There is a law that the wind will push an object in the direction it blows. But a poet pointed out:

> One ship drives east and another west,
> While the selfsame breezes blow;
> 'Tis the set of the sails and not the gale
> That bids them where to go.

> Ella Wheeler Wilcox

Water will not flow uphill, but that does not keep us from building bathrooms upstairs. You see, we have learned to manipulate natural laws and make them our servants.

There isn't anything evil about the laws that govern the universe. You plant a bulb in the fall, and it will grow and bloom in the spring. Take a high-powered automobile and drive it down the road at seventy miles an hour and ram it into a tree, and you are likely to get killed.

Natural laws do not handcuff God; rather, they are a part of God's intelligent plan for His universe. Prayer must be based on the faith that God is never baffled, never defeated, and never at His wits' end. He has a will in every set of circumstances, and if He cannot take us around the dark chasms of life, He will provide a little light by which we can walk safely through the shadows.

Aunt Jane advised Vanessa, "Don't be frightened, my dear. Trust God. . . . Life's a dangerous thing, my dear, and you can't escape the danger by staying in bed all day or making other people act for you. Don't expect things to be easy. Why should they be? God doesn't arrange the universe only for me—not for you, either . . . the way some people talk . . . you'd think that every time they have a toothache, God ought to be ashamed of Himself."

We often make requests that God refuses to answer. It is

when God says "No" to a fervent request that most of us begin to doubt. We wonder if God really hears us, and if He does, why does He refuse us? God's refusals reflect His love and wisdom.

Someone gave me a shiny knife once. When my son Randall was about three years of age, he saw it and wanted to hold it. I placed the knife in his little hand and he asked me to open it for him. I had to deny his request. He could not understand, and I am certain he thought that I did not love him. My refusal to let him have an open knife was based on my love and wisdom. I knew that someday he would understand that "No" was the only answer a wise father could give.

I am sure that each person who reads these lines has been disappointed in prayer, but I am also certain that many have had prayers answered. Some are ready to give up praying when God says "No" to a request. No good mechanic would give up after a first look if he failed to find the reason why the engine of a car skipped. No physician would quit practicing his profession if he failed to find the cause of a pain in his patient. No student would give up math if he did not get the right answer. I like the words of a poet who wrote:

> I've prayed many prayers when no answer came,
> Though I waited patient and long,
> But answers have come to enough of my prayers,
> To make me keep praying on.

Anonymous

When life's load gets heavy, you can do one of three things:

(1) You can give up. You can conclude that there is no help and you are defeated. Six months ago, I talked to a man who had given up. The load life had placed on his shoulders seemed too much. He was headed toward a drunkard's grave. He felt no one wanted or needed him. I told him God had a place for him if he would do his part. Today he is a changed

man. I saw him the other day, and that radiant look is coming back to his face.

(2) You can grit your teeth and walk on in sheer determination. You can resolve to win the battle with mere human strength. I like to see a person with courage and perseverance, but they will not take you very far down the road. You must have more.

(3) You can look up and ask God to help you. When you have exhausted your strength and done all you know how to do, you can come to God, and He will never fail you. I do not mean that He will lift from your shoulder the heavy weight you bear, but He will give you grace to bear it. I do not mean that He will take you around the valley of sorrow, but He will walk through it with you. I do not mean that He will keep you from getting hurt, but He will comfort you when you are wounded.

God does not want to disappoint us. He does not like to see His children hurt, but we cannot go through life without the scars of some hard battles. God knows that our disappointments will heal and they need not defeat us.

When I was a small lad, I asked for an electric train. That was just at the beginning of World War II, and there was a priority on steel. It was almost impossible to find an electric train. But I got the train that Christmas, and that was more than twenty-five years ago.

I didn't know until recently the demands I was placing on my father when I asked for the train. My father made less than twenty dollars a week, and he was trying to feed and clothe his five children. But he bought me a train. Just before Christmas, a very wealthy man called and asked to buy the train. Price was no consideration. My mother and father discussed selling the train. They could take the money and buy something else for me, and still have money left. It would take them a long time, paying a dollar a week, to pay for the train. They decided to keep the train and give it to me for Christmas. They didn't want to disappoint me. I still have that train. I prize it highly. It is mine because of a great sacrifice my parents made.

A long time ago God made a sacrifice for all of us. It cost Him more than we can imagine. He didn't want us to be disappointed in life, and He sent His Son to the cross in order to redeem us.

Roy M. Pearson wrote, "Prayer is not a lazy substitute for work. It is not a short cut to skill or knowledge. And, sometimes, God delays the answer to our prayer in final form, until we have time to build up the strength, accumulate the knowledge, or fashion the character that would make it possible for Him to say 'yes' to what we ask." We should think of prayer as a channel to discover God's will and never an aid to get what we want. It is human to pray for easy loads, but let us never forget to pray for strong backs. Some may pray to be excused from the battlefields, but let us always pray for the fortitude to stand as faithful soldiers as we face the inevitable battles of life. Madam Chiang Kai-shek once said, "I used to pray that God would do this or that. Now I pray that God will make His Will known to me."

When we commit our thoughts and wishes to God in prayer, we must learn to trust Him. James Hervey expressed it this way:

> Good when He gives, supremely good,
> Nor less when He denies,
> E'en crosses from His sovereign hand
> Are blessings in disguise.

Jesus taught us to pray, "Thy will be done." When we learn to pray with perfect trust, we can face life with perfect confidence, believing that God will give us what is best. We do not always want, or even know what is best for us.

Not long ago, little Richard had to go to the doctor. After a careful examination the doctor said, "I hate to do this, but he must have a shot of penicillin." Little Richard didn't want that shot, but because it was best for him he had to take it.

The man prays best who always prays, "Thy will be done." Prayer will be more satisfying when we think of God as a Father, and when we are willing to say, in the words of Eliza Hickok:

> I leave my prayer to Him alone
> Whose Will is wiser than my own.